# What Really Works With Universal Design for Learning

*Wendy Murawski would like to dedicate this book to her mother, Susan Farrell.*

*Mom—you are the strongest, smartest, most elegant woman I know.*
*You have always supported giving me choice, voice, and options…and only*
*mildly raised an eyebrow when my choices weren't ones you'd advise.*

*I love you and you are my role model. Wink.*

# What Really Works With Universal Design for Learning

*Editors*

Wendy W. Murawski
Kathy Lynn Scott

FOR INFORMATION:

Corwin

A SAGE Publishing Company

2455 Teller Road

Thousand Oaks, California 91320

(800) 233-9936

www.corwin.com

SAGE Publications Ltd.

1 Oliver's Yard

55 City Road

London EC1Y 1SP

United Kingdom

SAGE Publications India Pvt. Ltd.

B 1/I 1 Mohan Cooperative Industrial Area

Mathura Road, New Delhi 110 044

India

SAGE Publications Asia-Pacific Pte. Ltd.

18 Cross Street #10-10/11/12

China Square Central

Singapore 048423

Program Director: Jessica Allan

Content Development Editor: Lucas Schleicher

Senior Editorial Assistant: Mia Rodriguez

Production Editor: Amy Schroller

Copy Editor: Talia Greenberg

Typesetter: Hurix Digital

Proofreader: Dennis Webb

Indexer: Sheila Bodell

Cover Designer: Anupama Krishnan

Marketing Manager: Deena Meyer

Printed in the United States of America

*Library of Congress Cataloging-in-Publication Data*

Names: Murawski, Wendy W., author. | Scott, Kathy Lynn, author.

Title: What really works with universal design for learning / Wendy W. Murawski, Kathy Lynn Scott.

Description: Thousand Oaks, California : Corwin, [2019] | Includes bibliographical references and index.

Identifiers: LCCN 2018053220 | ISBN 9781544338675 (pbk. : alk. paper)

Subjects: LCSH: Inclusive education. | Instructional systems—Design. | Individualized instruction. | Educational planning. | Cognitive styles.

Classification: LCC LC1201 .M85 2019 | DDC 371.9/046—dc23 LC record available at https://lccn.loc.gov/2018053220

This book is printed on acid-free paper.

SUSTAINABLE FORESTRY INITIATIVE

Certified Chain of Custody
Promoting Sustainable Forestry
www.sfiprogram.org
SFI-01268

SFI label applies to text stock

19 20 21 22 23 10 9 8 7 6 5 4 3 2 1

# Contents

# SECTION III. WHAT REALLY WORKS WITH INSTRUCTION

# SECTION IV. WHAT REALLY WORKS WITH SPECIAL POPULATIONS

# SECTION V. WHAT REALLY WORKS BEYOND THE CLASSROOM

# *Preface*

Universal Design for Learning. UDL. Is this just another acronym education is foisting on teachers? Something to add to their baskets of RTI, MTSS, LRE, FAPE, and IEP? We think not. UDL is so much more than an acronym or the hottest trend in education. It is about equity and access for all students. That is why we are passionate about providing educators with a book on what *really* works with UDL across different settings, contexts, and students.

As with all of our books, our goal was to create a resource for educators that is evidence-based, reader-friendly, and chockful of strong, concrete, and meaningful strategies. We wanted a text that provided research but wasn't mired in it, as well as a text that had enough substantive examples to make UDL come alive for its readers. We did something a bit different in this fourth book of the *What Really Works* series. We added "Case in Point" examples to paint a picture of UDL in action. We added "Strategy Spots" that would exemplify ways that teachers at various grade levels could employ UDL principles. We also asked authors to help point out differences between UDL and differentiated instruction (DI), as those are often confused concepts.

We kept elements that were successful in our other three *What Really Works* books. Among other things, this text includes "Tech Tips," "Key Concepts," "Websites We Recommend," and "Apps We Love." Though we have moved away from the "Do This and Don't Do That" bulleted format in this book, we kept the narratives focused on practical applications of UDL. Each chapter is divided into three sections to align with the UDL framework: multiple means of representation, multiple means of engagement, and multiple means of action and expression.

We are honored to have Dr. Katie Novak write our introduction and co-author our final chapter on baby steps to using UDL. In addition, she was gracious enough to read and provide feedback on the book throughout its creation, ensuring that chapters were aligned and clearly articulated best practices. She also gave us suggestions for where we might find additional resources or even talk to individuals who are phenomenal exemplars of using UDL well in their schools. We are grateful for her input!

Reading the various first drafts of chapters for this book helped emphasize to us how truly important—and truly difficult—the use of UDL will be for many educators. Many of us still have a "differentiation" lens, one that is specific to individual learners with individual disability or special needs labels, as opposed to a proactive, all-means-all lens. It is possible this text continues to promote the differentiation lens by having chapters that focus on a particular ability label (e.g., students with emotional/behavioral disabilities, students who are gifted). Our intent is not to do so, but rather to use these chapters to help educators bridge the conceptual jump from the labels and research we already have on these populations, with the actions we can and should take proactively for *all* learners. It is these universally designed actions that will, in turn, also specifically support individuals with specific special needs.

The Center for Teaching and Learning in the Michael D. Eisner College of Education at California State University, Northridge, is the professional development and research arm of the college. We try to keep our finger on the pulse of what is cutting edge in education and provide resources to our local and national community to bridge gaps between research and practice. This fourth book in our *What Really Works* series with Corwin is the pinnacle of our work. We feel strongly that the more educators embrace Universal Design for Learning principles, the more all learners (truly *all*) will have an opportunity to succeed.

—**Wendy W. Murawski and Kathy Lynn Scott**

# *About the Editors*

 **Wendy W. Murawski, PhD,** is the Michael D. Eisner Endowed Chair and Executive Director for the Center for Teaching and Learning at California State University, Northridge (CSUN). She is a tenured Full Professor in the Department of Special Education, a past president of the Teacher Education Division (TED) for the Council for Exceptional Children, a former Teacher Educator of the Year for the state of California, and the recent recipient of the Outstanding Faculty Award for her university. She has authored ten books, as well as numerous chapters, articles, and handbooks in the areas of co-teaching, collaboration, inclusion, differentiation, and teaching. Wendy owns her own educational consulting company (2 TEACH LLC), loves to travel and speak nationally and internationally, and is a frequently requested keynote speaker. This year, her fourteen-year-old son Kiernan started high school and, as a former HS teacher, this petrifies her. Wendy and her fiancé, Donald, are trying to ignore the reality of passing time through travel, house projects, outdoor BBQs, movie nights, and even working out. It's not helping.

 **Kathy Lynn Scott, PhD,** is the Center Administrative Analyst for the Center for Teaching and Learning at California State University, Northridge. Kathy was trained as an old school darkroom photographer, but she fell in love with all things to do with education. After conducting research on art education and adult education in England and coordinating research on learning disabilities in New Jersey, Kathy jumped from coast to coast, finding a new home with the CTL, where she gets to do a little bit of everything related to education. When not acting as the "glue" for the CTL (as Wendy calls her), she's happiest just relaxing at home, learning to cook new dishes, watching *Jeopardy!*, and shouting out the (not always correct) answers.

# *About the Contributors*

**Rebecca M. Ashton, BFA,** currently serves as Education Director for the Area Stage Company and Conservatory in Coral Gables, Florida. Previously, she served as Director of Preschool Education at the Santa Monica Playhouse in California. She possesses fifteen years of experience in arts education. When she is not teaching or performing, you will most likely find her scuba diving, running, or hanging out anywhere that nature and animals are located.

**Tamarah M. Ashton, PhD,** holds degrees and credentials in music, education, counseling, and special education. She is currently a Professor in the Department of Special Education at California State University, Northridge. In her spare time, you will find her dancing and singing her heart out on local area stages. Froyo and the color purple are her current life's passions.

**Philip E. Bernhardt, EdD,** is an Associate Professor of Secondary Education and Associate Director of the Honors Program at the Metropolitan State University of Denver. When not teaching or writing, he loves spending time camping, traveling, eating, laughing, and watching Colorado Rockies baseball games with his wife and two wonderful children.

**Anne Brawand, PhD,** is an Associate Professor in the Department of Special Education at Kutztown University of Pennsylvania. Now that she has successfully achieved tenure and promotion, she would like to become proficient with gardening and interior painting. Meanwhile, she is content studying YouTube videos to learn how to implement her sons' crazy haircut requests.

**Caitlyn A. Bukaty, PhD,** is the Evaluation Coordinator and Analyst for the Florida Center for Students With Unique Abilities at the University of Central Florida. Her research interests include infusing technology and Universal Design for Learning to optimize students' in-school and postschool outcomes. When she's not busy developing her educational superhero skills, Caitlyn enjoys baking delicious things; pampering her two adorable furkids, Giselle and Bukets; and playing at the Disney Parks with friends.

**Zhen Chai, PhD,** is an Assistant Professor of Early Childhood Special Education (ECSE) at California State University, Northridge. She enjoys working with ECSE teacher candidates and seeing them become competent and confident teachers over the years. During weekends, she loves spending time with her family exploring different restaurants in and around Los Angeles.

**Ching-I Chen, PhD,** is an Assistant Professor in the area of early intervention/early childhood special education at Kent State University. Her research interests include the development and application of culturally and linguistically relevant assessments, and personnel development in early childhood intervention. During leisure time, she enjoys traveling with her family and serves as the housekeeping staff of her cat.

**Kyena E. Cornelius, EdD,** is an Assistant Professor in Special Education at Minnesota State University, Mankato. Her research interests include teacher preparation practices and the induction and mentoring of early career special educators. Her passions include spending time with her family, baking, wine, and traveling. She especially enjoys traveling if a winery is on the itinerary.

**Jaime True Daley, EdD,** has spent the past twenty years providing special education to children from pre-K through twelfth grade in multiple settings and states. She earned her doctorate from Johns Hopkins University and now teaches teachers and conducts research at the University of Delaware. She's researching a new order of operations that stops multiplying her kids' activities and dividing her time between multiple projects—while adding more time to play and subtracting gray hairs!

**Lauren A. Delisio, PhD,** is an Assistant Professor at Rider University in New Jersey. Her research interests include students with autism spectrum disorder, word problems in mathematics, and technology. When she's not working, cleaning, running, or doing CrossFit, Lauren enjoys reading, correcting other people's grammar, traveling, eating, and traveling to places to eat. Also, did she mention eating?

**Tesha Fritzgerald, EdS,** serves as Director of Federal Programs with the East Cleveland City School District. She has been a teacher and leader in urban schools for over eighteen years. Her life's work is to awaken, celebrate, and activate the brilliance of others to actualize achievement wherever it seems impossible. A self-proclaimed *Jeopardy!* enthusiast and imagination expert, she loves writing and dreaming out loud with her husband, two children, and committed educators who believe in academic success for all.

**Cathy (Cat) R. Gaspard, PhD,** is an Assistant Professor of Mathematics in the Department of Secondary Education at California State University, Northridge. Her entire career has been dedicated to math education, with fourteen years as a secondary mathematics teacher and five as a professor of math education. For the past ten years, her focus has been on how reducing stress and anxiety in students improves their mathematical learning. In her free time . . . (LOL) . . . she would enjoy cooking and surfing.

**Brittany L. Hott, PhD,** is an Associate Professor of Special Education at Texas A&M–Commerce. Her interests include school-based interventions and quantitative research methods. Brittany has designed numerous interventions to support two awesome toddlers who do not need sleep and three bird dogs that are not into birds. To date, most of her toddler and bird dog experiments have resulted in null effects.

**Claire E. Hughes, PhD,** is the Director of Education and Teacher Preparation at the College of Coastal Georgia. Previously, she was the Faculty Director of Special Education at Canterbury Christ Church in England. She is still slightly confused between "favorite" and "favourite" and which side of the road to drive on, but she does know how to invigilate!

**Kimberly M. Johnson, PhD,** is an Assistant Professor in the Department of Special Education at Minnesota State University, Mankato. Her research interests revolve around instructional design that facilitates the meaningful inclusion of students with high-incidence disabilities. In addition to running, cycling, and yoga, she enjoys sampling her co-author Kyena's creative baking endeavors.

**Janet Josephson, PhD,** is an Assistant Professor in the Department of Early, Middle, and Exceptional Education at Millersville University in beautiful Lancaster County, Pennsylvania. Because they say that teaching is one-quarter preparation and three-quarters theater, she can often be found on the local community theater stages in various musical productions . . . just in case the whole professor thing doesn't work out.

**Amy Kramer** is a doctoral candidate at Bowling Green State University in Leadership Studies. Currently a special education administrator, she has been a teacher, a principal, and a university instructor. Her research and expertise focus on inclusion and co-teaching. Considering her house is filled with all-males (a husband, three boys, and even a male dog), she relishes in those few-and-far-between moments of a clean house and a chick-flick.

**Amelia Martin, BS,** is a STRIDE Lab research assistant at Texas A&M–Commerce. When she's not supporting 8,000 research projects, Amelia dedicates her spare time to annoying her neighbors and tremendously spoiled cat by rehearsing her flute repertoire.

**Wendy W. Murawski, PhD,** is the Eisner Endowed Chair and Executive Director of the Center for Teaching and Learning at California State University, Northridge, and CEO of the educational consulting company, 2 TEACH. Her goals used to be to travel the world, write books, and give keynote presentations; now she just wants a glass of Merlot, some movie popcorn, and a personal masseuse.

**Sarah A. Nagro, EdD,** is an Assistant Professor in Special Education at George Mason University. Her research and teaching focus on preparing reflective, profession-ready special educators who effectively implement evidence-based practices to improve the learning experiences of all students. Sarah is planning to keep writing chapters in Wendy's books until she is finally able to write a witty bio. In the meantime, she will stick to being a new mom.

**Katie Novak, EdD,** is an internationally recognized expert in Universal Design for Learning (UDL) and a practicing administrator as an Assistant Superintendent of Schools in Massachusetts. As a mom of four little Novaks, she is a semi-pro flash light tag competitor, has perfected cottage cheese pancakes, and loves wearing red high heels. If anyone knows Christian Louboutin, hook a sister up.

**Ruby L. Owiny, PhD,** is an Assistant Professor in the Division of Education at Trinity International University in Deerfield, Illinois. She's recently revisited getting her workouts in the pool, where aqua aerobics keep her head above water but hide her lack of grace and coordination. However, her daughter's Fitbit Challenges also have her walking the neighborhood at all hours, thanks to her competitiveness!

**Kathy M. Randolph, EdD,** is an Assistant Professor at the University of Colorado–Colorado Springs. Her research interests include coaching teachers with technology to enhance teaching practices and interventions to support students with behavior issues. She spends her spare time and money at softball fields watching her twins play softball, and wishes she could get all three of her daughters, and husband, to put their dishes in the dishwasher without prompting. Paper plates for everyone!

**Carolyn Rethwisch,** a former National Science Teacher of the Year, is in her twenty-fifth year of teaching. Her passion for science and love of middle schoolers have led her out of her comfort zone to coach junior astronauts learning to launch and land the space shuttle in a flight simulator, as well as solve space engineering challenges where *failure is not an option*. At the end of most days, she can be heard saying, "Beam me up, Scotty!"

**Leila Ansari Ricci, PhD,** is an Associate Professor at California State University, Los Angeles. She is passionate about training general and special educators in co-teaching to include all kids. Teaching others to get along well comes naturally from many years as a mom to three daughters, three cats, and a dog—whose names she's been known to use interchangeably.

**Jacqueline Rodriguez, PhD,** is the Assistant Vice President, Programs and Professional Learning, at the American Association of Colleges of Teacher Education. Jackie is interested in education policy, high quality teacher preparation, and special education law. She was previously a faculty member at the College of William & Mary where she worked to increase supports for veterans and military affiliated students, directed the Holmes Scholar Program, and co-directed the Social Justice Graduate Fellows Program. If she's not watching CSPAN she's probably baking chocolate chip cookies or off trail running.

**Victoria Russell, EdD,** is an Associate Professor at the University of Mary Washington in Virginia. Her research interests include assessment and supporting general education teachers in developing inclusive mindsets and practices. Victoria's superpower in UDL–Action and Expression is the ability to carry on complete conversations with her co-author using only *Real Housewives* memes.

**Barbara Serianni, PhD,** is an Assistant Professor of Special Education at Georgia Southern University in Savannah, Georgia. Her research interests include co-teaching, inclusion, student engagement, culturally responsive teaching, and the tech tools and pedagogies that support those endeavors. As "Grammie" to ten digital natives ranging from eighteen months to fifteen years, she is forever challenged to remain relevant when it comes to her grands. . . . Keeping up is a bit like living inside of Temple Run!

**Jennifer D. Walker, PhD,** is an Assistant Professor at the University of Mary Washington in Virginia. She has presented and published articles and book chapters on classroom management, positive behavior interventions and supports, functional analysis, and working with students with emotional and behavioral disabilities. Jennifer's idea of paradise includes a day at the beach with a good book, a bushel of steamed crabs, and an evening on the couch watching reality television (*Real Housewives*, of course!).

# UDL

## An Introduction From Pizza Parlor to the World

Katie Novak

*Groton–Dunstable Regional School District*

*CAST Professional Cadre Member*

In the early 1980s, education news ruled the headlines. For one, the Reagan administration commissioned the report *A Nation at Risk*, which highlighted significant inequities and declining performance of students in the United States. The report charged, "If an unfriendly foreign power had attempted to impose on America the mediocre educational performance that exists today, we might well have viewed it as an act of war" (U.S. National Commission on Excellence in Education, 1983). Ouch.

At this same time, there was great promise in education, as Apple, led by Steve Jobs, released the first Macintosh personal computer and the *New York Times* declared, "It's poised for a stunning success" (Hayes, 1984). They got that right!

The good, the bad, and the ugly of those '84 headlines don't portray the whole story of how education was changing at that time. It's important to remember that amazing ideas, some that go on to transform the world, have humble beginnings that don't even make the news. Universal Design for Learning (UDL) is one such example. To highlight just how mundane

 **STRATEGY SPOT**

Are you inspired at your desk? No? Consider that your students may not be, either. You may not be able to let them all go out for pizza during an assignment, but you can let them choose where and how they sit, and with whom they interact. When we are comfortable, we all tend to be more inspired and inspiring!

the beginnings were, ask yourself: How many times have you and your friends gone out for pizza?

While Steve Jobs exploded onto the education scene and redefined future technology, five clinicians from North Shore Children's Hospital in Salem, Massachusetts—Anne Meyer, David Rose, Grace Meo, Skip Stahl, and Linda Mensing—went out for pizza. Over pitchers of soda and slices of cheese and pepperoni, these visionaries decided they wanted to change the outcomes for students with learning disabilities. That night, they conceived a company called CAST (Center for Applied Technolgy). Armed with passion, an anonymous grant of $15,000, and an inherent belief in the power of learning, these five colleagues asked a question: How can computer technology enhance learning for students with disabilities? (CAST, 2016). As they passed napkins and parmesan cheese, they identified their goal. They would find, adapt, and invent technologies that would allow students to access and engage with curriculum and instruction in inclusive classrooms with their peers.

Dinners like this were probably not unique. Many educators likely conspired to address the sobering realities presented in *A Nation at Risk* while capitalizing on new technology. Although there was nothing newsworthy about the original soiree, what has happened since is quite extraordinary.

As they followed their "patients" in their classrooms, the founders of CAST quickly realized they had a much bigger mission than they originally planned. They became convinced that many students faced barriers to learning, not because of their disabilities but because of the disabilities in curriculum. Stop for a moment and think about how powerful that idea was: *students are not disabled; schools are.*

It was soon clear to them that focusing only on learning disabilities and special education, as opposed to all learners and general education, oversimplified learner differences and failed to accurately represent the diversity of students (Meo, 2008). Their future work, therefore, would not be focused on helping students with learning disabilities to overcome barriers, but by helping teachers and schools eliminate those barriers through proactive curriculum design (Meyer, Rose, & Gordon, 2014).

This realization, that disability is contextual, was inspired by the work of architect Ron Mace, who coined the term *Universal Design* in 1988. Mace defined Universal Design as the "design of products and environments to be usable by all people, to the greatest extent possible, without the need for adaptation or specialized design" (Center for Universal Design, 2008). Buildings where all people could not enter were deemed "architecturally disabling."

Inspired by this concept, CAST defined Universal Design for Learning (UDL) in 1995 and addressed the reality that inflexible goals, methods, materials, and assessments provided barriers to learning (Hitchcock, Meyer, Rose, & Jackson, 2002). "Failure to learn," they argued, was not a measure of the inherent capacity or potential of the learner, but a reflection of learning systems that were not designed to meet the needs of all learners (Moore, 2007).

Dr. David Rose, one of the co-founders and a developmental neuropsychologist from Harvard University, ensured that the UDL evidence-based principles were grounded in neuroscience and aligned to the three main neural networks in the brain (Meyer et al., 2014). The activities of these networks parallel the three prerequisites for learning described by development psychologist Lev Vygotsky in 1962: recognition of the information to be learned, application of strategies to process that information, and engagement with the learning task (Rose & Meyer, 2002).

**Key Concept**

UDL is defined as the design and delivery of curriculum and instruction to meet the needs of all learners by providing them choices for *what* they are learning, *why* they are learning, and *how* they will share what they have learned.

In the first best-selling book on UDL, *Teaching Every Student in the Digital Age*, co-founders David Rose and Anne Meyer (2002) introduced the importance of the three networks in learning and how every individual brain differs substantially—a point, the authors note, that has critical implications for the design and delivery of learning experiences. Because learner variability, or how learners vary greatly in how they approach learning tasks, is systematic and predictable, UDL required that educators change the way they design and deliver curriculum and instruction (Hartmann, 2015; Rose & Meyer, 2002).

The three networks of the brain and their purpose in learning provide a foundation for the UDL framework and its principles (Rose & Meyer, 2002). Recognition networks enable learners to recognize, identify, and comprehend information, ideas, and concepts. Strategic networks enable learners to plan, execute, and monitor actions and skills, and affective networks specialize in attaching emotional significance to tasks.

The UDL framework translates an understanding of neural networks and brain-based learning into practice by providing three guiding principles (Figure I.1):

- Multiple means of engagement (the "why" of learning)
- Multiple means of representation (the "what" of learning)
- Multiple means of action and expression (the "how" of learning)

These principles also include a set of guidelines that support the design and delivery of curriculum and instruction to meet the needs of all learners by providing them choices for why they are learning, what they are learning, and how they will share what they have learned (Novak, 2016).

What started as a cozy meeting in a pizza parlor snowballed into the National UDL Task Force (National Center on UDL, 2017), which works

**Figure 1.1    UDL Brain and Principle Alignment**

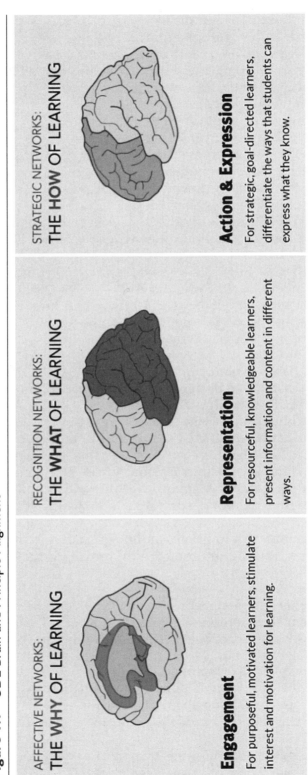

AFFECTIVE NETWORKS:
THE **WHY** OF LEARNING

**Engagement**

For purposeful, motivated learners, stimulate interest and motivation for learning.

RECOGNITION NETWORKS:
THE **WHAT** OF LEARNING

**Representation**

For resourceful, knowledgeable learners, present information and content in different ways.

STRATEGIC NETWORKS:
THE **HOW** OF LEARNING

**Action & Expression**

For strategic, goal-directed learners, differentiate the ways that students can express what they know.

to influence the presidential administration and Congress to adopt UDL principles in federal legislation and policy. The National UDL Task Force includes over forty organizations including, but not limited to, American Federation of Teachers (AFT), American Institutes for Research (AIR), Council for Exceptional Children (CEC), Easter Seals, Learning Disabilities Association of America (LDA), National Association of State Boards of Education, National Center for Learning Disabilities, Inc., National Down Syndrome Society, National Education Association (NEA), National PTA, National School Boards Association, PACER Center, and UDL—Implementation and Research Network (UDL-IRN).

This task force has successfully promoted the use of UDL to improve academic achievement and educational opportunities for all learners, as its mission. In 2008, UDL was endorsed in the Higher Education Opportunity Act (HEOA); in 2010, it was included in the National Educational Technology Plan and the Common Core State Standards; and in 2015, President Barack Obama signed the Every Student Succeeds Act (ESSA), which endorses UDL several times throughout the legislation.

Today, UDL is defined as "a scientifically valid framework for guiding educational practice that (a) provides flexibility in the ways information is presented, in the ways students respond or demonstrate knowledge and skills, and in the ways students are engaged; and (b) reduces barriers in instruction, provides appropriate accommodations, supports, and challenges, and maintains high achievement expectations for all students, including students with disabilities and students who are limited English proficient," in the Higher Education Opportunity Act (PL 110-135).

**Key Concept**

Critical elements of UDL are student *choice and voice.* Teachers need to provide *clear objectives* and then work with students to select ways to learn, engage, and demonstrate mastery of that objective that match each student's unique learning profile.

Personalized learning, through UDL, requires educators to provide this flexibility so students have options and choices throughout the design and delivery of instruction. Because variability is the rule, not the exception, we have to provide our students with options and choices so they can make decisions about why they are learning, what they learn, and how they share what they know (Novak, 2016). When educators implement UDL, research has shown that the framework increases access, participation, progress, attitudinal outcomes, and achievement for all learners, including those with significant disabilities (Katz & Sokal, 2016; Rao & Meo, 2016). These outcomes result from a focus on removing barriers and fostering expert learning in students.

Being an expert learner, which is a goal of UDL, is a lifetime goal. This goal is one that we will always work toward and never achieve. It's because it is not achievable. The word *expert* makes most of us think about someone with authoritative knowledge or skill but, as argued in *UDL Theory and Practice* (Meyer et al., 2014), "If we think a moment, we realize that expertise is never static. Developing expertise in anything is always a process of continuous learning—practice, adjustment, and refinement. In the context of UDL, we focus on learning expertise: the lifelong process of becoming ever more motivated, knowledgeable, and skillful" (p. 15).

If one goal of UDL is that students learn how to be learners, and learn how to make choices that will help them reach their goals and personalize their journey, always growing and improving, we as their teachers need to be committed to our own expert learning. Our goal is that *every* student needs to experience achievement, growth, and success. The UDL framework does not delineate between certain groups of students (Meo, 2008; Nelson, 2013). UDL is not blind to the fact that some students need significant support to participate with their peers, comprehend information, and express what they know (Nelson, 2013), but these students should be given opportunities to make choices and experience relevant, authentic learning opportunities that are meaningful to them as they work toward goals.

CAST and the National UDL Task Force aren't fighting this battle simply because test scores highlight the fact that our nation is still at risk, decades after the original Reagan administration report. The success that we're trying to achieve is not just on classroom assessments and standardized tests, but in life. How awesome of a task is that? And yet, we've been trying to reach that peak for decades. Educators throughout time have been trying to help all learners succeed. Just as we start closing gaps and improving the outcomes of all kids, the world around us spins, technologies change, students become more variable, we compete with robots, and we feel like we are slipping back. I am here to tell you that we are never slipping back.

UDL provides a blueprint, a trail map if you will, that will empower you to apply the UDL Guidelines to the four components of curriculum—goals, assessments, methods, and materials. This framework gives all educators a systematic way to design lessons that includes flexible pathways and supports and various options and choices to help all students progress toward mastery (Rao & Meo, 2016).

The UDL map will guide us on a different journey. So how do we accomplish this massive undertaking and epic adventure? How do we embrace the opportunity that is Universal Design for Learning (UDL)? This book will do just that.

In the next sections, I will break down the three major principles underlying the UDL framework, unpack them for you, and explain their importance in the classroom. My colleagues will then each take a chapter to apply these principles to specific areas of content, pedagogy, and educational situations. By the time you are done with this book, you too will be eager to create your own universally designed lessons, themes, practices, and programs. And maybe, just maybe, you will feel inspired to check out your local pizzeria, so you too can change the world.

## THE "WHAT" OF UNIVERSAL DESIGN FOR LEARNING: REPRESENTATION

The recognition network manages the *what* of learning. Its job is to receive information and translate it. Learners are unique in how they comprehend information. The *what* of learning needs to be age appropriate, aligned to a specific set of standards or goals, and well organized, and the content needs to be valuable or authentic (Novak, 2016). When the brain is viewed using specific technology, (i.e., brain imaging), scientists can literally see the brain "light up" when recognition is activated (Nelson, 2013). If we want to experience this stimulation, we cannot deliver curriculum and instruction in only one way.

Often, teaching is designed as a "one-size-fits-all" approach for the mythical average learner, someone who excels by listening to lectures and reading printed text (Meyer & Rose, 2002). Although these practices are appropriate for some students, they don't work for all of them. In an inclusive classroom that values all learners, students don't have to be educated in a different setting to get what they need. All students deserve to know *what* they are learning while sitting in class together.

Teachers don't need to assign the same text to all students, or require a class to watch the same film. Similarly, the same vocabulary words don't have to be assigned to a class, as if their background knowledge and levels of vocabulary are the same. Learners need options and choices about what materials they will use to learn knowledge, build critical vocabulary, and comprehend information.

To ensure that all students know what they are learning, educators need to provide multiple means of representation. This can be accomplished through the UDL Guidelines for Representation, Table I.1, excerpted from *UDL Now* (Novak, 2016), which unpacks the UDL Guidelines and provides translations to make them more accessible. You will also have multiple examples in each of the following chapters in the book.

**Table 1.1**    Representation Guidelines From *UDL Now!*

| Provide Multiple Means of Representation | Translations |
|---|---|
| Provide options for perception<br>• Offer ways of customizing the display of information<br>• Offer alternatives for auditory information<br>• Offer alternatives for visual information | • Provide digital copies of all class materials so students can access and personalize them.<br>• Don't just lecture to students. Provide visuals and hard copies so all students can access at least one of the media.<br>• Don't just have students read. Also provide audio, visuals, and things for them to manipulate. |
| Provide options for language, mathematical expressions, and symbols<br>• Clarify vocabulary and symbols<br>• Clarify syntax and structure<br>• Support decoding of text, mathematical notation, and symbols<br>• Promote understanding across languages<br>• Illustrate through multiple media | • Preteach vocabulary and math symbols in student-friendly language.<br>• Point out text structures (like compare/contrast), sentence structure, or math formulas if they are important for learning.<br>• If you provide reading, provide scaffolding to bring student attention to most important content.<br>• If English is a second language for students, offer instructions in their home language(s).<br>• Simplify complicated directions to make student friendly.<br>• Always offer visuals like charts, pictures, movies, audio clips, and things for students to touch and manipulate. |
| Provide options for comprehension<br>• Activate or supply background knowledge<br>• Highlight patterns, critical features, big ideas, and relationships<br>• Guide information processing, visualization, and manipulation<br>• Maximize generalization and transfer | • Remind students what they already know about the content. If nothing, teach the necessary information.<br>• Make it clear what the most important information is by modeling comprehension strategies such as monitoring, highlighting, asking questions, and note taking.<br>• Provide work exemplars, explicit directions, and scaffolds so students can persist through the lesson.<br>• Help students see how they can use the new information in other classes, units, or settings. |

# THE "WHY" OF UNIVERSAL DESIGN FOR LEARNING: ENGAGEMENT

The affective network of the brain needs to know *why*. Once learners know *what* they are doing, they need to know *why* they are doing it. In order to instill a sense of *why* and wonder and purpose in our students, we have to provide multiple means of engagement.

Great educators must engage all students by providing expectations that optimize motivation; minimize all the threats, distractions, and barriers that get in the way of success; and, most important, optimize relevance, value, and authenticity so students realize that learning can actually get them somewhere, regardless of where they started. To do this, we have to provide all students with options to make learning meaningful. We know this sounds simple, and we know most of you want—and try—to engage your students. So what does UDL offer that teachers haven't tried for years?

There has been a tremendous amount of research that demonstrates the old way of teaching is simply not working for all students (Novak, 2017). Lecturing and reading textbooks are not the best tools at our disposal to allow all students to meet rigorous standards. We simply cannot teach to the whole class in the same way, even when we are working toward the same goals. In a UDL classroom, goals are unlinked from the means to achieve them so that teachers can provide students with multiple options and choices to experience success (Rose, Meyer, & Gordon, 2014). Repeat—*the goals are unlinked from the means to achieve them.*

Making the kind of impact needed to give our children equal opportunities at success requires a more personalized approach to teaching and

## CASE IN POINT

If we were to write a Greek myth today, it could be penned like this:

The brave student warrior stands stoically at the base of the climb. A great prize is perched atop Mount Olympus, where it stands guarded by mythical beasts. The warrior is ready for the challenge. He or she steps forth, in full body armour, and asks, "Why, dear teacher, am I undertaking this journey?" The teacher, an Amazonian wonder with muscles rippling like white water rapids, whispers, "Because you need to pass the state standardized test," or better yet, "Because I told you to."

At this point, the warrior is like, "This is stupid," and that's the end of the story.

learning (Sheninger & Murray, 2017). It requires us to dig deep to ask the question, "Is the curriculum [really] designed to optimize learning for all students?" (Hartmann, 2015, p. 57).

Without UDL, the answer to that simple question is often "no." Many students are simply not engaged in their learning. According to research, 66 percent of surveyed students reported being bored in every class or at least every day in school. Of these students, 98 percent claimed the material being taught was the main reason for their boredom, 81 percent thought their subject material was uninteresting, and two out of three students found the material lacked relevance (Yazzie-Mintz, 2010). Students are screaming for change! Our nation is at risk. We need to listen.

UDL provides a foundation to show schools and teachers how to meet the needs of all of our learners while also teaching them important skills for the future like self-direction, creativity, and problem solving (Novak, 2016). These strategies give all students a voice in the design and delivery of their own education and, as they change and evolve as learners, their education will change and evolve with them, challenging them to reach further and accomplish more.

We need students to learn for so many important reasons. We have to be really clear about the value of everything we're teaching; we also need to be very clear about the expected outcomes and *why* those are so critical. If we want our kids to love learning, we have to recruit their interest and help them to identify a meaningful goal—one that is equally meaningful to them, so they know *why* effort is important. We all know that it is not enough for us to just get our kids' attention. Success, or anything that is worth achieving, requires significant effort, intrinsic motivation, and the ability to self-regulate or cope when things get challenging.

Recent empirical studies highlight that motivation is a key factor in increasing interest, academic achievement, and personal growth but also requires a growth mindset, or the ability to believe that sustaining effort and persistence is worth it (Ng, 2018). Because achievement and growth require both motivation and challenge, educators need to anticipate the need to scaffold the ability to self-direct, make appropriate choices, personalize learning, and persist. This isn't as simple as letting students make choices; it is a process, and it will take work to become a streamlined, individualized, successful, and new way of teaching. Expert learning is a journey for both teachers and students, but one that is worth the effort when it is personalized and connected to meaningful and authentic goals (Meyer et al., 2014).

Educators should prepare students for their journey by helping them to build effort and persistence so they can select the goals, methods, materials, and assessments that allow them to be successful. This can be accomplished through the UDL Guidelines for Engagement. Table I.2, excerpted from *UDL Now* (Novak, 2016), unpacks the UDL Guidelines for Engagement.

**Table I.2**  Engagement Guidelines From *UDL Now!*

| Provide Multiple Means of Engagement | Translations |
|---|---|
| Provide options for self-regulation<br>• Promote expectations and beliefs that optimize motivation<br>• Facilitate personal coping skills and strategies<br>• Develop self-assessment and reflection | • Offer students tips on how to stay motivated and provide resources to prevent frustration; allow students to work in groups, use mentors or coaches, or just provide tips on how to persist and work with a text.<br>• Prevent students from getting upset or quitting by giving them scaffolds, positive reinforcement, break time, and so on.<br>• Encourage students to assess their own learning by using checklists and rubrics. |
| Provide options for sustaining effort and persistence<br>• Heighten salience of goals and objectives<br>• Vary demands and resources to optimize challenge<br>• Foster collaboration and communication<br>• Increase mastery-oriented feedback | • Ask students to restate a lesson's standard or objective and remind them about it often throughout the lesson.<br>• Provide varying levels of challenge so students can pick assignments that are not boring or too difficult for them.<br>• Allow students to work together.<br>• Give feedback often throughout each lesson using various methods like self-reflection, peer review, and teacher feedback. Don't just give feedback on final assessments. |
| Provide options for recruiting interest<br>• Optimize individual choice and autonomy<br>• Optimize relevance, value, and authenticity<br>• Minimize threats and distractions | • Allow students to make choices so they are more likely to be engaged in the curriculum.<br>• Tell students at the beginning of a lesson why it will be relevant to them. Make the connection explicit.<br>• Create a classroom environment where students feel safe and can express knowledge in ways that are best and most engaging to them. |

# THE "HOW" OF UNIVERSAL DESIGN FOR LEARNING: EXPRESSION

Once the affective network is activated and children know *why* they are learning, and the recognition network has interpreted *what* they need to know, it's time for the strategic network of the brain. The strategic network creates a strategy so students can apply the new knowledge or skill in a way that it is clear *how* they are going to use that new information. Using this lens, all assessments should be meaningful options for students to meet the objective that you set out at the beginning of the lesson.

For example, many teachers assess students' knowledge using the traditional "one-size-fits-all" approaches like multiple-choice tests, worksheets, or essays. These narrow and inflexible assessments do not allow all students to communicate their knowledge or skills, and are especially unfair for students with diverse backgrounds or who have differences in their abilities to learn (Hartmann, 2015). Additionally, they are definitely not authentic products or ones that learners would use in the real world. How many of you have been given a multiple-choice test in your jobs recently? UDL reminds us to provide multiple means of action and expression so all students can create authentic products while working toward the same goal.

For example, if the goal is to "write informative text," that objective can be met in many different ways. Some students may choose to write an essay about butterflies, while others choose to write advertising copy, a history of Manchester United's best soccer players, a technological manual, or a series of informative tweets. Students can use tools like exemplars, graphic organizers, sentence frames, word banks, or assistive technology to complete their task. For example, all students could have the option to use tools like those in the "Tech Tips" box. They can also be provided with more engaging and fun options for formative assessments, like using exit slips on *Google Forms*, in-class games like *Kahoot*, or kinesthetic response cards like *Plickers*. The options are endless!

**Tech Tips**

*Dragon Naturally Speaking*, *iMovie*, and *Google Read & Write* help students to express knowledge while working collaboratively, receiving feedback, and accessing scaffolds.

The overall point of having multiple means of action and expression is to allow students different ways to demonstrate that they have, indeed, mastered the very clear objective that you set out at the beginning of the lesson. If the teaching objective is clear, the ways in which students can demonstrate mastery or attainment of that objective shouldn't be limited only by what a textbook or paper/pencil test or a teacher's own skills dictate.

To learn how to provide multiple means of action and expression to students, view Table I.3, excerpted from *UDL Now* (Novak, 2016), which unpacks these guidelines.

## BRINGING IT ALL TOGETHER

In 1984, five individuals who believed in the power of learning had a goal. They wanted to make learning accessible for all students. Because their goal was relevant, authentic, and meaningful, they were determined to

**Table 1.3**  Action and Expression Guidelines From *UDL Now!*

| Provide Multiple Means of Action and Expression | Translations |
|---|---|
| Provide options for physical action<br>• Vary the methods for response and navigation<br>• Optimize access to tools and assistive technologies | • Give students the option of composing with different media (writing, typing, physically manipulating objects, and so on) when completing assignments.<br>• Allow students to use technology to express knowledge like using speech recognition software, typing, and so on. |
| Provide options for expression and communication<br>• Use multiple media for communication<br>• Use multiple tools for construction and composition<br>• Build fluencies with graduated levels of support for practice and performance | • Give students choices about how they will respond. Instead of just writing a response, they could perform a skit, make a poster, create a PowerPoint, and so on.<br>• Provide students with the tools they need to complete assignment: dictionaries, thesauruses, computers with spell check, voice recognition software, calculators, handouts with necessary formulas, and exemplars.<br>• Build scaffolding into every assignment and provide feedback while students are working. |
| Provide options for executive functions<br>• Guide appropriate goal setting<br>• Support planning and strategy development<br>• Facilitate managing information and resources<br>• Enhance capacity for monitoring progress | • Begin all assignments with an objective and rationale and provide work exemplars, scaffolds, and checklists for every assignment.<br>• At the beginning of each assignment, give students tips and checklists to help them work through the assignment.<br>• Give students a lot of tips on how to stay organized while they are completing each assignment. Some students don't know how to organize things on their own.<br>• Have students reflect on their learning by asking questions, and always provide many opportunities for students to get feedback before completing final drafts. |

create a strategy and fight until they arrived at their destination. Now, all of us are a part of their journey, and we are called to create our own path to optimize options and choices for all of our students.

The UDL framework presents all of us with a structure for designing curriculum and instruction for learners of all variability as we embrace the varied ways in which the learning networks function for each individual (Rao & Meo, 2016). As much as creating those options and choices and guiding your students in self-reflection and self-direction will sometimes feel a little like pushing a rock up a mountain, I can tell you from experience, I wouldn't trade that adventure for anything in the world. As a practitioner, UDL has allowed me to embrace the journey to expert learning . . . for both me and my students. I have also realized that the choices I create and the options I provide students continue to get easier for me over time, and sometimes, in the middle of the night, I wake up with a great idea. When this happens, I start to feel a little hungry. Hey, anyone want to go out for a slice of pizza?

**Provide multiple means of Engagement →**

Affective Networks
The "WHY" of learning

**Provide multiple means of Representation →**

Recognition Networks
The "WHAT" of learning

**Provide multiple means of Action & Expression →**

Strategic Networks
The "HOW" of learning

Provide options for
**Recruiting Interest (7) →**

- Optimize individual choice and autonomy (7.1) ›
- Optimize relevance, value, and authenticity (7.2) ›
- Minimize threats and distractions (7.3) ›

Provide options for
**Perception (1) →**

- Offer ways of customizing the display of information (1.1) ›
- Offer alternatives for auditory information (1.2) ›
- Offer alternatives for visual Information (1.3) ›

Provide options for
**Physical Action (4) →**

- Vary the methods for response and navigation (4.1) ›
- Optimize access to tools and assistive technologies (4.2) ›

Provide options for
**Sustaining Effort & Persistence (8) →**

- Heighten salience of goals and objectives (8.1) ›
- Vary demands and resources to optimize challenge (8.2) ›
- Foster collaboration and community (8.3) ›
- Increase mastery-oriented feedback (8.4) ›

Provide options for
**Language & Symbols (2) →**

- Clarify vocabulary and symbols (2.1) ›
- Clarify syntax and structure (2.2) ›
- Support decoding of text, mathematical notation, and symbols (2.3) ›
- Promote understanding across languages (2.4) ›
- Illustrate through multiple media (2.5) ›

Provide options for
**Expression & Communication (5) →**

- Use multiple media (or communication) (5.1) ›
- Use multiple tools for construction and composition (5.2) ›
- Build fluencies with graduated levels of support for practice and performance (5.3) ›

Provide options for
**Self-Regulation (9) →**

- Promote expectations and beliefs that optimize motivation (9.1) ›
- Facilitate personal coping skills and strategies (9.2) ›
- Develop self-assessment and reflection (9.3) ›

Provide options for
**Comprehension (3) →**

- Activate or supply background knowledge (3.1) ›
- Highlight patterns, critical features, big Ideas. and relationships (3.2) ›
- Guide information processing and visualization (3.3) ›
- Maximize tranfer and generalization (3.4) ›

Provide options for
**Executive Functions (6) →**

- Guide appropriate goal-setting (6.1) ›
- Support planning and strategy development (6.2) ›
- Facilitate managing information and resources (6.3) ›
- Enhance capacity for monitoring progress (6.4) ›

Access

Build

Internalize

**Expert Learnesr** who are . . .

**Purposeful & Motivated**

**Resourceful & Knowledgeable**

**Strategic & Goal-Directed**

Goal

*Source:* CAST (2018). Universal Design for Learning Guidelines version 2.2. Retrieved from http://udlguidelines.cast.org.

## TOP FIVE WEBSITES TO SUPPORT YOUR UNDERSTANDING OF UDL

➜ Check out my website to learn about all things UDL: www.katienovakudl.com

➜ The UDL Guidelines have a new home. Check out an interactive version of the UDL Guidelines here: http://udlguidelines.cast.org/

➜ The UDL Progression Rubric is a useful self-assessment tool for UDL practice. For each guideline and checkpoint, the authors identify teacher progress as Emerging, Proficient, and Progressing toward Expert Practice. http://castpublishing.org/novak-rodriguez-udl-progression-rubric/

➜ Access the full text to the book *UDL Theory and Practice* with a free login. In this book, Meyer and Rose, along with David Gordon, provide the first comprehensive presentations of UDL principles and practices since 2002. This new look at UDL includes contributions from CAST's research and implementation teams, as well as their collaborators in schools, universities, and research settings. http://udltheorypractice.cast.org/login

➜ The UDL-IRN and CAST launched Learning Designed, an online global community platform and educators' resource bank. Learn more about UDL and connect with like-minded educators: https://www.learningdesigned.org

## APPS WE LOVE

➜ *Dragon Anywhere*: In full disclosure, I wrote most of this chapter on *Dragon Anywhere*, which is marketed as professional-grade mobile dictation that makes it easy to create documents of any length and edit. Format and share them directly from your mobile device; the accuracy is incredible.

➜ *Google Read & Write*: Wonderfully intuitive and easy to use, Read & Write for Google Chrome provides personalized support to make documents and web pages more accessible.

➜ *iMovie*: This is an app where students can make videos. The app provides students with the ability to add text to the video, which is why it is a great option for multiple means of action and expression.

➜ *Kahoot* allows you to transform student devices into powerful formative assessment tools. Plus, students think they are a fun game!

➜ *Plickers* is a powerfully simple tool that lets teachers collect real-time formative assessment data without the need for student devices.

# REFERENCES

CAST. (2016). *CAST through the years: One mission, many innovations.* Retrieved from http://www.cast.org/about/timeline.html

Center for Universal Design. (2008). *About the center: Ron Mace.* Retrieved from https://projects.ncsu.edu/ncsu/design/cud/about_us/usronmace.htm

Hartmann, E. (2015). Universal Design for Learning (UDL) and learners with severe support needs. *International Journal of Whole Schooling, 11*(1), 54–67.

Hayes, T. C. (1984, February 25). Strong sales seen in '84 for Apple's Macintosh. *New York Times.* Retrieved from https://www.nytimes.com/1984/02/25/business/strong-sales-seen-in-84-for-apple-s-macintosh.html

Hitchcock, C., Meyer, A., Rose, D., & Jackson, R. (2002). Providing new access to the general curriculum: Universal Design for Learning. *TEACHING Exceptional Children, 35*(2), 8–17.

Katz, J., & Sokal, L. (2016). Universal Design for Learning as a bridge to inclusion: A qualitative report of student voices. *International Journal of Whole Schooling, 12*(2), 36–63.

Meo, G. (2008). Curriculum planning for all learners: Applying Universal Design for Learning (UDL) to a high school reading comprehension program. *Preventing School Failure, 52*(2), 21–30.

Meyer, A., Rose, D. H., & Gordon, D. (2014). *Universal Design for Learning: Theory and practice.* Wakefield, MA: CAST Professional.

Moore, S. (2007). David H. Rose, Anne Meyer, Teaching every student in the digital age: Universal Design for Learning [Book review]. *Educational Technology Research and Development, 55,* 521–525. doi:10.1007/s11423-007-9056-3

National Center on Universal Design for Learning (UDL). (2017). *About the National UDL Task Force.* Retrieved from http://www.udlcenter.org/advocacy/taskforce

Nelson, L. L. (2013). *Design and deliver: Planning and teaching using Universal Design for Learning.* Baltimore, MD: Brookes Publishing.

Ng, B. (2018). The neuroscience of growth mindset and intrinsic motivation. *Brain Sciences, 8*(20). doi:10.3390/brainsci8020020

Novak, K. (2016). *UDL now! A teacher's guide to applying Universal Design for Learning in today's classrooms.* Wakefield, MA: CAST Professional.

Novak, K. (2017). *Let them thrive: A playbook for helping your child succeed in school and in life.* Wakefield, MA: CAST Professional.

Rao, K., & Meo, G. (2016). Using Universal Design for Learning to design standards-based lessons. *SAGE Open.* doi:10.1177/2158244016680688

Rose, D. H., & Meyer, A. (2002). *Teaching every student in the Digital Age: Universal Design for Learning.* Alexandria, VA: Association for Supervision and Curriculum Development.

Rose, D. H., Meyer, A., & Gordon, D. (2014). Reflections: Universal Design for Learning and the common core. *The Special EDge, 27*(2), 3–5.

Sheninger, E. C., & Murray, T. C. (2017). *Learning transformed: 8 keys to designing tomorrow's schools, today.* Alexandria, VA: ASCD.

U.S. National Commission on Excellence in Education. (1983). *A nation at risk: The imperative for educational reform: A report to the nation and the Secretary of Education.* Washington, DC: U.S. Department of Education.

Vygotsky, L. S. (1962). *Thought and language.* Cambridge, MA: MIT Press.

Yazzie-Mintz, E. (2010). *Charting the path from engagement to achievement: A report on the 2009 High School Survey of Student Engagement* [Electronic version]. Bloomington, IN: Center for Evaluation and Education Policy.

# SECTION I

## *What Really Works With Content Areas*

1

# *UDL and Literacy*

## *Providing Options for Language Success*

Ruby L. Owiny
*Trinity International University*

Anne Brawand
*Kutztown University*

Janet Josephson
*Millersville University of Pennsylvania*

## SETTING THE STAGE FOR UDL AND LITERACY

How in the world does Universal Design for Learning (UDL) apply to literacy? Doesn't one just give a book or a pencil and paper to a student and voilà, they're reading and writing? If you're reading this chapter, chances are you picked up on the sarcasm. Of course, there's more to literacy than that. Literacy, or English Language Arts (ELA), not only encompasses reading and writing, but also speaking, listening, viewing, and visually representing, both digitally and in traditional print. Updated literacy standards (International Literacy Association, 2017) include all of these components. Besides having firsthand experience with the enormity of trying to cover each literacy component, you know the challenge of teaching to mastery! The goal of this chapter is to help that task feel less daunting by giving you tools to implement the principles of UDL.

This chapter will focus on reading and written expression, primarily language in its multiple print and digital forms. Within these sub-areas, there are several elements. Reading includes five elements: phonological awareness, phonics, vocabulary, fluency, and comprehension. Written expression includes the rules of grammar, spelling, and mechanics, along with writing for various purposes and audiences.

ELA teachers must think in terms of "literacy," which focuses on meaning. Lê (2018) notes that there are multiple literacies and ways to find meaning, not just through printed text. Comprehension isn't always clear in messages being sent and received in an increasingly complex world. So, then, how do we help our students develop this "critical literacy"? The answer lies in the Introduction to this book! Novak notes that one goal of UDL is to train students to be efficient learners and to make wise choices to meet their goals. Critical literacy provides students with the ability to seek answers to questions they have while reflecting about the world around them (Cutler, 2018), which is ultimately the goal of reading and writing.

Do you want more "bang for your buck"? Do you want to help all students in your inclusive classroom access the general curriculum and succeed? Research supports that application of UDL principles increases achievement in reading and writing across grade levels and abilities (e.g., Coyne, Evans, & Karger, 2017). The National Assessment of Educational Progress shows that only 36 percent of the nation's eighth graders were reading at a proficient level in 2017. Reading proficiency is defined as summarizing a text, identifying themes, making inferences, connecting texts to make meaning, and analyzing text features for comprehension (National Center for Education Statistics, 2018). We've got some work to do!

The word *reading* might conjure an image of sitting at a desk with a book on the desktop and a student bent over the book, reading intently. The word *writing* might make you think of a student with a pencil and a notebook, sitting at her desk, writing with perfect handwriting. Is this what you envision when you think about students participating in reading and writing activities? These are not inaccurate images, but let's push the envelope a bit. What if reading could be in a bean bag with a friend reading a favorite blog, or writing could be a series of tweets while lying on a rug under a desk with a personal tablet? These images of reading and writing might be more in line with classrooms today. You might be asking how in the world UDL applies here. We'll get to that! Keep reading.

## PUTTING UDL AND LITERACY INTO PRACTICE: REPRESENTATION

A major principle of UDL is representation, or the "what" of learning. Providing multiple ways of approaching strategic tasks (e.g., perception and comprehension of new material) guides the design of learning environments as part of the UDL framework (Meyer, Rose, & Gordon, 2014). Consider how the guidelines of representation (perception, language and symbols, and comprehension) play a role in developing reading and writing skills.

## Perception

Encourage students to use more than one sense when engaging in literacy instruction, rather than having all instruction rely on written or oral language. Teaching literacy is a bit easier when we consider the bazillions (okay, maybe not that many) of types of media our students can access (e.g., vlogs, blogs, e-mails, print books, audio books, digital books, etc.). Text features, such as graphs, tables, pictures, and font sizes and styles, are all parts of text-based messages of various types. Here are some strategies for representation:

- **USE VARYING APPROACHES TO DEVELOP FLUENCY when reading various texts** (e.g., voice inflection to demonstrate emotions). Prosody, tone, and rate of speech are also important when teaching fluency. Students can record themselves to self-evaluate or peer-evaluate fluency based on the above characteristics.

- **INCORPORATE AMERICAN SIGN LANGUAGE (ASL) for students to practice spelling or vocabulary words.** It will reinforce English language skills while introducing a new language that will include students who sign as their primary language.

**Tech Tip**

Don't know ASL? Have your students learn alongside you by using:

- The ASL app
- Lifeprint.com
- Signingsavvy.com
- YouTube!
- Signingtime.com

- **UTILIZE TEXT FEATURES and other visuals such as charts and graphs to emphasize points.** Allow students to use text features in their work, too, rather than requiring only narrative descriptions. Digital versions also allow for enlargement of text, enhancing details of pictures, or text-to-voice. You may even want to introduce the "Accessibility" features on most smartphones. Many individuals do not even know they are there!

- **INCORPORATE THE SENSES when appropriate.** Using a variety of senses to help with description, narrative, characterization, and perception can make work far more interesting. Use a variety of lighting, fidgets, and seating with varying textures, or aromatherapy during writer's workshop or independent reading to help students engage more of their senses.

## Language and Symbols

This is where literacy and UDL really get heated up! When we think about representation in terms of language and symbols, we plan for instruction that provides multiple ways for students to interact with content-specific vocabulary and symbols. This includes idioms, slang, and notation symbols, to name a few. In addition, we must provide opportunities for students to work with the way words and phrases are arranged (syntax), which is necessary for all content areas (e.g., mathematics) and various literary forms (e.g., poems, fiction, nonfiction, including content-area specific texts). We must explicitly teach those forms to our students while also teaching the structures within those forms, including tables, graphs, etc. Decoding of text, in addition to providing opportunities for students to learn in their native language, is also important. Finally, we must provide students with opportunities to engage with content through multiple media. Here are some concrete tips for providing various methods of representation with language and symbols:

- **CREATE A WORD WALL FOR PERTINENT VOCABULARY** in which students take turns writing the word and representing the word graphically (Novak, 2016). Think how cool a student-driven word wall would be, at all grade levels!
- **PRACTICE IDIOMS OR FIGURES OF SPEECH through student-created skits using idioms, similes, or metaphors.** This allows for silliness and creativity! They can use iMovie to produce their work or create a cartoon using Pixton.com.
- **PROVIDE VOCABULARY WORDS and their definitions in the languages represented in your classroom or languages of interest to your students.** Couple that with visuals (lessonpix.com is a wonderful resource for this!) and you'll be helping your students who are English language learners, but your other students will learn new languages as well!

## Comprehension

This will come as no surprise to you—education is all about comprehension. In fact, this is the ultimate goal within representation. As Rose (2010) points out, this is the highest level of representation. Moving students to the point where they independently derive meaning from messages they receive, either by reading or listening, is the pinnacle of instruction. How do we promote comprehension within a UDL framework? Well, you're likely already doing many of these things. We must consider multiple ways to make learning accessible and explicitly teach students how to take that knowledge and use it appropriately. Think about how you might use these strategies to build comprehension skills in a variety of ways:

- **ACTIVATE PRIOR KNOWLEDGE before starting a new unit or reading a new text.** Do a "brain spill." Put chart paper on tables, give every student a writing utensil, and let them spill their ideas all over the paper, all at once. Want to increase choice? Let students choose their writing utensil or even how they want to "spill" their ideas (e.g., chart paper, Post-its, pictures, texting the teacher).
- **EXTEND LEARNING BEYOND THE LANGUAGE ARTS CLASSROOM.** Teach comprehension strategies in the content areas, and conversely, use content area text and media in the language arts classroom. This will help students generalize learning and see the big ideas more clearly.
- **PROVIDE LOTS OF EXAMPLES AND NONEXAMPLES verbally, written, pictorially, and through real objects.** Play games and use manipulatives to identify the examples from the nonexamples.

## CASE IN POINT

Ms. Walerczak is beginning a first-grade social studies unit comparing rural and urban life. She identifies background knowledge through a KWL chart for students to state what they already **know** and create questions about what they **want** to learn. Later, students will summarize their learning in the **learn** column. Students compare rural and urban life by choosing to watch a YouTube video of Jan Brett's book *Town Mouse, Country Mouse*; listen to it via the Audible app on their iPads; or read the book independently or with a peer. They complete a Venn diagram in groups to show similarities and differences, choosing their preferred method—digital, written, or drawing. Finally, students access their diagrams while viewing a Google slideshow with pictures of Ms. Walerczak's recent trip to Chicago and of her grandfather's farm in Kansas. They are encouraged to add to their diagrams as they view the slideshow. Students may look at the photos on the large screen or individual iPads via a shared link.

## PUTTING UDL AND LITERACY INTO PRACTICE: ENGAGEMENT

Let's continue with the principle of engagement, or the "why" of learning. Student engagement and motivation to learn are prompted by a variety of factors (Meyer, Rose, & Gordon, 2014). In thinking about engagement in literacy, we'll take a look at the influence of motivation, how to maintain effort, and the development of comprehension skills.

### Motivation for Reading and Writing

Capturing student interest by offering options for learning is one factor that leads to engagement in literacy. How many of us remember choosing books from libraries followed by an eagerness to read them? Providing choice of age-relevant content to be read, a context for guided practice and feedback, as well as opportunities to socialize in online discussions, are examples of how teachers have successfully increased student engagement and motivation (Coyne et al., 2017). Here are specific motivational strategies to incorporate student engagement into literacy:

- **HAVE STUDENTS CHOOSE THE STYLE in which they write (or type) a word, the color and size of the font, and how they graphically depict the meaning of that word. Based on experi-**ence, we recommend you state that the style must be legible. There are some very creative—and impish—students out there!

**Tech Tips**

Learn about Udio in the "Take a Tour" video: http://www.cast.org/our-work/research-development/projects/literacy-udio-center-emerging-technology-middle-school-disabilities.html#.Wv2KgcaZM6g

- **ENGAGE STUDENTS IN AN ONLINE UDL LITERACY ENVI-RONMENT** (e.g., Udio; Coyne et al., 2017). Students navigate the environment using embedded supports (e.g., audio-assisted reading) and teachers can assess progress through electronic usage logs and student-produced discussions.

- **PROVIDE CHOICE OF WRITING (e.g., factual essays, personal narratives) to increase motivation.** Simply be sure the objective of the writing activity is clear. Rubrics can help with this. Also, the spell check feature in Google Docs assists with word choice!

- **INCORPORATE A STUDENT RECOGNITION CEREMONY that acknowledges certain milestones achieved in reading.** Many classrooms use progress monitoring systems that have that data readily available. Some companies (e.g., Pizza Hut) offer incentives according to number of books or minutes read.

## Maintaining Student Effort

This brings us to our next task of maintaining student effort and interest. By teaching students to regulate their progress, they know how far they have come or need to go and are typically motivated by feeling that success or challenge. This self-regulation develops independent learners, which is the goal of a UDL-centered environment. Scaffolding is another way to maximize student effort by balancing knowledge of a student's learning strengths and weaknesses and knowledge of the curriculum demands (Dexter, Park, & Hughes, 2011). Examples of strategies to keep students engaged and executing increased effort with academic tasks in literacy include:

- **TEACH STUDENTS TO SET GOALS.** They can graph progress to show improvement or record a writing goal, compose a piece, and reflect on how they met their goal (or not).
- **CONSISTENTLY OFFER TIME FOR STUDENT PRACTICE for reading and writing progress.** Be sure to provide time for teacher feedback as well.
- **SCAFFOLD THROUGH SELF-REGULATED STRATEGY DEVELOPMENT** for any students requiring more explicit guided writing practice (Harris, Graham, & Mason, 2006). Several articles offer SRSD implementation tips in multiple settings for students of various ability levels (Gillespie Rouse & Kiuhara, 2017; Leins, Cuenca-Carlino, Kiuhara, & Jacobson, 2017; Mason, Harris, & Graham, 2011; Shora & Hott, 2016).

## Comprehension Instruction

An ultimate goal of literacy instruction is comprehension, which stems from the motivation of readers to efficiently apply comprehension strategies (National Reading Panel, 2000). Proficiency with comprehension strategies can also have a positive impact on writing quality. Some engaging UDL strategies for teaching comprehension strategies include reciprocal teaching (Hall, Cohen, Vue, & Ganley, 2015) and story mapping (Narkon & Wells, 2013). Specific examples for engaging students in reading comprehension instruction are:

- **ENGAGE STUDENTS IN PEER-TO-PEER MENTORING/ TUTORING through reciprocal teaching of comprehension strategies.** Be sure, however, that you are not inadvertently always having stronger or gifted students become de facto "tutors." It is important that all students receive appropriate challenge, support, and instruction.

- **CONDUCT INDIVIDUAL STUDENT CONFERENCES** to discuss the text and further improve reading comprehension while the rest of the class is engaged at learning stations. When collaborating with another educator, such as in a co-teaching situation, conferences can be done easily using the Alternative Teaching approach.

**Making Connections**

See Chapter 9 for more on UDL with Co-teaching.

- **USE INTERACTIVE STORY MAPPING** (e.g., Kidspiration) to increase engagement and interaction for students who have difficulty with reading and writing.

## PUTTING UDL AND LITERACY INTO PRACTICE: EXPRESSION

The final principle of UDL is action and expression, or the "how" of learning. When teachers provide options for students to show what they know, they are implementing the principle of action and expression (Meyer et al., 2014). By providing choices to students, they are also empowering them to become expert learners in identifying how they can best show what they know. By providing students with options for physical action, expression and communication, and executive function supports, you can pave the way to increasing students' access to literacy instruction.

### Options for Physical Action in the Literacy Classroom

When we think about making our instruction accessible to all students, we need to consider the learning, emotional, behavioral, social, and also physical needs of our students. Providing options for physical action in your literacy classroom can provide your students with more opportunities to show what they know (Harvey et al., 2017). Increasing the level of physical action in the literacy classroom is just one way to increase behavioral, social, and even emotional engagement.

- **VARY THE WAYS IN WHICH STUDENTS INTERACT WITH MATERIALS** to allow for physical action. Instead of providing one paper-and-pencil multiple-choice exam, students can choose how they take the exam (orally, on a computer, projected on the wall—the options are endless!). Also, students can create a class wiki, a screencast essay, or videos. They can tweet responses, post them on an electronic whiteboard, or tell them to a peer. The key is to allow students options that are physically accessible.

**Tech Tips**

- Learn more about Chat Stations by watching this quick video on how to make this work in your classroom: https://www.youtube.com/watch?v=eFUL4yP0vqo YouTube!

- **DIFFERENTIATE by providing access to adapted technology for those who need it.** This might include such items as alternative keyboards for writing activities (perhaps those that are enlarged or controlled by eye gaze). It is also important to teach keyboard shortcuts (cut/copy/paste) and how to utilize the built-in speech-to-text features for writing activities for all students.
- **USE TOTAL PHYSICAL RESPONSE (TPR),** well known by teachers of English as a Second Language (Asher, 2009), but beneficial for all students. TPR has students associate movement with a concept to aid memory and retention.

### Options for Expression and Communication in the Literacy Classroom

When teachers encourage the use of multiple forms of media, teach multiple tools for construction of ideas, and provide graduated levels of support for practice and performance, students learn how to communicate their learning more accurately. This allows teachers to more readily assess student learning. This next section provides tips for how you can provide options for expression and communication to support all students.

- **PROVIDE ALTERNATIVES TO PAPER-AND-PENCIL RESPONSE by changing how you write your objectives.** Instead of writing lesson objectives that begin with "Students will write," consider how a broader objective, such as "Students will create an example," can allow for more student choice and voice in how they demonstrate their learning.
- **CONSIDER THE INTEGRATION OF MULTIPLE TOOLS for construction of literature responses such as using the Udio online platform for sentence starters** (Coyne et al., 2017). To assist students with spelling, a variety of spell-checking programs and tools are available. Students can choose which one to use.
- **USE A SCREENCAST OR AUDIO RECORDING to provide differentiated feedback.** Students hear your voice, giving feedback as you refer to specific parts of their submission, eliminating much of the confusion of written feedback.

### Executive Function Supports for the Literacy Classroom

Executive functioning is about managing oneself and one's time to achieve a goal. When teachers provide students with options for goal setting, assist students in planning long-term

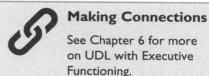

**Making Connections**

See Chapter 6 for more on UDL with Executive Functioning.

**Tech Tips**

Trello is an app that can be particularly helpful for long-term group projects. Students can assign tasks to each other and prioritize tasks. https://trello.com

projects, and teach students how to monitor their progress, students with literacy challenges are able to shine in the literacy classroom.

- **INTRODUCE BACKWARDS TIMELINES** and teach students how to create them from due date to project implementation using organizational apps, calendar reminders, written reminder, or other approaches.
- **PROVIDE EXPLICIT FEEDBACK using rubrics and check-lists** that can help students focus on specific areas to target for improvement.
- **ASSIST STUDENTS WITH INFORMATION MANAGE-MENT so they don't feel that they have to rely on their memory alone.** Students in all grades typically research and present their findings on a topic. Teaching students techniques for keeping track of what they have learned allows them to choose a method that works best for them.

### CASE IN POINT

Mr. Markel teaches ninth-grade Literature. He knows that his students have great ideas, but these ideas are hardly ever captured in the work they submit. Mr. Markel introduces the class to iMovie and gives students the choice of completing their upcoming papers via iMovie as a video journal. Some of the students had been using iMovie for years and chose to use alternatives such as Filmora, VirtualDub, and Adobe Premiere Pro for additional challenge, while others had never used iMovie before. Mr. Markel includes a long-term timeline to help all students monitor their progress and meet the assignment deadline. Mr. Markel continues to assess students' language conventions and the structure of their writing in this alternative format.

## BRINGING IT ALL TOGETHER

Whew! This was a lot of material to cover! We hope that you are ener-gized to use the UDL principles in your classroom to enhance student literacy in all content areas. Remember: the goal is to develop comprehension, executive functioning skills, and self-regulation to move students from dependence on you, as the teacher, to independently making meaning from messages they receive and to clearly articulate messages they send, in a variety of formats. Student choice and taking advantage of the plethora of resources now available via apps and the web, while continuing the use of more traditional materials, will increase the use of UDL while improving the literacy skills of your students. We started your list of application ideas in Table 1.1; now it is up to you to keep adding to it!

**Table 1.1**   Implementing UDL in Your Literacy Environment

| UDL Principle | Examples | Implementation |
|---|---|---|
| Representation | Remind | Students can text responses or questions to the teacher without sharing phone numbers. |
| | Twitter | Students can tweet to summarize learning or to answer questions in a discussion. |
| | Pixton or Powtoon | Students (or the teacher) can create cartoons to illustrate concepts. |
| Engagement | Kidspiration | Students can summarize story information while reading through an interactive story map. |
| | Storyboard That | Students can plan and organize writing and add scenes/props to the storyboards they create. |
| | Google Docs/ Drive | Students can access the Google Intelligent Spellchecking feature, which provides word choices. |
| Action and Expression | Padlet | Students can share their thoughts in a number of modalities including text, image, link, audio, and video. |
| | Jing, Screencastomatic, or iMovie | Students can use Jing to create original screencasts as a means for showing what they have learned. |
| | Mendeley, EndNote, or RefWorks | Students can learn how to select and use a document management system that works best for them. |

## TOP FIVE WEBSITES TO SUPPORT LITERACY

→ http://lessonpix.com

→ https://www.newsela.com

→ https://www.readinga-z.com

→ http://www.readwritethink.org

→ https://rewordify.com

## APPS WE LOVE

→ iReady (K–12)

→ IXL (preK–12)

→ Lexia (K–12)

→ MobyMax (K–8)

→ ReadWorks (K–12)

## RECOMMENDED READINGS

Dalton, B., & Proctor, C. P. (2007). Reading as thinking: Integrating strategy instruction in a universally designed digital literacy environment. In D. S. McNamara (Ed.), *Reading comprehension strategies: Theories, interventions, and technologies* (pp. 421–439). Mahwah, NJ: Lawrence Erlbaum.

Rapp, W. H. (2014). *Universal Design for Learning in action: 100 ways to teach all learners.* Baltimore, MD: Paul H. Brookes.

# REFERENCES

Asher, J. J. (2009). *Learning another language through actions* (7th ed.). Los Gatos, CA: Sky Oaks.

Coyne, P., Evans, M., & Karger J. (2017). Use of a UDL literacy environment by middle school students with intellectual and developmental disabilities. *Intellectual and Developmental Disabilities, 55,* 4–14.

Cutler, L. (2018). Challenging the familiar: Using fractured fairy tales to introduce critical literacy. *Literacy Today, 35*(6), 36–37.

Dexter, D. D., Park, Y. J., & Hughes, C. A. (2011). A meta-analytic review of graphic organizers and science instruction for adolescents with learning disabilities: Implications for the intermediate and secondary science classroom. *Learning Disabilities Research and Practice, 26,* 204–213.

Gillespie Rouse, A., & Kiuhara, S. A. (2017). SRSD in writing and professional development for teachers: Practice and promise for elementary and middle school students with learning disabilities. *Learning Disabilities Research & Practice, 32,* 180–188. doi:10.1111/ldrp.12140

Hall, T. E., Cohen, N., Vue, G., & Ganley, P. (2015). Addressing learning disabilities with UDL and technology: Strategic reader. *Learning Disability Quarterly, 38,* 2–83.

Harris, K. R., Graham, S., & Mason, L. H. (2006). Improving the writing, knowledge, and motivation of struggling young writers: Effects of self-regulated strategy development with and without peer support. *American Educational Research Journal, 43,* 295–340.

Harvey, S. P., Lambourne, K., Greene, J. L., Gibson, C. A., Lee, J., & Donnelly, J. E. (2017). The effects of physical activity on learning behaviors in elementary school children: A randomized controlled trial. *Contemporary School Psychology,* 1–10.

International Literacy Association. (2017). *Standards for the preparation of literacy professionals 2017.* Retrieved from https://www.literacyworldwide.org/get-resources/standards/standards-2017

Lê, M. (2018). All the time is story time: The power of picture books in literacy education. *Literacy Today, 35*(6), 30–31.

Leins, P. A., Cuenca-Carlino, Y., Kiuhara, S. A., & Jacobson, L. T. (2017). The flexibility of self-regulated strategy development for teaching argumentative text. *Intervention in School & Clinic, 53,* 81–87. doi:10.1177/1053451217693367

Mason, L. H., Harris, K. R., & Graham, S. (2011). Self-regulated strategy development for students with writing difficulties. *Theory Into Practice, 50,* 20–27. doi: 10.1080/00405841.2011.534922

Meyer, A., Rose, D. H., & Gordon, D. (2014). *Universal Design for Learning: Theory and practice.* Wakefield, MA: CAST Professional Publishing.

Narkon, D. E., & Wells, J. C. (2013). Improving reading comprehension for elementary students with learning disabilities: UDL enhanced story mapping. *Preventing School Failure, 57,* 231–239. doi:10.1080/1045988X.2012.726286

National Center for Education Statistics. (2018). The NAEP reading achievement levels by grade. Retrieved from https://nces.ed.gov/nationsreportcard/reading

National Reading Panel. (2000). *Teaching children to read: An evidence-based assessment of the scientific research literature on reading and its implications for reading instruction* (National Institute of Child Health Pub. No. 00–4769). Washington, DC: National Institute of Child Health and Human Development.

Novak, K. (2016). *UDL now! A teacher's guide to applying Universal Design for Learning in today's classrooms*. Wakefield, MA: CAST.

Rose, D. (2010). UDL guidelines structure. Retrieved from https://www.youtube.com/watch?v=wVTm8vQRvNc

Shora, N., & Hott, B. (2016). Write on: Improving persuasive writing using the POW+TREE strategy. *Beyond Behavior, 25,* 14–20.

# 2

# *UDL and Mathematics*

## *Making Algebra Accessible*

Sarah A. Nagro
*George Mason University*

Jaime True Daley
*University of Delaware*

Cathy R. Gaspard
*California State University, Northridge*

## SETTING THE STAGE FOR UDL AND MATH

Wait, what? Algebra is the gatekeeper for math success? Say it isn't so! But yes, algebra serves as a gateway to advanced math courses in the short term and advantages in college and career opportunities in the long term (Watt, Watkins, & Abbitt, 2016). In 1997, The U.S. Department of Education published a paper titled "Mathematics Equals Opportunity" and explained that mathematics generally and algebra specifically are the "key to college entrance and success in the labor force" (p. 5). Fast-forward to 2019, and the most recent national math performance data are showing our students at fourth, eighth, and twelfth grades are failing at math (U.S. Department of Education, 2015, 2017). When it comes to algebra specifically, our students are able to demonstrate understanding of only the most basic concepts. For example, students in fourth grade are not able to determine a proportional relationship (e.g., if Bryce sells grilled cheese sandwiches at the deli for $2.50 each, then he sells two sandwiches for $5.00). There is a clear gap between the skills necessary to be proficient in algebra and the skills of the average student. Yikes! The idea that algebra is an essential aspect of every student's education is not new, but what can we do to help our students who are struggling?

Wendy Ward Hoffer, a nationally board-certified math teacher, shared this quote in 2015:

> If we believe that math is difficult or inaccessible, that the important work of math is memorizing and following procedures, and that some kids are born capable and others not, we create classrooms where . . . failure is an acceptable option for some. . . . Yet, if instead we believe that all students can and must learn math, that the important work of math is thinking, and that all learners are capable of mastery, we create classrooms where teachers serve as coaches, students engage as a community of learners, and all can "get it" together. Creating such communities takes courage, effort, and patience, but the payoffs are tremendous.

Improving student outcomes through effective mathematics instruction remains the key. The Every Student Succeeds Act (ESSA) of 2015 explains what effective instructional activities look like. ESSA emphasizes that states should

- offer well-rounded educational experiences for all students;
- include increased access to and improved engagement and achievement in mathematics;
- support the learning needs of all students using the principles of universal design for learning;
- provide increased access to personalized, rigorous learning experiences;
- improve instruction and personalize learning using technology; and
- develop or use strategies that are innovative or evidence-based.

That's a lot to accomplish. So what does this all mean? When we are teaching math it is important to personalize our instruction, leverage our students' strengths, and allow them to engage in learning through flexible learning environments supported by research. Universal Design for Learning (UDL) is an approach to accomplishing this goal. A universally designed learning environment accounts for the learning objective, potential barriers for students working toward this objective, and supports and structures necessary for students to have frequent opportunities to demonstrate their understanding of the objective (Novak, 2016).

The purpose of this chapter is to explain how research-based practices, within a UDL framework that includes multiple modes of presentation, expression, and engagement, can be used to teach math effectively. We will focus on algebra, the gatekeeper, but show how these approaches can be used across the math curriculum with some thoughtfulness and planning. Specific practices such as including opportunities for student choice while meeting learning objectives, embedding movement into instruction, and incorporating visual supports will be shared. Additionally, concepts such as empowering students to be flexible thinkers by using heuristics or mental shortcuts, asking students to discuss their math reasoning, and sequencing or providing a range of examples are effective math practices that will be discussed (Gersten et al., 2009). When teachers use math activities such as games or peer learning that are self-directed, appropriately challenging (i.e., not at students' frustration level), and grounded in content, students have the opportunity to extend their math reasoning and thinking in engaging ways.

## PUTTING UDL AND MATH INTO PRACTICE: REPRESENTATION

Tasks that create opportunities for students to analyze multiple representations simultaneously can help students make sense of math connections. Creating a task where students are exposed to multiple representations also provides varying entry points for students with different levels of knowledge, therefore increasing engagement (National Center on Intensive Intervention, 2016). Multiple representations can be used in a variety of ways during math instruction. Great news! This list of strategies will allow you to facilitate your students' self-directed learning. Try these:

- **GENERATE A CUSTOMIZED VIDEO LIBRARY.** Start by creating your own Schoology, Edmodo, Canvas, Google Classroom, or other learning management system with a folder designated for video links and downloads. Create folders for each of the mathematical processes in your state standards. Use Khan Academy, Teaching Channel, BrainPOP, BrainPOP Jr., and other video resources to search for and add specific videos to each folder. Generate a table of contents and provide full access to your students so they can self-direct their research but find vetted resources.
- **REPRESENT CONCEPTS IN VIDEO.** Record yourself (with students, if appropriate) teaching concepts. For example, you might read math-related stories (e.g., *Math Curse,* by J. Schezka), demonstrate use of concrete manipulatives to solve an equation,

or demonstrate the steps to solving an algorithm. Provide twenty-four-hour access to instructional videos via your library so students can self-guide their pre-learning and re-learning as needed. You might add video models of math think-alouds you create or allow students to record their thinking by talking about their selected approach to solving a problem.

- **FLIP YOUR CLASS.** During face-to-face class time, mathematical problem solving and communicating in collaborative partnerships and groups must be maximized. One way to achieve maximum student engagement is to represent the concepts the night before class as homework. Provide your instruction via video that students can watch as many times as they need in order to begin understanding the concept (Sams & Bergmann, 2012). During class, provide many opportunities for students to practice problem solving and communicating their thinking with your facilitation and personalized coaching, rather than lecturing the whole class.

- **READ MATH STORIES.** Entire math libraries are available for purchase through companies such as Scholastic, but your school library may have titles as well. Marilyn Burns's *Math Reads* website provides lists of twenty-five books per grade level, such as *Can You Count to a Googol?* Math teachers who display fiction and nonfiction books and magazines help reluctant learners to access math content in a socially meaningful, familiar format that demonstrates concepts' authentic applications.

- **PROVIDE MULTIPLE SOLUTIONS TO ONE PROBLEM.** Aim to ask open-ended math problems with multiple solutions, and provide ample time for students to discuss various approaches. Asking open-ended questions does two things for students. First, it helps them understand that there isn't a definite "this way is the right way" to answer math questions. Second, it allows you the opportunity to say, "Tell me more" so that you can check the metacognitive strategies that students are using to solve problems.

For example, you can give everyone in class the same math word problem to solve: "A football team is down by six points with four minutes left in the game. Show one set of plays they can make in order to progress 75 yards to make a touchdown

> **Tech Tips**
>
> Students might also benefit from virtual manipulatives as one of the multiple means of representation. Check out the National Library of Virtual manipulatives, http://nlvm.usu.edu/en/nav/topic_t_2.html

and win the game. Solve the problem using an approach that works for you." Students should have access to multiple pathways for solving this problem such as using concrete manipulatives like colored tiles, or pictorial representations like a number line, or even algorithms modeled on an anchor chart to support their preferred approach to solving this word problem.

- **MODEL CONCEPTS USING WEB-BASED MATH TOOLS.** Websites such as www.geogebra.com and www.desmos.com allow you to customize math instruction for innumerable concepts. For example, you can model, then guide learners to select self-guided instruction in their individual areas of need using GeoGebra, while providing coaching as needed. Using DesMos, you can provide multiple representations of concepts that students can manipulate, question, discuss, and justify with your guidance.

- **PROVIDE MULTIPLE ENTRY POINTS.** Graduated instructional sequences, such as concrete-representational-abstract (CRA), help students build bridges between various representations of the same mathematical concept promoting comprehension as opposed to strict memorization. Through CRA, students are able to better generalize math skills and understand processes (Gersten et al., 2009; Jones, Inglis, Gilmore, & Evans, 2013) and CRA allows students multiple entry points to the same question. The CRA sequence includes multiple exposures to concrete demonstrations, representational or pictorial depictions of the same probes or problems, and abstract depictions or symbolic notations. The CRA sequence is often referred to as the bridge between abstract mathematical theory and active student engagement in learning. So think of the UDL approach as a Segway that allows students to transport back and forth over the bridge with greater ease. Figure 2.1 on the next page illustrates one way teachers can use a graphic organizer to help students solve problems using the CRA sequence.

Overall, the goal is for all students, regardless of their proficiency on a given math topic, to be empowered to engage in the lesson, participate in strategy development, experience problem solving, articulate their reasoning, and understand their solutions (Buchheister, Jackson, & Taylor, 2017). Mental flexibility is a desirable learning characteristic in math because students who can approach one problem from multiple entry points are more likely to take academic risks, generalize concepts across topic areas, and exhibit perseverance in learning (Gurganus, 2017).

**Figure 2.1**    Multiple Representation Graphic Organizer With CRA Embedded

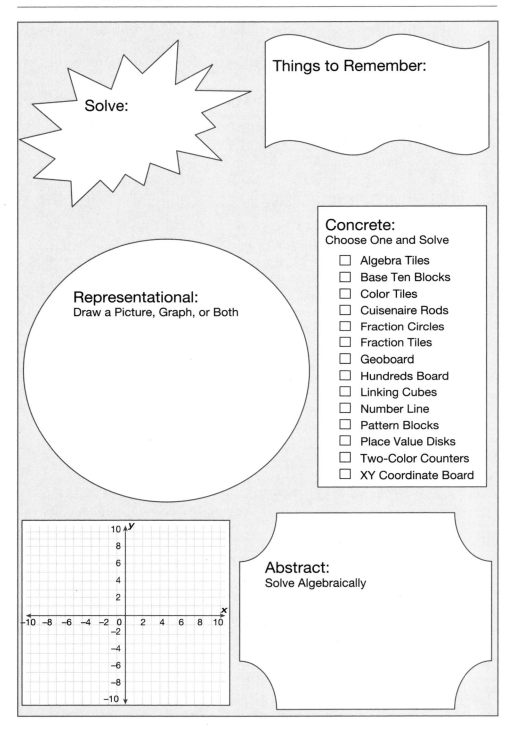

# PUTTING UDL AND MATH INTO PRACTICE: ENGAGEMENT

To emphasize a sense of belonging, teachers commonly use students' names when talking, combine scholastic and nonscholastic dialogue into daily exchanges, and make thoughtful connections to students' interests and backgrounds. What does this look like in math class, and how does this fit into UDL? A highly engaged math class upholds one major UDL tenet: teachers design multiple structures to engage every student throughout the learning process. While many students may engage in problem-solving activities enthusiastically, other students face stifling barriers while learning math. Math teachers need to consider cognitive, physical, emotional, academic, health, and sensory barriers during lesson planning. Great news . . . here are research-based approaches to planning engaging math lessons! Harbour, Evanovich, Sweigart, and Hughes's (2015) review of research-based, high-engagement teaching practices were applied to a math context for the purpose of this section.

## STRATEGY SPOT
### HINT CARDS

**Word Problem.** George and Summer worked on weeding a garden one afternoon. George weeded one-fifth of the garden; Summer weeded some of the garden as well. When George and Summer finished that afternoon, two-thirds of the garden still needed to be weeded. What fraction of the garden did Summer weed? Explain your answer two ways.

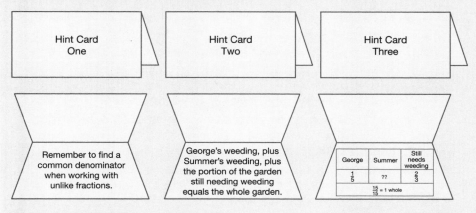

To see another example of using math hint cards, watch this quick video: https://www.teachingchannel.org/videos/hint-cards.

- **REDUCE COGNITIVE BARRIERS by teaching the math concept and the math thinking involved in solving the problem.** For example, write a problem and solve it, paying careful attention to each step you take to articulate the process. Next to each step, script a prompting statement or question you might say to a student to guide his or her learning. Pay close attention to areas that may cause frustration and therefore disengage students. For even greater effect, record yourself solving the problem, pausing between steps to think aloud the next procedure (prompt), and provide video and audio access to this type of scaffolding to students during guided practice. A low-tech version of this can be achieved using hint cards. Provide a series of hints that include prompts for students to remove barriers and create multiple entry points to engaging in problem solving.
- **REDUCE PHYSICAL BARRIERS.** Start by acknowledging barriers such as low hand strength for gripping manipulatives or writing numerals in place value columns and then take steps to reduce barriers. For example, adopt flexible seating arrangements. Provide various types of seats and standing stations with various types of writing utensils: remember that dry erase markers are easier to use than pencils because they require less hand strength! Provide two- and three-dimensional manipulatives. *Example:* Algebra tiles tend to be translucent, flat plastic tabs, which can be slippery and difficult to manipulate. Provide plastic blocks, such as Legos, but require students to assign different sizes and colors to place values and variables.
- **REMOVE EMOTIONAL BARRIERS (math anxiety!) by using specific, nonjudgmental feedback.** MacSuga and Simonsen (2011) recommend teachers provide students with two positive feedback statements per minute. Specific, positive, and timely feedback helps to increase specific behaviors that demonstrate progress toward a goal. This type of feedback draws clear connections between student actions and the feedback, thus limiting confusion. Corrective feedback that can include redirection is also an important part of math. Setting up the learning environment so that corrective feedback is not perceived as punitive but rather part of the learning process will also help combat math anxiety.
- **GET 'EM MOVING!** After barriers to learning are considered, reduced, or—even better—removed, there is still the challenge of maintaining student engagement. Embedding movement into instruction promotes sustained student engagement, learning endurance, and even improved academic performance (Nagro, Fraser, & Hooks, 2018). There is a relationship between

movement and attention, visual and language systems, and memory, which are all critical components to learning (Jensen, 2005). Specifically, embedding movement in a math lesson can support cognitive processes including predicting, sequencing, ordering, and timing (Jensen, 2005). Students might physically walk a number line to demonstrate gaining (adding) and losing (subtracting) yardage in a football-based word problem. Another example is that students may work in group to find an algebraic expression posted on one of the classroom walls, retrieve the algebraic expression, and then solve the expression using the life-sized number line or by standing at a poster-sized number line and making progress "on the field" with a dry erase marker or Velcro football icon. Better yet, on a nice day, the class might go to the football field during their math lesson and bring their clipboards to work in small groups, or individually if they so choose.

- **GET 'EM COLLABORATING!** Consider giving students voice regarding who they work with; they can choose to work alone, with one partner, or with a small group of up to four to five peers. Working on these tasks collaboratively enhances opportunities for students to increase engagement because peers can explain and justify their reasoning as they form conjectures and critique the reasoning of others. Teachers also benefit from collaborative tasks by learning from different perspectives and approaches to the same prompt represented by varied modeling schemes and verbal communication. Another benefit to peer learning is the opportunity for students to generalize informal thinking to formal concept development.

## PUTTING UDL AND MATH INTO PRACTICE: EXPRESSION

Structuring learning environments that emphasize student choice creates an authentic learning experience similar to what students face when problem solving in the real world (Nagro et al., 2018). Promoting choice making while students work toward academic objectives has resulted in greater learning independence and confidence as well as reduced disruptive behaviors (Flowerday & Schraw, 2003). Students pick up skills faster and are better at generalizing these skills across the curriculum when they are empowered through choice making (Toussaint, Kodak, & Vladescu, 2016). Hard-to-reach students (e.g., the nonstarters, those who avoid tasks, or those who are easily frustrated) will benefit from having a learning environment that accounts for their strengths and challenges. Strategies summarized in this section were adapted from the Collaboration for Effective Educator Development, Accountability, and Reform (CEEDAR) Center's anchor presentation on Universal Design for Learning (2015) and the National Council of Teachers of Mathematics' (n.d.) web post ("clip") on Video Games in the Math Classroom.

**Table 2.1**   From Discrete Tasks to Multiple Modes of Learning

| Moving from | Moving to |
| --- | --- |
| • Read<br>• Listen<br>• Write<br>• Speak<br>• Manipulate calculations<br>• Remember concepts<br>• Remember procedures<br>• Solve problems | • Take in information<br>• Express information<br>• Demonstrate understanding of processes<br>• Demonstrate understanding of concepts and ideas<br>• Show what you know through personally accessible formats<br>• Create a representation of what you know |

*Source:* Adapted from the Collaboration for Effective Educator Development, Accountability, and Reform (CEEDAR) Center (2015). *Anchor presentation on universal design for learning.* Retrieved from http://ceedar.education.ufl.edu/wp-content/uploads/2015/05/UDL-Facilitation-Guide.pdf

- **GET GAMING.** As technology becomes more accessible (and varied) within classrooms, video games and simulations are increasing in availability for math classrooms. For example, PhET (https://phet.colorado.edu/), partially funded by the National Science Foundation and developed at the University of Colorado, is free and offers interactive STEM simulations. Gizmos (https://www.explorelearning.com/) boasts interactive simulations that allow students to manipulate variables, visualize and graph data, and explore "what ifs" in math across Grades 3–12. Gizmos offers free games worth exploring to test for fitness with your classroom and student needs. Additional teacher-recommended games can be found through GameDesk's Educade, Common Sense Media's Graphite, MinecraftEdu, and Playful Learning.
- **MAKE THE SHIFT.** Teachers can shift the way expectations for learning are shared with students. This shift in articulating expectations demonstrates UDL principles in practice and emphasizes student-led learning.
- **PROVIDE CHOICE; ENCOURAGE CHOICE MAKING.** Choice making requires individuals to select from several options and accept the consequences of their choice (Shevin & Klein, 2004). Choice making is a teachable skill. Embedding student choice into math class creates an authentic learning experience similar to what students face when problem solving

in the real world (Berry, 2012). Ultimately, students who engage in choice making while meeting learning objectives have demonstrated greater independence and confidence, reduced disruptive behavior (Flowerday & Schraw, 2003), accelerated skill acquisition (Toussaint et al., 2016), and increased task engagement and skill generalization (Shevin & Klein, 2004). Embed choices into math lessons whenever possible. Simple choice making templates include a tic-tac-toe board where students choose three math problems to complete to successfully win the tic-tac-toe game. Steps for providing student choice opportunities include

○ setting up a learning environment that offers and allows for engagement in choice making,
○ providing various types of choices (e.g., choosing materials, roles, access),
○ offering appropriate choices with verbal modeling of appropriate choices,
○ allowing students time to think through options and use expressive communication (e.g., gesture, vocalization, written form) to make a choice, and
○ reinforcing appropriate choice making by providing desired choices (Cote Sparks & Cote, 2012).

## BRINGING IT ALL TOGETHER

Simple strategies such as using CRA to provide multiple representations; embedding movement and student choice; using games, graphic organizers, and manipulatives; and promoting peer learning are strategies and approaches to teaching math that will support a universally designed classroom and help all students. Leveraging technology and combining a variety of strategies will promote engagement and flexible math thinking. These approaches require some planning, but they can help students access, enjoy, and sustain learning.

## TOP FIVE WEBSITES TO SUPPORT MATH

→ http://www.abhortsoft.hu/functionvisualizer/functionvisualizer.html

→ https://www.mathgames.com/algebra

→ http://www.nctm.org

→ http://www.projectmaths.ie/for-students/learn-to-use-calculators/

→ http://www.transum.org/Software/SW/Starter_of_the_day/Similar .asp?ID_Topic=7

## APPS WE LOVE

→ Algebra Champ

→ Easel Algebra

→ HMH Fuse Algebra 1 Common Core Edition

→ Proportion Solver

→ Shuttle Mission Math

# REFERENCES

Berry, D. C. (2012). Authentic learning and student choice: Is there a place to allow athletic training students to set their own learning destiny? *Athletic Training Education, 7*(4), 205–210.

Buchheister, K., Jackson, C., & Taylor, C. E. (2017). Maths games: A universal design approach to mathematical reasoning. *Australian Primary Mathematics Classroom, 22*(4), 7–12.

Collaboration for Effective Educator Development, Accountability, and Reform (CEEDAR) Center. (2015). *Anchor presentation on Universal Design for Learning.* Retrieved from http://ceedar.education.ufl.edu/wp-content/uploads/2015/05/UDL-Facilitation-Guide.pdf

Cote Sparks, S., & Cote, D. L. (2012). Teaching choice making to elementary students with mild to moderate disabilities. *Intervention in School and Clinic, 47,* 290–296. doi:10.1177/1053451211430123

Every Student Succeeds Act (ESSA) of 2015 P.L. 114–95. (2016).

Flowerday, T., & Schraw, G. (2003). Effect of choice on cognitive and affective engagement. *Journal of Educational Research, 96,* 207–215. doi:10.1080/00220670309598810

Gersten, R., Chard, D. J., Jayanthi, M., Baker, S. K., Morphy, P., & Flojo, J. (2009). Mathematics instruction for students with learning disabilities: A meta-analysis of instructional components. *Review of Educational Research, 79,* 1202–1242.

Gurganus, S. P. (2017). *Math instruction for students with learning problems* (2nd ed.). New York, NY: Routledge.

Harbour, K. E., Evanovich, L. L., Sweigart, C. A., & Hughes, L. E. (2015). A brief review of effective teaching practices that maximize student engagement. *Preventing School Failure, 59,* 5–13. doi:10.1080/1045988X.2014.919136

Hoffer, W. W. (2015). *Our beliefs shape our classrooms.* Retrieved from https://blog.heinemann.com/wwh-cultivating-wkshop-model

Jensen, E. (2005). *Teaching with the brain in mind* (2nd ed.). Alexandria, VA: Association for Supervision and Curriculum Development (ASCD).

Jones, I., Inglis, M., Gilmore, C., & Evans, R. (2013). Teaching the substitutive conception of the equals sign. *Research in Mathematics Education, 15*(1), 34–49.

MacSuga, A. S., & Simonsen, B. (2011). Increasing teachers' use of evidence based classroom management strategies through consultation: Overview and case studies. *Beyond Behavior, 20,* 4–12.

Nagro, S. A., Fraser, D. W., & Hooks, S. (2018). Lesson planning with engagement in mind: Proactive classroom management strategies for curriculum instruction. *Intervention in School and Clinic.* Advance online publication. doi:10.1177/1053451218767905

National Council of Teachers of Mathematics. (n.d.). *Video games in the math classroom.* Retrieved from https://www.nctm.org/Research-and-Advocacy/Research-Brief-and-Clips/Video-Games-in-the-Math-Classroom/

National Center on Intensive Intervention. (2016). *Principles for designing intervention in mathematics.* Washington, DC: Office of Special Education, U.S. Department of Education.

Novak, K. (2016). *UDL now! A teacher's guide to applying Universal Design for Learning in today's classrooms* (2nd ed.). Wakefield, MA: CAST Professional Publishing.

Sams, A., & Bergmann, J. (2012). *Flip your classroom: Reach every student in every class every day.* Eugene, OR: International Society for Technology in Education.

Shevin, M., & Klein, N. (2004). The importance of choice-making skills with students with severe disabilities. *Research and Practice for Persons with Severe Disabilities, 29*(3), 161–168. doi:10.2511/rpsd.29.3.161

Toussaint, K. A., Kodak, T., & Vladescu, J. C. (2016). An evaluation of choice on instructional efficacy and individual preferences among children with autism. *Journal of Applied Behavior Analysis, 49*(1), 170–175. doi:10.1002/jaba.263

U.S. Department of Education. (1997). *Mathematics equals opportunity.* White paper prepared for U.S. Secretary of Education Richard W. Riley. Retrieved from https://files.eric.ed.gov/fulltext/ED415119.pdf

U.S. Department of Education, Institute of Education Sciences, National Center for Education Statistics, National Assessment of Educational Progress (NAEP). (2015). *2015 Mathematics Assessment.*

U.S. Department of Education, Institute of Education Sciences, National Center for Education Statistics, National Assessment of Educational Progress (NAEP). (2017). *2017 Mathematics Assessment.*

Watt, S. J., Watkins, J. R., & Abbitt, J. (2016). Teaching algebra to students with learning disabilities: Where have we come and where should we go? *Journal of Learning Disabilities, 49*(4), 437–447. doi:10.1177/0022219414564220

3

# UDL and Social Studies

## *Applying Project–Based Learning*

Philip E. Bernhardt

*Metropolitan State University of Denver*

## SETTING THE STAGE FOR UDL AND SOCIAL STUDIES

How can you ensure the authentic integration of UDL principles into your social studies lessons? Do you feel you sometimes miss opportunities to utilize UDL because this educational framework is not an integral part of how you have traditionally planned, instructed, and assessed students? Consider integrating the core characteristics of Project Based Learning (PBL), with which you are already probably familiar, as a way to cement UDL practices into your social studies classroom (or really, any classroom!). Not only does PBL make UDL easier to implement, but it also provides an effective instructional approach for bringing social studies to life for your students in authentic and meaningful ways. Hall, Meyer, and Rose (2012) position UDL as a guide for the development of a flexible learning environment that optimizes choice for students, accommodates and supports learning differences and preferences, and increases access by reducing cognitive, physical, and organizational barriers. This approach to teaching and learning is at the heart of PBL and reflects a deep understanding of the day-to-day reality in our classrooms—no matter what grade or content we teach, there is always variability in how our students learn!

## Key Concept

Project Based Learning (PBL) engages students in a project over an extended period of time—a few days, a week, and even a semester—and requires solving a real-world problem or answering an open-ended, complex question. Students demonstrate their knowledge, understandings, and skills by developing a public product or presentation for a relevant audience. Through the process, students have opportunities to develop deep content knowledge as well as critical thinking, creativity, and communication skills in the context of doing an authentic, meaningful project (Buck Institute for Education, 2018).

Project Based Learning can be implemented in any grade and with any content within social studies, and when used effectively, PBL is beneficial for all students (Barton & Levstik, 2011; Darling-Hammond et al., 2015; Han, Capraro, & Capraro, 2015). Additionally, PBL can be designed to support any instructional unit, curricula, or set of academic standards. In fact, there is evidence demonstrating that PBL aligns well with the Common Core State Standards (Boss, Larmer, & Mergendoller, 2013; Lenz, Wells, & Kingston, 2015; Weiss & Belland, 2016). This chapter specifically focuses on how UDL principles can be more consistently integrated within your social studies classroom through a close alignment with PBL. To start, though, it makes sense to identify the core purpose and primary characteristics of PBL and examine how PBL aligns with UDL principles.

## YOUR PBL PRIMER

Project Based Learning is a student-driven, mastery-oriented instructional framework that enables students to engage in the creation of inquiry-based projects that reflect their knowledge, understandings, experiences, and design choices (Bell, 2010; Buck Institute for Education, 2018; Noguera, Darling-Hammond, & Friedlaender, 2015). PBL requires that students develop projects that tackle challenging problems and questions that do not have simple answers. Successful projects require systematic planning and research, critical and creative thinking, formative feedback, individual reflection and monitoring of progress, and a presentation of findings to share what was learned. Doesn't this already sound like it fits perfectly with UDL? PBL provides an ideal context for student learning that embodies relevance, scaffolding, the application of knowledge and purposeful use of technology, and opportunities to interact with classmates, as well as potentially connect with professionals from the community.

For example, imagine the varied learning opportunities associated with elementary students conducting extensive research on Native Americans and then developing and curating a minimuseum of Native American culture that highlights both the past and the present to teach and educate members of the school and local community. Similarly, consider the excitement of engaging secondary school students in a unit focusing on thought-provoking political issues and facilitating opportunities for students to interact with local politicians, journalists, and organizations to advocate for change. These are real possibilities with PBL (and each of these projects can support the UDL principles)!

It is also important to note that the National Council for Social Studies (NCSS) Vision of Powerful Teaching and Learning (NCSS Board of Directors, 2016) aligns well with the core purpose of PBL:

> The vital task of preparing students to become citizens in a democracy is complex. The social studies disciplines are diverse, encompassing an expansive range of potential content. This content engages students in a comprehensive process of confronting multiple dilemmas, and encourages students to speculate, think critically, and make personal and civic decisions on information from multiple perspectives. (p. 180)

Used purposefully and implemented well, PBL provides students with opportunities to develop invaluable intellectual and reasoning skills, apply the academic content they are learning, and develop the dispositions and critical thinking capacities necessary for the challenges, dilemmas, and expectations they will encounter outside of school and in postsecondary education.

The next important question to consider is how PBL provides an ideal instructional context for supporting the integration of UDL into your planning, instruction, and assessment. The three principles of UDL can be seamlessly integrated into a social studies classroom committed to PBL. To start, it is important to highlight that both UDL and PBL provide accessible learning opportunities for *all* students through their focus on critical thinking and use of authentic contexts for learning. For example, when engaged in PBL, students are able to draw on their own backgrounds, experiences, and interests to connect with academic content, make choices in how their understandings are demonstrated, and select from a range of tools, methods, and mediums to apply and share their learning. Yes, UDL and PBL are a perfect match!

Second, the central tenets of PBL and UDL reflect the understanding that children have a broader range of capabilities, skills, and interests than they are typically asked to use and demonstrate in more traditional classrooms. With PBL, learning differences are approached as assets. To this end, students are required to utilize a variety of modalities and strategies as they research a challenging problem or question; establish goals and objectives for developing their project; monitor progress; and at the end of the process, present and communicate ideas to an audience. Additionally, PBL works well for recruiting student interest because choice and autonomy are central parts of the learning process. When students are genuinely interested and invested in what they are learning and encouraged to draw on personal interests and areas of strength, they typically achieve at higher levels.

Lastly, PBL creates meaningful opportunities for self-regulation and the development of intrinsic motivation through self-assessment, peer review, and formative feedback. Within a PBL approach, students have consistent opportunities to measure their learning and identify areas for further development as they reflect on goals, objectives, and project expectation and timelines. Additionally, because PBL relies on the use of effective rubrics as a tool for examining progress, goal setting is an integral part of the learning process.

To discuss and provide concrete examples of UDL practices within social studies, the subsequent three sections will discuss multiple means of representation, engagement, and expression through three of PBL's core characteristics. This approach creates a practical context for providing specific tips, examples, strategies, and ideas that can be directly integrated into your classroom. The following characteristics will be utilized to consider how to effectively put UDL and social studies into practice:

1. **Authentic Context (*multiple means of representation*).** Students are presented with challenging problems and questions that utilize open-ended questions and facilitate critical thinking as central to the learning process. These problems and questions are areas of inquiry encountered in life and/or faced by professionals in specific fields. Additionally, the audience for sharing and presenting what was learned is typically more than just the teacher.

2. **Performance Assessment (*multiple means of engagement*).** Students are tasked with designing quality products and/or performances in which they get to make a variety of choices related to topic, design, structure, and format for representing their learning. This assessment is completed as students design and engage in a planned, systematic process.

3. **Formative Development (*multiple means of action and expression*).** Class structure provides opportunities for meaningful feedback, from both the teachers and peers, to monitor progress.

## PUTTING UDL AND SOCIAL STUDIES INTO PRACTICE: REPRESENTATION

Creating a social studies classroom that draws on *authentic contexts* is an effective way to facilitate critical thinking and engage students in classroom tasks that have varied solutions, answers, and modes of inquiry.

The more opportunities for students to engage with authentic problems, questions, and issues, the more variety in ways a learner can engage with content. When universally designing, consider the following:

- **VARY YOUR SOURCES** to include images, graphics, audio, video, and text. It is also important to provide clear, succinct descriptions of selected sources to ensure they are accessible to all learners and provide the necessary context. Think about how easy it would be to utilize both primary and secondary sources to teach about important events and people associated with the Civil Rights movement.
- **ENSURE KEY VOCABULARY AND CONCEPTS ARE PRE-IDENTIFIED AND INTRODUCED** prior to teaching challenging content to promote connections to learners' experiences and develop background knowledge. For example, if we want students to make connections between the Cold War and current international events, there are definitely vocabulary and concepts that students need to know, understand, and be able to apply.
- **IDENTIFY THE STUDENTS WHO ALREADY KNOW** the vocabulary and concepts and respect that knowledge by asking them more challenging questions or having them share their knowledge.

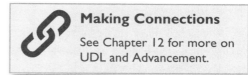

**Making Connections**

See Chapter 12 for more on UDL and Advancement.

- **SHARE OPPOSING VIEWPOINTS WITH STUDENTS** from a variety of sources across the political spectrum. For example, this can be done when using current events (print or video) in your civics class. This helps students identify relevant examples and nonexamples as well as consider critical patterns and concepts.
- **SELECT REAL-LIFE SCENARIOS AND DILEMMAS** drawn from history to make authentic connections to content. Students can be tasked to analyze and evaluate these scenarios and dilemmas to apply what they are learning. Real-world examples not only reflect the complexity and unpredictability of history, and as such can stimulate critical thinking, but they also highlight the need for thoughtful and nuanced approaches to problem solving at all grade levels.
- **UTILIZE PHYSICAL EXAMPLES** to help students make connections. For example, within classroom lessons focusing on archaeology, fossils, and artifacts, real fossils can connect to the work of archaeologists. You can even take items and bury fossils and artifacts in an area around the school to create an archaeological site. Students can then dig up items to develop a more concrete and tangible understanding of scientific fieldwork.

- **BE PREPARED WITH MULTIPLE VERSIONS OF MATERIALS.** For example, when engaging students in a station activity focused on analyzing political cartoons for meaning, make sure to use both color and black-and-white images, enlarge text included in the cartoons (as it is often difficult to read), and provide multiple copies of cartoons at each station so each student has a copy when working collaboratively. Ensure the cartoons are high quality, and it would be beneficial to enlarge them from the typical 8½ x 11 printout when possible. It also makes sense to have iPads or laptops at each station with political cartoons displayed to offer options for the visual display of information.

## CASE IN POINT

Ms. Weichel and Mr. Kiernan, co-teachers, review the objectives for a fifth-grade lesson that is part of a social studies PBL unit focusing on water quality. *Students will identify the importance of water quality and steps for examining water quality, use provided kits to test the quality of water from the Platte River, and share observations about water quality.*

To represent important issues related to water quality in varied ways, the two fifth-grade teachers wanted their students to be exposed to stories about the significance of water to diverse communities across the world. First, they provided different options for stories as well as how the stories were presented. Some students could have a teacher read to them, while others read on the computer, listened to audio stories or podcasts, or looked at a newspaper or magazine. Next, local experts visited the classroom to talk with students about local water issues. These experts, who included local activists and environmental science faculty from a local university, shared water poetry, colorful images of important water sources, and enlarged graphs and charts highlighting important research findings related to water quality issues. After some introductory discussion, students got the opportunity to test a variety of water sources. The environmental science faculty brought water-testing kits and water samples from a variety of local rivers, streams, and lakes; they even collected water from the elementary school water fountain.

Students were provided with lab notebooks to illustrate key vocabulary, draw the water testing tools they would use, record their observations and any relevant data, and synthesize findings. Though graphic organizers were available to the class, a few specific students were given adapted versions to support their notes because of specific learning disabilities, which demonstrated differentiation for their needs. Students were organized into groups of four, and a teacher or local expert facilitated each group. This activity created opportunities for students to engage in many of the same processes scientists utilize to study water quality and its impact on local communities. Students were able to interact with, touch, and use all the tools necessary for testing water quality. Once the water-testing process was complete, students shared observations with group members and created a visual synthesis of their findings to present to the class, teachers, and the local experts visiting the classroom.

- In the prior "Case in Point," the teacher might **PROACTIVELY PROVIDE ILLUSTRATED EXAMPLES of some of the vocabulary words,** which may not be appropriate for all students but  would be supportive of emerging bilingual students or those students with cognitive disabilities. By doing so, the teachers are *differentiating* to set students up for success and by ensuring they have important background knowledge and can visualize examples to help them complete an illustrated vocabulary assignment that is part of the water quality activity.
- **USE AN ONLINE RESOURCE like Newsela to differentiate reading levels of nonfiction text to accommodate the reading levels in your class.** In addition to the database of current events, it has a library of primary documents and other historical readings, all adapted to different reading levels.
- **LEVEL YOUR RESOURCES.** For example, when introducing students to excerpts from the journals of Lewis and Clark or narratives written by former slaves or military veterans, you may need to simplify the language while maintaining meaning and context. You can use an online resource like Rewordify to accomplish this goal and meet the needs of *all* your students.

> **Tech Tips**
>
> Find out more about Newsela by going to https://newsela.com/or watching the video at https://www.youtube.com/watch?v=SiKvLWaQPtQ

## PUTTING UDL AND SOCIAL STUDIES INTO PRACTICE: ENGAGEMENT

Another core principle of PBL is the use of performance assessments. This strategy requires that students develop a product and/or a performance to demonstrate their learning and that fits well with the Engagement section of UDL. As teachers, we know that learners differ in the ways in which they can be engaged or motivated to learn. Hence, it is important that when designing PBL we ensure all students in our classroom can access the information, resources, and materials necessary for them to succeed. Additionally, students need support in figuring out how to manage information they are collecting and how to develop materials that will ultimately be shared with others. Without this clarity, some students will struggle to integrate their research and what they have learned to create a project that demonstrates their understanding and meets the project's expectations and objectives. Ultimately, we need to remember that there is no one particular method of engagement that will be optimal for all learners in your classroom. Want to engage students in varied and meaningful ways? Try these strategies:

**Making Connections**

See Chapter 6 for more on UDL and Executive Functioning.

- **PROVIDE STUDENTS WITH A LIST OF POSSIBLE TOPICS** that span across political, social, cultural, and economic issues as you help them decide how to focus their culminating projects focusing on the Civil War or World War I or II. Let students have as much choice and autonomy as possible when selecting topics. Providing a list of options will help students narrow and focus their efforts and help you ensure they are on target.

- **HAVE STUDENTS SET CLEAR ACADEMIC GOALS for their work as they begin to develop their project ideas.** Help them identify what supports are necessary to ensure they can meet expectations. For example, what materials and resources will they need? What timelines will they set for completing various parts of their project? What challenges do they envision? What do they hope to learn and get out of the experience?

**Tech Tips**

Find out more about Prezi by going to https://prezi.com/ or watching the video at https://www.youtube.com/user/PreziVideoChannel

- **MAKE SURE STUDENTS UNDERSTAND THERE IS FLEXIBILITY in how they develop and display their own projects.** This would include text, format, graphics, layout, and the integration of multiple modalities: visual, auditory, kinesthetic, and tactile. Encourage them to move beyond basic PowerPoints that many have been doing since first grade. Using past exemplars as models is also a great idea!

- **PROVIDE MASTERY-ORIENTED FEEDBACK to students on their work during the process (not just after).** For example, if part of a project requires students to write narratives highlighting what life was like for colonists during the American

Revolution or Native Americans during the bloody years of westward expansion, there need to be multiple opportunities to provide students with feedback that is timely, relevant, descriptive, and developmental. This will ensure students are making progress and will allow you to identify the students who are struggling and those who might need additional resources to extend their thinking.

- **PROACTIVELY PROVIDE A TEMPLATE** for organizing ideas and research. In the Case in Point example below, the teacher might have a template related to the development of their legistlative bill. An example is provided in Table 3.1 on the next page. Some students might receive a version of the template that includes key vocabulary to help them craft the narrative portion of the assignment that other students would not need. This *differentiation* is designed to ensure that an emerging bilingual student or a student with a specific disability has the necessary scaffolds for success.

## CASE IN POINT

Ms. Gonzalez's tenth graders are engaged in small-group projects where they are to identify an interesting issue that is currently being debated in Congress or their state legislature; identify and review materials associated with this issue (committee bills, policy papers, news articles, videos, etc.); and then, ultimately, write a bill that will be shared with classmates as well as state and local politicians. As students move toward the end of their summative project, Ms. Gonzalez knows it is important to facilitate opportunities for students to share their work to help foster collaboration and community.

To support this ongoing classroom goal, Ms. Gonzalez puts two things into action. First, to help students edit and further develop their draft bills, she encourages students to get into collaborative groups so they can share their progress and challenges and receive peer feedback. Students are provided with clear expectations and guidelines via a rubric for working together, as well as for how to provide feedback about the content, clarity, structure, and feasibility of draft legislative bills.

Second, once work on the project is complete, students get the opportunity to share their final bills with a panel of local experts that includes politicians and journalists. Student groups were provided with autonomy in the design of their final presentations. As groups developed their presentations, they were encouraged to utilize a variety of media, illustrations, pictures, video, and so forth to communicate information and ideas. After the presentations, there was also an opportunity for both experts and students to ask questions and provide feedback.

**Table 3.1**    UDL Lesson Plan Organizer for Social Studies

Grade Level:
Content Area Within Social Studies:

| State Level Academic Standards and/or Common Core State Standards addressed in <u>this lesson plan:</u> | |
| --- | --- |
| Big Ideas This Lesson Addresses: | Essential Question for This Lesson: |
| Anticipating Potential Misunderstandings: *What might students misunderstand in this lesson?* | Relevant Guiding Question(s) for This Lesson: |

How does this lesson connect to and support Project Based Learning?

**LESSON OBJECTIVES**
*What should the student be able to DO [demonstrate] by the end of the lesson?*

Essential Knowledge: *What specific content do you want students to learn by the end of <u>THIS</u> lesson?*
LIST essential knowledge to be learned here: Students will know . . .

Essential Skills: LIST/UNPACK the academic skills to be learned in this lesson. *What specific skills do you want students to learn by the end of <u>THIS</u> lesson?* *Higher-Order/Critical Thinking should be emphasized!
LIST essential skills to be learned here: Students will be able to . . .

**UNIVERSAL DESIGN for LEARNING**
What will you focus on during this lesson? How will you focus on UDL Principles?

1. Multiple Means of Representation: What will you provide options for and what will it look like in practice?
2. Multiple Means of Action and Expression: What will you provide options for and what will it look like in practice?
3. Multiple Means of Engagement: What will you provide options for and what will it look like in practice?

*Be sure to visit CAST.org to help align lesson with Universal Design Principles:* www.udlguidelines.cast.org/?utm_medium=web&utm_campaign=none&utm_source=cast-about-udl

# PUTTING UDL AND SOCIAL STUDIES INTO PRACTICE: EXPRESSION

Developing a social studies program that consistently integrates *formative assessment* as a primary component of the instruction is an effective way to help students reflect on their understanding of content, identify what they are misunderstanding, and determine the support they may need. We know that some students may process information quicker than those with learning or sensory disabilities or those with language or cultural differences. Hence, teachers need to provide opportunities for students to think about their strengths; identify areas for development; and, in conjunction with their teacher, identify further supports they may need. Consider how UDL strategies can be used to enhance opportunities for students to self-reflect and assess and receive meaningful feedback to improve their work.

- **RUBRICS ARE ESSENTIAL!** Whether it's elementary students creating small businesses as they learn about money, purchasing power, and commodities; middle school students developing projects for National History Day; or high school students simulating an important

**Tech Tips**

Find previously created rubrics and tools to help out with rubric development at Rubistar: http://rubistar.4teachers.org or iRubric: https://www.rcampus.com/indexrubric.cfm?

gathering in the United Nations, students need to have a guide that outlines academic expectations and performance criteria so they can plan their work, monitor progress, and make necessary changes.

- **USE A DIVERSE RANGE OF MODELS AND EXEMPLARS to help students develop understanding about what is expected.** For example, if students are expected to create visual representations of important contributions associated with ancient Greek, Roman, or African civilizations, these models and exemplars help to create effective benchmarks that can not only inspire creativity, but also provide tangible scaffolds to support learning.

- **USE CONCEPT OR MIND MAPS to help students construct and focus their ideas and interests.** These tools can be created electronically, with paper and pencil, or even using concrete manipulatives. This process will make student thinking

**Tech Tips**

Find concept/mind mapping tools at:
MindMup: https://www.mindmup.com
Mindomo: https://www.mindomo.com
Coggle: https://coggle.it

STRATEGY SPOT

GALLERY WALKS

Use gallery walks as a method for students to interact with their peers. A gallery walk is an instructional tool that gets students out of their seats and actively engaged with each other as they walk throughout the classroom discussing and analyzing meaningful questions, problems, texts, images, and/ or documents. This super strategy can also be used by teachers to help check student understanding. Within social studies, there are so many opportunities to utilize gallery walks in meaningful ways. For example, gallery walks can be used to debrief after completing challenging reading to support understanding, to examine historical documents or images, to determine students' prior knowledge before starting a new topic, to facilitate opportunities for peer feedback, and to generate ideas, share perspectives, and reflect.

more visible and help you guide students to select appropriate and relevant topics. Studying topics like the Holocaust, Anne Frank, or racial segregation at the elementary school level can be daunting. It can be even more challenging to get students to select meaningful project ideas related to these topics because they are complicated. Concept and mind maps will help students develop and refine their ideas.

- **VARY THE WAYS IN WHICH FEEDBACK IS PROVIDED when giving students feedback on their projects at the start, during the process, and after completion.** While written feedback is important, physically meeting with students is also important, as this allows for questions and responses from both students and the teacher. Additionally, it is wise to identify methods for providing feedback via e-mail or a learning platform, so feedback is timely and the digital copy can assist both students and teachers in tracking development and progress.

- **PLACE STUDENTS IN GROUPS TO PRACTICE PRESENTATIONS and to receive targeted feedback.** For example, when students are preparing oral presentations as part of their projects on impactful leaders of the 20th century, providing opportunities to practice presenting will help move students toward mastery and create a forum for students to share their goals for the project and discuss progress toward these goals. Have a student with identified anxiety or a phobia of public speaking? If you want most students to present to their peers in class, you may choose to allow that one student with an identified special need to present to the teacher alone or to videotape his or her presentation to be viewed by the class. This is an example of differentiation and demonstrates how, even with great strategies such as group presentations, teachers need to be ready to be flexible given students' needs.

## BRINGING IT ALL TOGETHER

This chapter focused on the ways in which UDL and PBL can be utilized together to create learning environments that embody personalized learning, culturally responsive pedagogy, authentic learning contexts, and instructional accessibility and differentiation. The core principles and guidelines of both UDL and PBL support the design and delivery of instruction to meet the needs of all learners by providing choices for why students are learning, what they are learning, and how they will share what they have learned (Novak, 2016). Together, these two well-established learning models can be used to effectively support students' academic, social, and emotional development. Both instructional approaches are flexible, student-centered, and can be adapted to meet the constantly evolving needs, desires, and interests of students at all points of the learning spectrum.

## TOP FIVE WEBSITES TO SUPPORT UDL AND SOCIAL STUDIES

→ https://www.docsteach.org/
→ https://www.nationalgeographic.org/education/
→ https://www.nationalww2museum.org/
→ https://rmpbs.pbslearningmedia.org/socialstudies/
→ https://www.tolerance.org/

## APPS WE LOVE

→ Back in Time
→ Google Earth
→ Icivics
→ The Pyramids
→ World Atlas

## RECOMMENDED READINGS

Larmer, J., Mergendoller, J., & Boss, S. (2015). *Setting the standard for Project Based Learning*. Alexandria, VA: ASCD.

Meyer, A., & Rose, D. (2005). *The future is in the margins: The role of technology and disability in educational reform*. Wakefield, MA: CAST.

## REFERENCES

Barton, K. C., & Levstik, L. S. (2011). *Doing history: Investigating with children in elementary and middle schools.* London, England: Routledge.

Bell, S. (2010). Project-based learning for the 21st century from The Collaboration for Effective Educator Development, Accountability, and Reform (CEEDAR): Skills for the future. *The Clearing House, 83*(2), 39–43.

Boss, S., Larmer, J., & Mergendoller, J. R. (2013). *PBL for 21st century success: Teaching critical thinking, collaboration, communication, and creativity.* Novato, CA: Buck Institute for Education.

Buck Institute for Education. (2018). *What is PBL?* Retrieved from http://www.bie.org/about/what_pbl

Darling-Hammond, L., Barron, B., Pearson, P. D., Schoenfeld, A. H., Stage, E. K., Zimmerman, T. D., . . . Tilson, J. L. (2015). *Powerful learning: What we know about teaching for understanding.* Hoboken, NJ: Wiley & Sons.

Hall, T. E., Meyer, A., & Rose, D. H. (Eds.). (2012). *Universal Design for Learning in the classroom: Practical applications.* New York, NY: Guilford Press.

Han, S., Capraro, R., & Capraro, M. M. (2015). How science, technology, engineering, and mathematics (STEM) project-based learning (PBL) affects high, middle, and low achievers differently: The impact of student factors on achievement. *International Journal of Science and Mathematics Education, 13*(5), 1089–1113.

Lenz, B., Wells, J., & Kingston, S. (2015). *Transforming schools using project-based deeper learning, performance assessment, and common core standards.* Hoboken, NJ: Wiley & Sons.

NCSS Board of Directors. (2016). A vision of powerful teaching and learning in the social studies: A position statement of the National Council for the Social Studies. *Social Education, 80*(3), 180–182.

Noguera, P., Darling-Hammond, L., & Friedlaender, D. (2015). Equal opportunity for deeper learning. Students at the center: Deeper learning research series. Boston, MA: Jobs for the Future.

Novak, K. (2016). *UDL now! A teacher's Monday-morning guide to implementing Common Core Standards using Universal Design for Learning.* Wakefield, MA: CAST Professional Publishing.

Weiss, D. M., & Belland, B. R. (2016). Transforming schools using project-based learning, performance assessment, and Common Core standards. *Interdisciplinary Journal of Problem-Based Learning, 10*(2), 4.

# 4

# *UDL and Science*

## *Integrating STEM*

### Barbara Serianni
*Georgia Southern University*

### Carolyn Rethwisch
*Savannah–Chatham Public Schools*

## SETTING THE STAGE FOR UDL AND SCIENCE

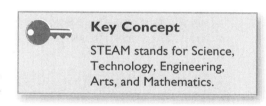

**Key Concept**

STEAM stands for Science, Technology, Engineering, Arts, and Mathematics.

Today's high-stakes testing focuses primarily on reading and mathematics, so why is STEM education such a hot topic? How can UDL support STEM integration as well as science instruction? Since the Russian launch of *Sputnik* in 1957 ignited a fear that America was falling behind the rest of the world in scientific advancement, educators have turned their focus toward science, technology, engineering, and math (STEM), long before the acronym was coined by the National Science Foundation (NSF). What began at NSF as SMET (science, math, engineering, and technology) in the early 1990s was later dubbed STEM. Today, schools are starting to hear about a move toward STEAM (STEM + Art) to acknowledge the creative aspect of the discipline. This evolution has occurred in concert with a growing preK–12 initiative to expose more students to STEAM content and careers in preparation for their future in

21st century jobs in those fields. For the rest of this chapter, however, the acronym used will be merely STEM, not to avoid the integration of the arts, but merely for simplicity's sake.

"STEM is an approach to learning that removes the traditional barriers separating the four disciplines and integrates them into real-world, rigorous, relevant learning experiences for students" (Vasquez, Sneider, & Comer, 2013, p. 4). This definition of STEM is a bit reminiscent of education before 1983, when *A Nation at Risk* sparked a movement to narrow the curriculum and create curricular silos. Today, things are changing; 21st century STEM initiatives are poking holes in the walls of those silos again, creating interdisciplinary learning where students can learn, apply, create, and make sense of the world in which they live.

UDL and STEM have a symbiotic relationship; their similarities make them perfect partners. UDL provides the ideal framework for integrating the interdisciplinary content of STEM across the curriculum. Think about UDL as an information highway for STEM content. It allows multidirectional travel and exploration, complete with express lanes for students who move faster than others and slow lanes for those who need a more leisurely pace to allow learning to occur. The UDL highway provides on-ramps, which offer multiple access points that allow students to enter learning at a place that matches their needs and readiness, and off-ramps that allow students to stop and dig deeper into areas of interest, explore interesting rabbit trails, rest and refuel, or access support services.

By its very nature, UDL supports accessibility, student voice, and student choice. Students can make their own what, how, when, and where decisions related to how they access content, engage with content, and express or demonstrate their learning. The partnership between STEM and UDL supports the development of deeper learning by providing opportunities for students to engage in higher-level cognitive tasks (Basham & Marino, 2013) and creative expression.

## CASE IN POINT

Ms. Miller told her sixth-grade class they were about to become architects and designers! With the objective of understanding world history and geography while infusing STEM concepts, she encouraged every student to pick their own favorite famous monument. Students were allowed to choose their monument and report on its history and geography using posters, videos, and technology. They could work alone or with a partner to build a scale model, using math skills (scales and measurement), technology (3D printers, computer designs, and Word documents), engineering (materials and design), creativity and art (aesthetics), and science (environment and principles of physics). The results were impressive, and the students were actively engaged!

One of the most exciting prospects of a STEM–UDL partnership is how STEM can expand the context for students to exhibit their learning. Demonstrating literacy skills is not bound to traditional literature found in English language arts (ELA) or reading curricula, but with UDL can expand to include students' interests in all areas, including STEM content (Donegan-Ritter, 2017; Israel, Maynard, & Williamson, 2013). Mastery of mathematics skills can be demonstrated through algorithm-based problem solving or through STEM integration that may include authentic engineering or problem-solving tasks that embed targeted math skills (Basham & Marino, 2013; Vasquez et al., 2013). Science and social studies classrooms can support not only student engagement in literacy activities, but they can also contain a host of opportunities for students to demonstrate mastery of literacy skills in the context of their content. Conversely, ELA classrooms can draw from the content of other disciplines to support learner variety and provide voice and choice in expression (Gravel, 2018). Voice and choice gives students ownership of their learning and supports our ultimate goal of building self-directed learners, prepared for postsecondary opportunities in the real world.

We are preparing students to learn, live, and work in a global society where factors such as time, distance, and geopolitical borders are mitigated by technology. STEM skills are critical for successful engagement in this environment, and therefore schools need to prioritize the development of these skills (National Education Association, 2014). The effective integration of STEM requires teachers, schools, and districts to step outside of the steel box forged by a high-stakes-driven, siloed curriculum and move forward to engaging, authentic, STEM-focused interdisciplinary learning supported by today's extraordinary technology and UDL principles.

## UDL IN ACTION: REPRESENTATION IN SCIENCE AND STEM

So how do we put it all together and teach universally designed science curricula or use UDL principles to integrate STEM into other academic disciplines? The answer is in the beauty of the STEM–UDL partnership. UDL is about student voices and

**Tech Tip**

A great site to help with STEM literacy is www.readingrockets.org/ reading-topics/stem-literacy

choices, and STEM content can provide those choices, regardless of the curricular area. STEM is about "real-world, rigorous, relevant learning experiences" (Vasquez et al., 2013, p. 4), so it is in the context of those experiences that we can talk about integrating STEM with UDL into any content area.

**Tech Tip**

Use technology to access free online leveled reading passages to make content accessible to learners.

- https://newsela.com/
- https://www.readworks.org/
- https://www.rif.org/literacy-central/collections/leveled-reading-passages

## Integrating STEM and UDL Into English Language Arts (ELA)

The content for reading and writing can be either informational or narrative in nature. Both science and engineering provide countless pages of informational text that include myriad science topics, engineering marvels, new and future technologies, as well as hometown projects and heroes. Any of these can be used to build reading comprehension and writing skills while engaging with real-world STEM content.

The UDL framework provides accessibility options for students. Some may choose to read, while others prefer to listen or watch to engage with content. Technology supports the accessibility needs and reading level variations of students, allowing each to access content at an appropriate level of rigor. Even narrative texts about future technologies, inventions, engineering feats, and space exploration are options for reading material and writing inspiration. These topics pique the interest and imagination of students, especially when they have a choice.

- **LET STUDENT INTERESTS DRIVE CHOICE in reading and writing about STEM topics.**
- **LET STUDENT NEEDS DICTATE MECHANISMS for accessing content.** Ask students, "How will you learn something about [insert STEM topic of interest] today?" Bookmark STEM sites on student devices or create an anchor chart that lists science/STEM websites for students to explore. Have students fly their red flag for a question or one-on-one time with a teacher. If you need to have  time for specially designed instruction with a particular student for an Individualized Education Program (IEP) goal or objective, there can even be choice by the student in when or where that occurs and can be tailored to their individual science/STEM interests.
- **GIVE STUDENTS TIME AND FLEXIBILITY to deepen STEM learning through research and wide reading.** Have a regular STEM time each week. Options for STEM time can include library or reading time, extended computer time, cooperative learning time, web quests, and scavenger hunts focused on local or internationally relevant STEM topics.

## Integrating STEM and UDL Into Social Studies

In the United States, the subject of social studies became a content area used as a catch-all for various content that did not fit into other areas of the school curriculum, such as ELA, math, and science (Dunn, 1916). In today's classroom, that content includes history, geography, political science, and the humanities. These broad areas present tremendous opportunities to integrate all four disciplines of STEM in one way or another. Some examples of STEM integration in social studies include having students do the following:

- Explore ancient buildings and infrastructure through engineering and design.
- Investigate time and distance, natural resources, topography, latitude and longitude, and other STEM disciplines as part of the study of places.
- Relate celestial events and meteorological events to geopolitical events and history.
- Design tools to improve the human condition in third world countries.
- Communicate with people across the globe through various technological applications.
- Use Google Earth to identify topographical features in a region and contextualize where "home" is in relation to the state, our nation, and the world.

### Integrating STEM and UDL Into Math

One of the challenges of mathematics is the variation among learners in a given classroom. These variances are most pronounced in student strengths and learning differences, as well as present level of performance or level

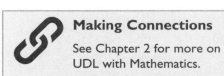

**Making Connections**

See Chapter 2 for more on UDL with Mathematics.

of readiness. In the mathematics classroom, technology and other tools can support learners who don't have the necessary background knowledge or skills or are not yet ready for the day's instruction. As students work toward Common Core's Standard for Mathematical Practice #5, *use appropriate tools strategically*, UDL can provide a collection of tools to choose from as students access mathematics content.

Technology can provide multiple means of representation through apps such as WolframAlpha. This app allows students to enter variables and calculate solutions to mathematics, science, and technology problems, as well as see solutions in multiple representations. Multiple means of representation are invaluable to learners struggling with conceptual

**Tech Tip**

Use http://www .wolframalpha.com/ to create multiple representations of math and science problems providing multiple access points to meet the needs of all learners.

understanding in mathematics and science. Diagrams, plots, problem-solving steps, visualizations, and concrete models can help them make the connection and move beyond the surface learning of procedures to the deep conceptual understanding that will build a foundation for learning new concepts and skills.

Connecting an engineering concept during the introduction of a mathematics concept can set the stage for the use and development of models as part of learning. Students may more easily connect to topics such as ratios, scales, or conversions when they are couched in real-life, engineered models such as the blueprint of their school or other places of interest (malls, parks, neighborhoods). The introduction of content in this way can set the stage for students to engage in constructing their own concrete or representational models as a part of their learning.

### Integrating STEM and UDL Into Science

Can we live on Mars? How will we get food? Can we grow food in Martian soil? Can we take a cow to space? Will she produce milk? Student questions drive engagement and learning and more questions. The cycle is dynamic and endless, limited only by time and resources. There are countless ways that students can use questions like these as a starting point for inquiry.

Collaborative learning is a great way to give students opportunities to brainstorm any of these questions and identify questions and topics that need further research. Aligned questions and topics that result from these sessions can be offered as options for further exploration by students. Once students choose topics, they can elect to narrow their focus by working independently or broaden their approach to a topic by working in affinity groups. Driven by their own questions and curiosity and supported with access to a variety of resources, students will actively engage in building their understanding of a topic in a search for the answers to their own questions. It is fascinating to watch this process, as students often find they develop an endless list of new questions that often have no answers.

**Figure 4.1   Integrating UDL Into Science**

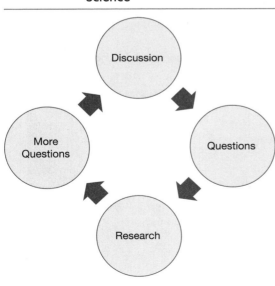

- **USE THE INTERNET TO EXPLORE topics of interest.** NASA has content of particular interest to students at all levels. Students can take virtual field trips through Discovery Education™ online or learn about science and environmental issues at Ducksters™.
- **USE VIDEO CONFERENCING or video presentations to bring experts into your classroom.** Get experts live online or to answer student questions in a short video recording. Use websites such as TED Talks, NASA, Discovery Education, or YouTube to provide multiple means of representation of science content.

**Tech Tip**

**NASA for Students**: https://www.nasa.gov/audience/forstudents/index.html

**Virtual Field Trips**: http://www.discoveryeducation.com/Events/virtual-field-trips/explore/index.cfm?campaign=flyout_students_virtual_field_trips

**Science for Kids**: https://www.ducksters.com/science/e

**TED Talks for Kids**: https://www.ted.com/playlists/86/talks_to_watch_with_kids

**SCISHOWKIDS**: https://www.youtube.com/user/scishowkids

## UDL IN ACTION: ENGAGEMENT IN SCIENCE AND STEM

By definition, science is about exploring questions about the world around us. What better setting for inquiry-based instruction through UDL? There is nothing like the authentic questions of students to engage them in the

**STRATEGY SPOT**
BRING IN LOCAL STEM EXPERTS!

Explore your own community for organizations and individuals who live and work with the topics you are teaching. Imagine an actual astronaut speaking to your students about the physical challenges of living in zero gravity. Do you know a local farmer who can talk about the problem of pollinating crops when bee populations decline due to mosquito spraying by local health authorities? Often, you don't need to look further than your school family. You may have parents or guardians who are engineers, scientists, pilots, electricians, mechanics, builders, architects, artists, writers, travelers, or have a host of other occupations or hobbies that bring STEM into your class.

learning process (Colburn, 2000). Inquiry-based instruction in science is about not only teaching but *doing* by incorporating the activities in which students engage to develop knowledge of subjects and understanding of scientific ideas (National Research Council, 2012). Colburn (2000) defines inquiry-based instruction as "the creation of a classroom where students are engaged in essentially open-ended, student-centered, hands-on activities" (p. 1).

### Engagement and UDL in Science

Inquiry-based instruction occurs on a spectrum ranging from student-driven open inquiry to teacher-led guided inquiry. Inquiry-based instruction lends itself well to the application of UDL principles to engage diverse learners with varying interests and strengths, as well as academic and support needs in inclusive settings (Watt, Therrien, Kaldenberg, & Taylor, 2013). Even students who feel they "hate science" can be engaged when they are the ones asking the questions!

- **MAKE CONNECTIONS TO OTHER STEM AREAS to activate and maintain student engagement.** The Next Generation Science Standards (NGSS; www.nextgenscience.org) provide connections to related engineering practices and math standards for each standard.
- **ALLOW STUDENTS TIME TO EXPLORE those math, engineering, and/or technology connections until they begin asking their own questions.** You will never find time to individualize learning or integrate other content if you don't provide a structure where it can occur. Look at your day and prioritize a bit of STEM time!
- **USE STUDENT LIFE EXPERIENCES to relate science content and promote student inquiry** (e.g., a student's problem at home with an ant infestation could lead to questions about the habits and habitats of ants).
- **HAVE A STEM CAREER DAY** and bring in community partners and local speakers who work in science and STEM jobs.
- **USE BADGES AND CHECKPOINTS to keep students on task and engaged.** Checkpoints, badges, progress charts, and game boards can maintain momentum. Create custom desk badges to go along with a webquest on the solar system. As students meet your objectives for each planet, have them add it to their desk sticker board to mark their progress. This serves not only as a form of motivation, it also allows learners track their own progress.
- **USE MIND MAPS AND THINKING ORGANIZERS to scaffold exploration and track learner progress.** Real-time mind

maps and web walls can provide a pictorial representation of
student exploration and direction. Give students a space on
the wall to visually represent the
milestones in a long-term project. Students collecting insect
specimens may create a web
wall in their space, organizing

**Tech Tip**

Use MindMup https://www
.mindmup.com/
Find great tips for how at
https://www.makeuseof
.com/tag/try-mindmup-mind-
mapping-via-google-drive/

insect targets by class and order. This is a great way to incorporate creative expression into a project.

- **USE SOCIAL MEDIA to engage students in discussion.** Try
  using student blogs, tweets, breaking news, and other forms of
  live updates to highlight student progress to maintain engagement and foster inquiry (using student handles, create a no-tech
  twitter wall where students can "tweet" about their research).
  Check out how to use Paper Twitter at http://decentralisedteach-
  ingandlearning.com/low-tech-teaching-2-paper-twitter/

- **VARY THE LEVEL OF CHAL-
  LENGE.** Allow students to
  choose from a range of STEM
  activities that vary in difficulty
  or complexity. Students studying weather may take a virtual

**Making Connections**

See Chapter 12 for more on
UDL with Advancement.

field trip to connect with weather (Discovery Education), make
their own barometer, monitor daily weather characteristics,
gather regional data on weather patterns, create pictorial representations of weather data to share with peers, or analyze
weather data to identify long-term trends.

## CASE IN POINT

A group of students gathered around a child on the playground who
held a cup containing a captured caterpillar. Returning to the classroom,
Mr. Gordon talked to the students about how the caterpillar would die in
the cup if it were not set free. The students wanted to keep the caterpillar
and make it a home, which led to a class project to learn about caterpillar
and butterfly habitats and how to build one. Knowing that caterpillars were
not part of this year's curriculum, but wanting to build on students' interests,
Mr. Gordon decided to integrate various skills that were part of grade-level
curriculum into learning about caterpillars.

*(Continued)*

(Continued)

> The students used computers and the Internet (technology) to find the information they needed and discovered that their new friend would soon form a chrysalis and emerge a couple of weeks later as a Monarch butterfly (science). To get ready, the students made a list of the materials and plants, researched costs, and created a budget (math). They measured and computed the area of the little plot of ground needed and then designed (engineering; art) their garden in a design program. Once budgeting and planning were complete, they raised money and went shopping for materials (math). While they were planning and planting, the students placed their caterpillar in an aquarium with a milkweed branch and some water so it would be safe while they worked (science).
>
> One morning, they discovered their caterpillar morphed into a chrysalis, attaching itself to the side of the aquarium. Once the habitat was ready, the students gently opened the aquarium and placed the branch and chrysalis plants among the milkweed plants so when the butterfly emerged, it could fly free in the garden. This very personal adventure provided a context for learning that no textbook or worksheet could ever do. STEM integration at its best!

## UDL IN ACTION: EXPRESSION IN SCIENCE AND STEM

Learning deepens when students have the opportunity to actively engage in activities that involve practice and application of the knowledge and/or skills central to the learning objective. Real-world problems and authentic tasks provide engaging opportunities for students to demonstrate that they have mastered these skills. Science lends itself nicely to the real-world problem-solving scenario since by its very nature it involves identifying and answering questions about the world around us. Science and STEM content provide countless opportunities for student action and expression.

### Expression in Universally Designed Science

In life science class, students learn to use a dichotomous key to identify living and nonliving things. One way to actively engage students in practicing the use of a dichotomous key is the classic Jelly Belly® identification project. In this activity, students use a dichotomous key that contains color and marking criteria to identify the flavor of the jelly bean. They confirm their hypothesis by tasting each jelly bean. Once students have a grasp of how a dichotomous key works, they can then apply that skill to an authentic question in their own world. When students can apply new knowledge and skills to answer their own questions, they are demonstrating a deep understanding of not only the content, but its function in real-world science. Use some of these strategies to enable students to take action and express their learning in a variety of ways:

- **USE LABS so students can demonstrate an understanding of the application of content.** Both real and virtual labs can provide opportunities for students to engage with science content. Check out forty science lab ideas (https://www .scholastic.com/teachers/articles/teaching-content/40-cool-science-experiments-web/) or free online labs (https://bloom board.com/users/elizabeth-kaplan/collections/virtual-science-experiences-labs-with-no-clean-up/de053d3e-9069-4e70-a5f1-7a395a26a491).
- **ENCOURAGE SCIENCE FAIR PARTICIPATION to get every student involved in "doing" science.** Countless choices of topics and types of research make science fairs UDL friendly. Here are 1,154 ideas to get you started (https://www.sciencebuddies .org/science-fair-projects/project-ideas/list).
- **USE BLOGS AND SOCIAL MEDIA to connect with experts and express an understanding of the latest in science topics.** Check out blogs by NASA (https://blogs.nasa.gov/), tech blogs (http://insidetech.monster.com/benefits/articles/8537-10-best-tech-blogs), or all types of science blogs (https://blog.feedspot .com/science_blogs/), which are all great ways to get current information in these areas. Check out these science handles on Twitter @NASA, @science, @EPA, @CurrentBiology, or search for other science topics of interest.

### Expression in Universally Designed STEM Integration

The cross-curricular connections of STEM integration can strengthen and deepen content area learning, be powerful motivators, and serve to maintain student engagement. Additionally, STEM integration adds a host of action and expression options that can allow students to demonstrate their learning. In language arts classrooms, typically reluctant writers find the ability to express themselves when writing about a topic that fascinates them. An avid skier struggling with understanding the concept of "slope" may make the connection in an engineering problem requiring the construction of a ski lift. Check out the Case In Point below for STEM integration in nonscience classes.

- **THE SCIENTIFIC METHOD provides structure for inquiry and discovery.** Use it to engage students in STEM-related research in nonscience classrooms with questions that connect history and engineering, or literature and technology, or music and mathematics. It all begins with a research question.

**CASE IN POINT**

"Which is the largest of the ancient pyramids?" Armed with just this single question, students set out to identify the world's largest pyramid. The Internet provided a start, but the assignment required that they identify "the best" way to compare pyramid size. Students were required to defend their choice of measurement after calculating and comparing those values for the five largest pyramids previously identified by archeologists. As they brainstormed measurement options, students considered size in terms of height, length, width, weight, volume, surface area, number of blocks, and mass. They researched to find formulas and determine if the information they needed for the calculations was available. They could use photos, satellite images, and digital tools to get a closer look at various pyramids, making note of irregularities that might be a factor in their calculations.

Students used Internet sources to find established dimensions of the targeted pyramids and performed various calculations with the information available to determine multiple measures of size for comparison purposes. Some groups built scale models, others used CAD programs to create 3D images for visual comparison, while others put pencil to paper and sketched. In the end, six groups of students reached independent conclusions, justifying their calculations and measures. These projects demonstrated a deep understanding of size, dimensions, similarity, comparisons, polyhedrons, polygons, bases, lateral faces, congruence, angles, and vertices . . . and yes, a deep appreciation for the seemingly impossible task of constructing these structures without modern machines and technology.

- **SOCRATIC SEMINARS provide a structured format to integrate STEM into discussions** to promote the use of STEM language and understanding in other curricular areas. Check out http://www.readwritethink.org/professional-development/strategy-guides/socratic-seminars-30600.html
- **BLOGS PROVIDE AUTHENTIC AUDIENCES for students to express their learning around a variety of topics, to include STEM ones.** Wordpress, Squarespace, and other hosting sites make blogging accessible to anyone. Get tips for how to blog at https://www.bloggingbasics101.com/how-do-i-start-a-blog/

## BRINGING IT ALL TOGETHER

Make relevant connections among science, STEM, and your students. Do everything you can to bring authentic science and STEM experiences into the classroom. Leverage *Star Wars,* community partners, and industry to bring in STEM experts. Build background knowledge through these experts or through authentic video experiences.

To bring student culture into the classroom, watch what they watch, listen to their music, and read what they read. Look for science and STEM connections in everything (find the real science in sci-fi) and make learning feel like an extension of their world. Are your students playing Fortnite, talking about escape rooms, watching Marvel or *Star Wars,* or reading *Hunger Games*? How can you connect these interests to science or STEM-related topics?

Many of tomorrow's opportunities are in STEM fields or require STEM skills. Our most vulnerable students (economically disadvantaged, minorities, and students with disabilities) continue to be grossly underrepresented in STEM careers, and few find accessible opportunities to engage in science and STEM in school. A science class every year is not likely to change this disturbing statistic, but STEM integration across various subjects in a universally designed manner can change those odds. Couched in the framework of UDL, STEM integration can free science, technology, engineering, and mathematics from their curricular silos. The more universally designed exposure our students have with STEM content, skills, and careers, the more likely they are to pursue STEM options in school and postsecondary settings.

**Table 4.1    STEM Integration Matrix**

|  | *Multiple Means of Engagement WHY* | *Multiple Means of Representation WHAT* | *Multiple Means of Action and Expression HOW* |
|---|---|---|---|
| **SCIENCE** | Can students choose topics based on their interest, a question they have, or a problem they want to solve? | What resources are available for students to access science content or science connections? | Can students choose to use strengths and interests in science as they demonstrate learning? |
| **TECHNOLOGY** | Do students have the opportunity to choose tools and apps to support their learning? | What tools are available to support learner variability and needs in accessing content? | Do students have tech options for creating products and demonstrating learning? |
| **ENGINEERING** | Can students choose where and how to incorporate planning, design, or construction in this lesson? | What options are available for accessing related engineering content/skills to support this lesson? | Are students incorporating planning, designing, or construction? |
| **MATH** | Does the essential question prompt a mathematics connection? Is there an authentic mathematics application? | Where and how can students find math connections and acquire information on how to apply those connections? | How are students incorporating math in this lesson? (e.g., calculations, logic, reasoning, data, SMP) |

## TOP FIVE WEBSITES TO SUPPORT STEM

➜ http://barbarabray.net/2017/06/08/design-thinking-process-and-udl-planning-tool/

➜ https://www.ck12.org/student/

➜ http://www.egfi-k12.org/engineer-your-path/

➜ https://www.nationalgeographic.org/education/stem-education/

➜ https://www.teachengineering.org/

## APPS WE LOVE

➜ Educreations

➜ PanterTechnology

➜ Sketchup

➜ Tinkercad

➜ WolframAlpha

# REFERENCES

Basham, J. D., & Marino, M. T. (2013). Understanding STEM education and supporting students through Universal Design for Learning. *Teaching Exceptional Children, 45*(4), 8–15.

Colburn, A. (2000). An inquiry primer. *Science Scope, 23*(6), 42–44.

Donegan-Ritter, M. (2017). STEM for all children: Preschool teachers supporting engagement of children with special needs in physical science learning centers. *Young Exceptional Children, 20*(1), 3–15.

Dunn, A. W. (1916). *The social studies in secondary education: A six-year program adapted both to the 6–3–3 and the 8–4 plans of organization.* Report of the Committee on Social Studies of the Commission on the Reorganization of Secondary Education of the National Education Association. Bulletin, 1916, No. 28. Bureau of Education, Department of the Interior.

Gravel, J. W. (2018). Going deep: Leveraging Universal Design for Learning to engage all learners in rich disciplinary thinking in ELA. *Teachers College Record, 120,* 030303.

Israel, M., Maynard, K., & Williamson, P. (2013). Promoting literacy-embedded, authentic STEM instruction for students with disabilities and other struggling learners. *Teaching Exceptional Children, 45*(4), 18–25.

National Education Association. (2014). Preparing 21st century students for a global society: An educator's guide to the "Four Cs." Washington, DC: Author.

National Research Council. (2012). *A framework for K–12 science education: Practices, crosscutting concepts, and core ideas.* Washington, DC: National Academies Press.

Vasquez, J. A., Sneider, C., & Comer, M. (2013). *STEM lesson essentials, Grades 3–8: Integrating science, technology, engineering, and mathematics.* Portsmouth, NH: Heinemann.

Watt, S. J., Therrien, W. J., Kaldenberg, E., & Taylor, J. (2013). Promoting inclusive practices in inquiry-based science classrooms. *Teaching Exceptional Children, 45*(4), 40–48.

# 5

# UDL and the Performing Arts

## *Inspiring Creativity*

Rebecca M. Ashton
*Area Stage Company, Coral Gables, FL*

Tamarah M. Ashton
*California State University, Northridge*

## SETTING THE STAGE FOR UDL AND THE PERFORMING ARTS

Why is it that arts in the classroom are almost always associated only with the early years of education, or as a diversion or "break" from more traditional teaching methods?

> [I]n any civilization—ours included—the arts are inseparable from the very meaning of the term "education." We know from long experience that no one can claim to be truly educated who lacks basic knowledge and skills in the arts. (Adapted from the National Core Arts Standards, 2014, Adopt the Arts Foundation)

Depending on your era, it is likely that as you were growing up, you were familiar with "edutainment" programs like *Mister Rogers'*

*Neighborhood, The Magic School Bus,* or even that lovable purple dinosaur, *Barney,* to name just a few. Each of these shows has promoted the concept that music and drama make learning fun! For instance, have you ever considered making a math problem into a song for a group of sixth graders? How about rapping a Canterbury Tale? Probably not. Let's allow those ideas to settle for a bit while we explain the structure of our chapter.

In this chapter, we will discuss the three main disciplines of the performing arts: acting, singing, and dancing, and how they might be integrated into your classroom teaching using the principles of UDL. The arts are a vast and ever-growing field, and there are many more art-related activities you might wish to include in your lesson plans (e.g., drawing, painting, cartooning, sculpture), but here, the performing arts (acting, singing, and dancing) will be our focus.

It may be helpful for you to think of the performing arts not as something you must "fit in" with your UDL strategies, but as something that naturally supports and bolsters your efforts. Remember that you want to minimize barriers and maximize learning for all of your students (Ashton, 2015). So, for example, what better way to reach an auditory learner than through rhythm and music? How about devising a memorization game for kinesthetic learners—connecting simple dance steps to the words they must memorize? The performing arts involve all your senses at once!

Additionally, you can often use one performing arts activity to reach multiple students with different learning profiles. Teaching the periodic table of elements? Why not turn it into a goofy little song? (We would personally add some tap dancing, but that's totally up to you!) Print out the lyrics so students can read along while they sing along, and have everyone get on their feet to clap and stomp out the rhythm! Are you worried about looking or feeling foolish while implementing such an activity with your students? Well, that's the point! Help your students get out of the day-to-day monotony of the classroom to engage them. You will all feel silly together.

Through this one activity, you are able to engage learners of multiple types. Not only that, but these activities can be adapted easily and on-the-fly in order to accommodate students with special needs. Perhaps one of your students participating in the periodic table activity is particularly sensitive to loud sounds. Let any students who want them have access to noise-canceling ear buds (even a pair of earmuffs will do to dull the sounds and help students feel safe and included) and let them continue dancing it out at their comfort level. You see, the performing arts truly are the perfect way to include UDL in any lesson you teach!

The benefits of including the arts in a well-rounded education plan have long been studied, with the general consensus that students who are exposed to the arts show stronger academic performance than those who are not (e.g., Caterall, 2009; Fiske, 1999). There is even strong evidence that there is a direct link between inclusion of the arts in education and graduation rates (Center for Arts Education, 2009).

The benefits of artistic instruction do not stop with the classroom. Through artistic instruction, students improve cooperation and leadership skills while gaining confidence in themselves and their abilities. The arts help students connect to the larger world and their place within it, improving community function and cohesion (McCarthy, Ondaatje, Brooks, & Szanto, 2005). Correlations have been measured between exposure to the arts and students' values, such as tolerance and empathy. Outcomes suggest that students' awareness of the world, and different people and places within it, was increased through their exposure to the arts, ultimately making them more empathetic and tolerant people (Greene et al., 2014).

We could continue to list the exceptionally strong evidence supporting the vital importance of the arts in schools (e.g., Rapp-Paglicci, Stewart, & Rowe, 2011). However, despite this strong evidence, there continues to be a disparaging dearth of artistic instruction in schools across the country. Funding for the arts continues to lessen while students' scores on arts education assessments, such as on the Nation's Report Card (2016), continue to fall. It is up to us as educators to take it upon ourselves to include the arts in the classroom. Just as UDL is a mindset, and not merely a set of instructions, the arts are a mindset as well. Artistic aspects can be included in just about any lesson plan.

Here, we will outline just a few of the ways in which this can be accomplished. But we challenge you to be creative! Find new and engaging ways to incorporate the arts in your classroom each and every day. As Michelle Obama (2015) said, "Arts education is not a luxury, it's a necessity. . . . It's how we get kids excited about getting up and going to school in the morning. It's how we get them to take ownership of their future."

So, why not just put on a *Schoolhouse Rock* video and call it "music integration"? Well, if integrating the arts into the classroom is brand new to you, then that might not be a bad place to begin. But you can do better! Simply playing a video for your students will not improve engagement and universal access to learning as much as you would like, because your students will not actually be doing anything outside the norm for them. They will be watching and listening—which is what you ask of them each day when you begin class.

Perhaps you grew up with *Schoolhouse Rock* or *Sesame Street* and you absolutely love them. Great! You may not have realized it at the time, but those shows were teaching you content through all the silly songs! Remember the *Schoolhouse Rock* multiplication song? It may have seemed like just a fun activity, but setting those multiplication tables to a melody and beat helped you learn and retain the material. So why not try it with your

**Tech Tip**

Have access to your "oldies but goodies" through YouTube! Every student should learn how a bill becomes a law through *Schoolhouse Rock*. (https://www.youtube.com/watch?v=FFroMQlKiag)

students? Show the video several times, encouraging students to sing along as they become more familiar with the melody and lyrics. Once they become proficient at singing along, turn off the video's sound, hand out instruments, and have the students play and sing the song together just as a band would do. It doesn't have to sound perfect! Try turning on the captions to keep your new band on beat. For other students, why not set those same lyrics to a rap beat? Ask for a student volunteer to beatbox, and have the other students take turns rapping the lyrics over the beat. Through rhythm and music activities like these, students truly learn and retain the material because they are actively doing something and not passively watching and listening.

Do you have to be a Broadway performer in order to put these ideas into practice? No! However, most of us possess certain performing arts talents, whether we admit it or not. Did you take tap lessons when you were eight? How about piano? Or participate in drama club in high school? Even if you have never done a single one of those things, do you enjoy listening to any type of music? Are you a Shakespeare aficionado? Even if absolutely none of these connects with you, do you at least recognize that some of your students are artistically inclined or driven by performance? Whew. Good! That alone makes you qualified to guide your students and include the arts in your universally designed lessons.

You can learn along with them, and expand your horizons as an educator in the process. Those are all skills you can draw upon to put UDL principles and arts instruction into practice. It is not about you demonstrating the perfect performance technique; rather, the goal is to engage your students. Make yourself vulnerable, and your students will recognize that your classroom is a safe space to experiment and identify their own best ways to learn. Demonstrate, be the first to try, and lead by example. Then, encourage your students to "do"!

## PUTTING UDL AND THE PERFORMING ARTS INTO PRACTICE: MULTIPLE MEANS OF REPRESENTATION

Because we are discussing ways in which we might *utilize* the three main disciplines of the performing arts as *tools* to convey general education material, and not ways in which we would provide an education in the artistic practices themselves, remember that it is okay to act, look, and feel silly. You, the teacher, need not be an expert in acting, singing, or dancing. There are many ways you can employ these disciplines as means of representation for your students.

### Acting

Acting is a wonderful discipline to begin with if you are apprehensive about arts integration. Most acting exercises, games, and tools are very adaptable and accessible to everyone—including those who have no prior experience.

- **UTILIZE ROLE-PLAYING!** Dress up in full costume (this does not have to be expensive; just use things already in your closet). Adopt an accent, if appropriate. Stay in character for the duration of the lesson. Portray fictional and real-life characters. Encourage students to do the same when they are doing presentations.
- **HAVE STUDENTS INTERVIEW YOU** while you are role-playing. Supply them with a list of questions they might ask to get them started, but then encourage them to ask other questions they think might be relevant based on the character you are portraying.
- **APPLY ROLE-PLAYING TO OTHER DISCIPLINES (like science and math), not just in presenting historical material.** There is no reason you cannot role-play as an animal, cell, or even as a math equation. You have not lived until you have heard seventh graders role-play mitosis!

## Singing

Singing and rhythm are some of the best tools for improving retention. In fact, there is evidence suggesting a strong correlation between involvement in music education and test scores in elementary school students (Johnson & Memmott, 2006).

## CASE IN POINT

Ron prepares to teach a lesson on the signing of the Declaration of Independence. He chooses to integrate role-play in the representation of the material and decides to portray John Adams. He arrives in the classroom fully decked out in attire of the time period. As students enter his classroom, he asks them to line up and greet him formally with a bow and a handshake, just as they would have done in 1776. He also plays chamber music from his computer to immerse students into the atmosphere as much as possible. To further represent the material, he provides handouts listing each of the most prolific signers of the Declaration, a few important facts about each, and a few questions to which the students must compose answers throughout their interview with him. Students begin the interview, first asking questions suggested on the handout, and then some of their own. At the conclusion of the interview, students are asked to guess which of the Founders their teacher is portraying. Ron's students all scored well on their pop quiz the next week, after having learned from John Adams himself.

- PROVIDE A BACKGROUND SOUNDTRACK for each of your activities throughout the day. This is one of the simplest methods for integrating music into your classroom representation. As illustrated in the Case in Point, this can be very useful in setting the mood for a new activity. Music can also have a very calming and focusing effect. Consider always having the same playlist going during the same activities each day, cuing your class to prepare and focus for the next activity.

- EMPLOY VISUAL AIDS, such as a musical staff drawn on a whiteboard with magnetic notes to represent the musical rhythms. If you do not read music, and have never seen a musical staff, don't worry! A simple Google image search will guide you. You might also ask your students who study music to help you. Through musical rhythms, you can teach mathematical concepts such as addition, subtraction, and division. Believe it or not, music—something that students enjoy—is a useful method for teaching math. Did you study music theory or piano as a child? Fantastic! Now is the time to use that knowledge.

- CREATE A SONG OR A RHYTHM (or encourage your students to create their own) that can be spoken over and over again to assist with memorization when teaching something repetitive that would normally be learned by rote (e.g., mathematical formulas, dates, etc.). Employ a call-and-response tactic with your students, "singing" the song or rhythm over and over again. Encourage students to clap along, or even provide them with instruments with which to keep the rhythm. Maracas and tambourines work great! Yes, even for high school students. Simply ask them to mimic the beat from their favorite Kanye West song, and they will be more engaged than you have ever seen them.

### Dancing

Here is another opportunity for integrating your abilities into your lessons. Many of us participated in some form of dance training throughout our school years. Why not dance for your students? You do not have to be a prima ballerina to make this fun and engaging. (In fact, it is sometimes more engaging and fun to watch teachers who can't dance than those who can!)

- INTEGRATE DANCE WITH THE RHYTHM-BASED, CALL-AND-RESPONSE ACTIVITY discussed above by adding a specific foot-stomping pattern to the rhythm or song you create. Even high school students might appreciate a little stomp and clap action to break up the day!

- Have a day where you push tables and desks to the sides of the classroom and TEACH A DANCE TO YOUR STUDENTS. This is easily integrated into historical or language arts lessons. Learn the waltz when reading and discussing fairy tales, or try a bit of ballet if learning about the Renaissance.
- WATCH CURRENT MUSIC VIDEOS of popular songs. Let students select songs of interest to them (as long as they are teacher-approved). Have students connect their content to the dance video. You may have them write descriptive paragraphs, create a scientific problem to solve, design a math equation, or even pretend they are sociologists from the future who have come upon this video and need to determine what the dance moves are meant to express.

## PUTTING UDL AND THE PERFORMING ARTS INTO PRACTICE: MULTIPLE MEANS OF ENGAGEMENT

"To engage with the performing arts on a deeper level, students must have the opportunity to explore the process of artistic creation" (Floberg & Brown, 2013, p. 51). Engagement is the area in which integration of the performing arts truly shines. The above quote, from a study conducted to explore the most effective means of student engagement in the arts, further illustrates our earlier point that students often learn best by doing. For example, your ski instructor can explain and show you exactly the technique needed to make it down the steepest run on the mountain, but until you try it yourself, you will not learn. The arts expand your opportunities for "doing" in the classroom.

### Acting

Introduce games and strategies not as "acting" or "performing arts games," but rather flow into them naturally from previous activities. This will encourage students to think of these exercises as games, and to engage in them with enthusiasm and without self-consciousness.

- CREATE A QUESTIONS GAME. Ask for a few student volunteers and have them stand up in front of the class. Let them know that they will be improvising a short scene, but that they will only be able to ask questions of their scene partners. They may not utilize any other type of sentence, only questions. This activity is quite useful in teaching different sentence types (e.g., interrogative or declarative). The game can be adapted to fit multiple other learning objectives by changing what students are allowed to say during the improv.

**STRATEGY SPOT**
THE CLAPPING GAME

Are your students often hyperactive and unfocused before recess? Or is your after-lunch period usually lethargic and uninterested? Consider beginning each new class period with the Clapping Game. To ensure students are relaxed, focused on the task at hand, and fully engaged, employ this activity. Have students stand in a circular formation, and have one student begin the clap. They will pass it to their right or left, around the circle. To pass the clap, they will look the other student in the eye, and clap at exactly the same moment. Encourage the students to focus on keeping the rhythm steady and to block out all other distractions. Once they are comfortable here, they can begin reversing the direction of the clap, or even passing it across the circle. You will find that this game involves multiple aspects of the performing arts, and is useful for engaging all types of learners. Once students are focused, centered, and engaged, they are in the prime mindset for learning any content you wish to teach—and it only takes a few minutes!

- **DIRECT YOUR STUDENTS IN A SCENE.** Ask for volunteers, and assign them characters from the lesson. Then, proceed to narrate the sequence of events, asking students to act out the scene as it goes.
- **ALLOW YOUR STUDENTS TO EXPRESS THEIR CREATIVITY AND SILLINESS.** They may have a tendency to take history into their own hands, and your reaction might be to call for quiet and focus. But acting is truly all about playing. Allow students to influence the activity, while still maintaining the direction, and while keeping the learning objectives in mind. When students present ideas during an acting exercise, always try to say, "Yes, and . . . ," rather than "No, but. . . ."

## Singing

Singing, music, and rhythm are part of most contemporary students' daily lives without them even realizing it. Kids today know the words to every pop song on the radio and can sing them on command. To engage them through music, you need only tap into that already existing passion.

- **EMPLOY SONGS AS WRITING PROMPTS.** Either choose an appropriate contemporary song that you know your students enjoy or let them select their own. Then ask students to write a paragraph inspired by that song. Or why not play their favorite music during a stream of consciousness writing activity?

- **GUIDE YOUR STUDENTS' GROUP MOOD THROUGH MUSIC.** Imagine a scene from a movie that always makes you cry. Now imagine that scene without any music. It loses power. Music influences our moods and emotions whether we realize it or not. Try playing calming music during a group activity, and see how the energy in the room is different than it is without music. You will likely see a decrease in extraneous talking among groups.
- **UTILIZE TECHNOLOGY!** Create mood playlists on Spotify and download music visualization iPad apps (e.g., Singing Fingers, Sound Drop, and Novation Launchpad) to offer students more choices in their learning.

### Dancing

Dancing is extremely useful for improving engagement because it truly involves your entire being. While dancing, your visual, auditory, and kinesthetic senses are all fully employed. Therefore, if you dance something, you *will* learn it!

- **PLAY "STATUES."** Put on some fun, upbeat music that your students enjoy, and call out themes, vocab words, parts of speech, dates, or anything else that is relevant to your learning objectives. Once you call out the word, students should strike a strong pose—or "statue"—that represents that word for them. You can encourage them to find a different statue of their own for each word to help with memorization and retention!
- **PLAY THE MIRROR GAME to help students increase their cooperation skills when about to work on a class project in groups or with partners.** Partners stand facing each other (groups stand in a small circle), and a leader is chosen. The leader then begins slow and controlled movements of their choosing, and the "mirror(s)" must follow as precisely as they can. It is useful to play music during this activity to assist with the interpretative movement and to increase focus. Partners and groups will become more comfortable working together and will learn about cohesion, thereby taking their minds off the partner or group aspect of the activity, and allowing them to focus on learning the content.
- **CHANGE THE PHYSICAL CLASSROOM ENVIRONMENT.** Change the configuration of desks and/or tables in your classroom every few weeks to ensure there is always adequate open space in the center, or to the sides for movement games and activities. Recruit students to help you reconfigure the room.

- USE GONOODLE.COM for interactive dance and movement activities that are perfect for the classroom!

**Tech Tip**

Find out more about GoNoodle by going to https://www.gonoodle.com/or watching the video at https://www.youtube.com/user/GoNoodleGames

- ALLOW FOR ANONYMITY. Have reluctant dancers in your group? Try playing some slow, calming music and having students move to it with their eyes shut. This will allow those students who might feel self-conscious or silly to move in their own way, without fear of being mocked.

## PUTTING UDL AND THE PERFORMING ARTS INTO PRACTICE: MULTIPLE MEANS OF ACTION AND EXPRESSION

At the end of the day, the performing arts are about performance. Once acting, singing, and dance activities are integrated into your representation and engagement toolboxes, you have the ability to expand action and expression options for your students.

### Acting

Any performer will tell you that acting is all about storytelling. Encourage your class to express its knowledge through a story in the classroom!

- HAVE STUDENTS DO THE ROLE-PLAYING by flipping the interview activity around! Write the names of several people, places, or things you are currently learning about on some sticky notes. When students take their turn, place a sticky note on their forehead so the class can see who or what they are, but they cannot (similar to the game HeadBandz). The class must then answer their questions pertaining to the person, place, or thing they are representing. The student in the hot seat has three tries to guess who or what he or she is based on the responses from peers.
- INSTRUCT STUDENTS TO WRITE AND PERFORM A SCENE. Divide your class into small groups of four or five and ask students to work collaboratively to express what they have learned throughout the lesson. This can be adapted for shy students, English language learners, or even nonverbal students. Have them serve as the director of the scene, or as a writer or critic or stage manager, if they are too anxious to perform.

UDL v. DI

- PLAY "SCENES FROM A HAT." Instead of giving your class a test on *To Kill a Mockingbird,* why not have them act out the story

## STRATEGY SPOT
### REENACTMENT RUBRICS

Provide students with a clear rubric of learning objectives prior to having them commence in any action and expression activity. If given only general instructions, students are likely to get caught up in the fun and creativity of expression, and lose sight of the specifics. For example: if you are asking them to write and perform a scene about the Louisiana Purchase, and would like to ensure they know the key dates, places, and people involved, then be certain to list these specifics on your rubric.

instead? Two students will go first, and will draw a prompt from a hat. You will write the prompts beforehand, and they should be short sentences describing a scene from the book. The two students will then act out a short scene, expressing their knowledge of the learning objectives. One student will sit down, and another will stand, cycling through the class until all students have had a turn.

Singing

- **INTEGRATE TECHNOLOGY INTO YOUR MUSIC CURRICULUM.** When asking students to create an individual composition, such as a poem or an essay, it is a great idea to give them the option of creating a song instead. Choice is critical to a universally designed classroom. There are a variety of websites that can help students compose music quickly and easily. Check out the Tech Tip for a few suggestions.

- **HAVE STUDENTS CREATE MUSIC VIDEOS** to express what they have learned. Encourage students to work in groups and suggest possible positions within the group to give all students an option that appeals to them personally. Suggestions can include videographer, editor, director, choreographer, singer, composer, and so forth. As previously mentioned, be sure to make the requirements clear, and then give students freedom in how they express those requirements.

 **Tech Tip**

Find out more ways for students to share their learning through musical compositions by going to

- www.incredibox.com
- or by watching the video at https://www.youtube.com/watch?v=qkmtRu-ceYc

Dancing

- **EXPRESS A STORY learned during class through dance and movement.** Rather than telling students they must dance, ask them to express themselves through movement. Tell them the only rule is they cannot use words during the movement piece.
- **SHARE STUDIES OF VARIOUS CULTURES AND SOCIETIES through dance or movement.** Dance is a very social concept, so allow students who enjoy demonstrating different types of movement to share their own personal culture or knowledge they have gleaned about other societies through movement.
- **USE DANCE TO BRING DIFFERENT QUALITIES OF MOVEMENT TO LIFE.** Imagine studying different qualities of movement—say, among different types of insects. How much more interesting would it be to have those students who are inclined to actually dance those movements, while others may choose to create videos, draw examples, or describe the movement in writing? *Pro Tip:* Try this with dinosaurs . . . you will laugh all the way home in the car. Trust us—so cute!

## BRINGING IT ALL TOGETHER

We began our chapter by reminding you of some of your positive childhood memories related to learning experiences and how music, dance, and acting might have engaged you personally. We hope that now that you will begin to ponder new ways to utilize the performing arts in your daily curriculum, all in the name of Universal Design for Learning. Whether or not you are a performer at heart is not the point—UDL emphasizes multiple methods of representation, engagement, and expression so that your students have options to show their stuff. And some of them might just be the next Gene Kelley, Barbra Streisand, Justin Timberlake, George Clooney, Gloria Estefan, or Ariana Grande! So dust off your zither, get your bongo drums out of your mom's garage, or do whatever you need to so you and your students can start having fun while actively representing, expressing, and engaging with and through your academic content via UDL and the performing arts!

## TOP FIVE WEBSITES TO SUPPORT UDL AND THE PERFORMING ARTS

→ http://creativitypost.com

→ http://www.mswholeschools.org/research/universal-design-for-learning

→ https://www.psarts.org/universal-design-learning-udl-arts-embracing-variability-learners/

→ https://www.vermontartscouncil.org/uploads/Grants/Arts%20Education/Sample%20Arts%20Integration%20Lesson%20Plans.pdf

→ http://wonderteacher.com

## APPS WE LOVE

→ Comic Life

→ Explain Everything Whiteboard

→ GarageBand

→ iMovie

→ WordFoto

# REFERENCES

Ashton, T. M. (2015). Unique Universal Design for Learning. In W. W. Murawski & K. L. Scott (Eds.), *What really works in secondary education* (pp. 170–182). Thousand Oaks, CA: Corwin.

Caterall, J. S. (2009). *Doing well and doing good by doing art: The effects of education in the visual and performing arts on the achievements and values of young adults.* Los Angeles, CA: Imagination Group/I-Group Books.

Center for Arts Education. (2009). *Groundbreaking study links high h.s. graduation rates to strong arts education programs.* Retrieved from https://centerforartsed .org/mediareleases/groundbreaking-study-links-high-hs-graduation-rates-strong-arts-education-programs

Fiske, E. B. (1999). *Champions of change: The impact of the arts on learning.* Washington, DC: Arts Education Partnership.

Floberg, J. L., & Brown, A. S. (2013). *Engaging next generation audiences: A study of college student preferences towards music and the performing arts.* Hanover, NH: Dartmouth College.

Greene, J. P., Kisida, B., Bogulski, C. A., Kraybill, A., Hitt, C., & Bowen, D. H. (2014). Arts education matters: We know, we measured it. *Education Week, 34*(13), 24. Retrieved from https://www.edweek.org/ew/articles/2014/12/03/13greene.h34.html

Johnson, C. M., & Memmott, J. E. (2006). Examination of relationships between participation in school music programs of differing quality and standardized test results. *Journal for Research in Mathematics Education, 54*(4), 293–307. doi:10.1177/002242940605400403

McCarthy, K. F., Ondaatje, E. H., Brooks, A., & Szanto, A. (2005). *A portrait of the visual arts: Meeting the challenges of a new era.* Santa Monica, CA: RAND Corporation.

Nation's Report Card. (2016). *Arts assessment.* Retrieved from https://www .nationsreportcard.gov/arts_2016/#/

National Core Arts Standards [adapted]. (2014). Retrieved from https://artsedge .kennedy-center.org/educators/standards

Obama, M. (2015). *Remarks by the First Lady at National Arts and Humanities Youth Program Awards.* Retrieved from https://obamawhitehouse.archives.gov/the-press-office/2015/11/17/remarks-first-lady-national-arts-and-humanities-youth-program-awards

Rapp-Paglicci, L., Stewart, C., & Rowe, W. (2011). Can a self-regulation skills and cultural arts program promote positive outcomes in mental health symptoms and academic achievement for at-risk youth? *Journal of Social Service Research, 37,* 309–319. doi:10.1080/01488376.2011.564067

# SECTION II

## *What Really Works With Behavior*

# 6

# *UDL and Executive Functioning*

## *Unlocking the Capacity for Learning*

Jennifer D. Walker

Victoria Russell

*University of Mary Washington*

## SETTING THE STAGE FOR EXECUTIVE FUNCTIONING AND UDL

Executive functioning (EF) skills are a set of cognitive capabilities or mental processes that guide critical thinking and self-regulation. These skills act like the traffic control center of the brain by organizing and planning, directing and regulating attention, initiating tasks, self-monitoring, and regulating emotions. Going through life without these skills might be like taking a road trip without packing, consulting a map, or even—gasp—traveling without GPS on your phone. Generally, researchers include the skill sets of working memory, inhibitory control, and cognitive flexibility in the characteristics of EF (e.g., Diamond, 2013; Meuwissen & Zelazo, 2014).

Let's break each of these characteristics down one by one. *Working memory* controls the ability to retain and manipulate multiple pieces of information over a short amount of time (Smith & Jonides, 1999). A student who struggles with working memory may have difficulty decoding unfamiliar words and also comprehending for meaning while reading, or remembering to carry the tens digit on a multiplication problem while also remembering multiplication facts. Essentially, working memory is the ability to hold onto one piece of information in our brains while we simultaneously work on another task.

**Key Concept**

Executive Functioning (EF) includes cognitive flexibility (can I switch gears quickly?), working memory (will I be able to remember information while you tell me something new?), and inhibitory control (can I keep myself from reacting immediately and without thinking?). Students may need differing levels of support with each component of EF.

*Inhibitory control* is the ability to focus attention on a task, person, event, or other stimuli without becoming distracted by unrelated stimuli in the environment (Diamond, 2013). For example, a student with strong inhibitory control can maintain focus on a teacher's instructions while other students pass by in the hallway. Students who struggle with inhibitory control may be distracted by external factors (e.g., a bird chirping outside the window, another student's sparkly earrings, or a clock ticking) or internal factors (e.g., hunger, thoughts about what to play at recess, or an itch).

In addition, these students may act impulsively as they respond to external or internal factors without first processing and deciding if their response is timely or appropriate. If they see a bird outside the window, they may suddenly announce it to the class, even if the class is quietly working. When completing assignments, these students may skip over directions or jump into work before checking to make sure they are on track. Working memory and inhibitory control have a reciprocal relationship in that both functions support one another. Working memory helps students to remember what to inhibit or hold back. Then, to put information together for working memory, they must resist focusing on external stimuli in order to make sense of material in front of them.

Finally, *cognitive flexibility* or flexible thinking refers to the ability to shift between different ideas, tasks, or demands. Cognitive flexibility builds on both working memory and inhibitory control (Davidson, Amso, Anderson, & Diamond, 2006). In a classroom, this may manifest itself in the inability to understand that a math problem can be solved in multiple ways (e.g., $10 \times 2$ is the same as $10 + 10$), that letters of a word are pronounced differently in different words (e.g., *ear*, *tear*, and *heart*), or that rules of grammar have exceptions (e.g., *talk* and *talked* versus *go* and *went*). Imagine learning to make change for a purchase. First, a student must focus on the task of subtracting the cost from the amount tendered. Then, the student must shift to remembering values of money (i.e., a quarter is 25 cents), and finally, the student must shift his or her thinking to counting out the money to make the right change. In order to reduce the mental load of these shifts, students with these challenges may be rigid in their approaches to learning, only focusing on one way or method of learning information. As one can imagine, students with poor cognitive flexibility don't always respond positively to novel stimuli or new changes to approach mastered tasks.

A student facing EF challenges often runs into significant learning barriers during day-to-day academic activities, particularly in areas like mathematics and reading that demand a great deal of executive function (Zelazo, Blair, & Willoughby, 2016). Struggles to remember and connect information, manage tasks, and regulate behaviors can lead to an inaccessible learning experience. But there's good news! Academic achievement and improvement with EF skills have reciprocal generalizability (Melby-Lervag, Redick, & Hulme, 2016). Let's see how UDL can break down those barriers and support a student with EF challenges.

## PUTTING UDL AND EXECUTIVE FUNCTIONING INTO PRACTICE: REPRESENTATION

Being a strategic and goal-directed learner puts working memory and cognitive flexibility into overdrive! Recall of prior knowledge, understanding of new information, and the connection between large concepts and identifying details are all required to successfully navigate curriculum. How teachers present and make information accessible to students is

### CASE IN POINT

Ramona has struggled with EF since preschool. Now that she's in ninth grade, her parents can look back and clearly see how issues with working memory, inhibitory control, and cognitive flexibility manifested in school, home, and the community. In school, Ramona's poor working memory creates challenges with reading comprehension and multistep math problems. While she has good reading fluency, she doesn't remember what she reads because her attention is on decoding words, not understanding for meaning. Similarly, Ramona does well with single-step math problems, but once she has to remember information from one step to the next (e.g., long division), she misses important steps or becomes bogged down in processes. Socially, Ramona often says things to her peers that aren't well received. Although she doesn't intend to come across as rude, her inhibitory control is limited and she often shares what is on her mind without considering the consequences. Finally, Ramona's parents see how her cognitive inflexibility has impacted her success in sports. In soccer, Ramona does best when she is in one position, like goalie, where the job stays the same. When placed as the midfielder, it is difficult for her to toggle between playing defense and offense.

the difference between "getting it" and being lost in class. Try these strategies to support representation:

- **BUILD CONNECTIONS between prior knowledge and new topics.** K-W-L charts completed at the beginning of a new unit or lesson generate recall (*what do I already know?*) and encourage students to consider connections between ideas (*what do I want to know?*). A chart can be kept on a bulletin board or in an electronic file accessible to all students. Students can add to the L-column (*what did I learn?*) as a summative review.

- **OFFER MULTIPLE WAYS for students to learn information.** Books, songs, pictures, dance—consider formats that are most accessible to meet individual student needs but also a variety of formats to support repetition of information for the entire class. This helps all learners, but is critical for those with executive functioning needs.

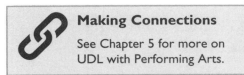

**Making Connections**

See Chapter 5 for more on UDL with Performing Arts.

- **MATCH GRAPHIC ORGANIZERS to the type of information you want students to learn.** A graphic organizer is "any visual structure or symbol that is used to represent knowledge or concepts and any relationships among them" (Rapp, 2014, p. 101). Graphic organizers are designed to serve specific functions—sequencing events, connecting details to main ideas, and concept comparisons are just a few examples. The templates these organizers provide make it easier to "see" information (versus a sea of words on the page) and set a structure to organize information that may be easier to remember (Ellis & Howard, 2007). This helps reduce that cognitive load called working memory!

- **ENCOURAGE STUDENTS to show off their talents by summarizing topics in their own style.** Class artists can produce sketch notes, budding authors can write summaries as newsletter articles, and future actors can reenact key concepts in short infomercials—the possibilities are endless! Students utilize choice in how they present information to the class while the class receives multiple representations of key content. Students take turns sharing their creations, which can be posted on a class website for review at a later date.

- **CHUNK INFORMATION into manageable "bites" and give students time to digest new information.** Depending on your students' attention levels, follow five to fifteen minutes of instruction with a check-in—have them tell you what they just learned and how it connects to past information. These periodic

**CASE IN POINT**

In middle school, Ramona's teacher, Ms. Frankel, wanted her students to take notes. She told them they could use any format they preferred, but she also gave them a two-column note-taking template to use if they wished. The first column had bulleted ideas with blanks. Those students who chose to use the form could fill in the blanks during instruction. Those who wanted to use a different note-taking format were allowed to do so as well. Every five to ten minutes, Ms. Frankel would pause the class for a "think check." She encouraged students to identify any ideas that were confusing or needed clarification. She taught the class a strategy to use if they thought it would be helpful—to place a sticky note in the second column of the template to flag any areas of confusion. Students were allowed to work with partners to address the "sticky" parts of the lesson, if they wished. Prior to removing the sticky notes, students were encouraged to write a clarifying note or draw an image to help them remember the correct information. Those who already had strategies for taking notes and retaining new content were allowed to choose their own formats, but because Ramona did not already have her own strategies, she found Ms. Frankel's template and sticky note strategy very helpful.

check-ins break up the lesson and allow you to formatively assess student understanding. Furthermore, students have time to process information and ask questions.

- **PROVIDE A QUIET READING NOOK or "concentration corner" where students can go to read or listen to information without environmental distractions,** such as windows or chatty classmates. Remember the inhibitory control challenges? The ability to focus is often related to the immediate environment. Help students learn to choose environments that are most conducive to their own success.

- **USE MNEMONICS AND RHYMES to support student recall of information and support working memory** (Scruggs, Mastropieri, Berkeley, & Marshak, 2010). While you can provide some classics to your students (e.g., ROY G BIV for the colors of the rainbow), student-driven creations draw on an individual's background and interests, which heightens engagement and better scaffolds new learning to prior knowledge. When students create their own memory strategies, they are more meaningful to them and the students will tend to remember them longer.

**STRATEGY SPOT**
CLICK OR CLUNK

During reading, students can use the *Click or Clunk* strategy to monitor their comprehension (Klingner & Vaughn, 1998). After reading a section of text, students identify ideas they understand (clicks) and ideas or words that are confusing or unknown (clunks). Once clunks are identified, students employ fix-up strategies to determine the meaning.

- **TEACH STUDENTS SELF-MONITORING COMPREHENSION STRATEGIES to support all facets of EF.** This is particularly important *while* students are reading because it helps them to focus for short periods, check understanding, and test recall of information (Joseph & Eveleigh, 2011).

A major barrier for many students is learning new vocabulary. It is particularly difficult for students with working memory challenges—words are either "right on the tip of their tongue" or too difficult to recall. Students who struggle with cognitive flexibility may confuse multiple meanings of individual words or not efficiently process clues signaling correct pronunciation (e.g., *tears on my face* versus *tears on my paper*). Students may also not understand how a word fits into the curriculum when learned in isolation. If the word isn't taught in context, it may be "stuck" in vocabulary purgatory. Teaching and reinforcing vocabulary in context are key for all students, but especially students with EF challenges (Bryant, Goodwin, Bryant, & Higgins, 2003).

- Novak (2016) offers a variety of methods for the **DIRECT INSTRUCTION OF VOCABULARY USING CONTEXT CLUES**. Notable and easy-to-implement ideas include picture clues, fill-in-the-blank activities, playing games, and clarifying idioms. All of these suggestions push beyond simple memorization and ask students to use language for practice and greater awareness of context clues.

**Making Connections**

See Chapter 1 for more on UDL with Literacy.

UDL v. DI

- **WORD WALLS are a common feature in classrooms.** Expand your wall's reach by including a "virtual wall" on the class website that includes audio pronunciation and definitions. Students can also create "portable word walls" by attaching hole-punched cards to a large O-ring. Portable word walls can be differentiated for individual students based on weekly assessments or on Individualized Education Program (IEP) goals and objectives—word walls can reflect different vocabulary based on student needs and learning goals.

- **BRING OUT THE KNOCK-KNOCK JOKES!** Jokes, riddles, and puns base their humor on layers of word meanings. These can be great ways to start a lesson by engaging students while reinforcing cognitive flexibility. Strengthen that flexibility by asking students to draw literal pictures of this word play or encouraging them to create their own language-based humor. Post student examples on the class website or create a class book at the end of the year.

## PUTTING UDL AND EXECUTIVE FUNCTIONING INTO PRACTICE: ENGAGEMENT

An engaged learner independently monitors progress and understanding while persisting through difficult parts of a lesson. Independence and persistence can be challenging for students with EF challenges. Environmental and instructional supports offer structure and organization so that students can focus on navigating the learning environment as well as managing their own behaviors.

- **LABEL MATERIALS to match specific tasks.** For example, you can color code folders so that all homework is in red folders and all take-home papers are in blue folders. Be careful—color coding is not always an effective way to help students differentiate spaces. Clear, bold labels with words and/or pictures can be just as effective, but even more important is to teach students different strategies for organization and to have them each select what works for them!
- **ESTABLISH "ZONES" in your students' learning spaces for specific activities and materials.** Zones for homework, missed work, daily agenda, and equipment are predictable reference points for students. For younger children, transition zones set a physical orientation for moving from one space to another. For example, giant footprint stickers along a classroom wall can indicate where students should stand while waiting to go to recess or the restroom. Older students may benefit from cooldown or quiet zones to de-stress when they feel overwhelmed. The more options for learning in the room, the better.
- **MAKE TIME for students to fill out planners each day, and monitor the accuracy of what they write!** While students with working memory challenges want to keep up, sometimes they struggle to simultaneously write down assignments, pack up their materials, and listen to last-minute teacher announcements. Keep an up-to-date work calendar on a class or electronic bulletin board that students can use to double-check their planners. At the beginning of each week, review the class calendar and highlight upcoming due dates and events. For older students,

**CASE IN POINT**

UDL
v. DI

In elementary school, Ramona's teachers used labeling and color coding to help Ramona and her classmates stay organized. In high school, though, Ramona was suddenly responsible for her own materials among five different classes. The first weeks of school were full of tears when Ramona forgot her books, materials, and homework because she left things in her locker after grabbing the wrong sets of items. Ramona's homeroom teacher sat and talked with her about her frustrations. They came up with a plan to keep all of her books and materials for classes before lunch on the top shelf of her locker and all of her afternoon materials on the bottom shelf. Ramona would only take materials she needed for a specific portion of her day and swap everything during a locker visit right before lunch. At the end of the day, Ramona used a reminder checklist taped to her locker door to sort through her planner so that she pulled folders and books she needed for studying at home. Although most of her peers did not need this additional organizational support, it reduced Ramona's frustration and increased her success in school!

consider using a calendar app that will message due date reminders. Multiple calendar formats support student preferences while providing the entire class multiple supports for planning.

- **HELP STUDENTS MANAGE THEIR CALENDARS by learning how to prioritize their work.** A planner on its own is not a foolproof solution. How many times have you written a long to-do list only to be overwhelmed with all the tasks? Students can sort tasks as "A" (urgent) and "B" (must be done, but have some time) based on due dates or assignment difficulty—from their perspectives. At the start of each week, note your suggestions for task codes on the class calendar. This helps address both cognitive flexibility and inhibitory control.

- **PROVIDE TIME MANAGEMENT ASSISTANCE.** When confronted with a task, students with EF challenges may

**Tech Tips**

Use Remind.com to:

- Send text messages to students and parents through an outside server.
- Update coded calendars and test, quiz, and assignment due dates after unexpected delays or days off from school.
- Send reminders for upcoming assignments or activities. These can be set ahead by weeks, days, or hours.
- Provide quick "class priority lists" for students and parents to reference.

be overwhelmed with both how to start the assignment and how to manage time. During in-class activities, assign directions in chunks, stopping groups after each set of steps to check on progress and necessary revisions in process. Use cueing systems (e.g., digital timer, call and response, light dimmer) to notify students how much time is left for a specific task. Provide students with task checklists for longer class assignments.

- **WORK WITH INDIVIDUAL STUDENTS to establish private cues for stopping or changing behavior that impacts learning.** Students may become overwhelmed or agitated during a lesson—lack of inhibitory control can lead to negative behaviors, such as off-task chatter, daydreaming, or task avoidance. For example, a teacher can pull her earlobe to indicate to a student that he needs to reduce his interruptions of classmates during discussion. This private visual cue can help students become more aware of behaviors and monitor their actions.

**UDL v. DI**

- **LOOK FOR GAMES that promote strategy development, turn taking, and clear directions.** EF skills can be practiced in fun ways by playing board games. Many common board games can be adapted to fit the age and content needs of your learners. For example, Wright (n.d.) shares eight board games that promote working memory, inhibitory control, and cognitive flexibility. These games include AnimaLogic, Distraction, Jenga, Max, Mindtrap, No Stress Chess, Quiddler, and Snake Oil. Have times when students can choose to engage in a game to reinforce content, and have multiple game types available.

## PUTTING UDL AND EXECUTIVE FUNCTIONING INTO PRACTICE: EXPRESSION

You put together a fun, creative assignment for your class that provides multiple options. You are excited for the students to show off their knowledge; they seem excited not to take a test! However, you notice a few students are struggling with the project options. One student is overwhelmed and anxious—she is not sure where to start and has changed her topic three times already. Another student is all over the map! He starts and stops different parts of the project, not making progress on any section. A third student lost her research index cards, found them in her locker, but now they are out of order and she forgot to note the source for each fact. There's a week to go before the projects are due, and you are not sure if these three are going to have something to submit.

Building supports into your assignment design offers the tools and structure students with EF challenges need to plan, execute, and monitor tasks (Lodewyk, Winne, & Jamieson-Noel, 2009). Simple strategies can go a long way in making an assignment more accessible for students:

- **BREAK ASSIGNMENTS INTO PIECES with individual due dates for those who need or want them.** Remember how hard it is for some students with EF challenges to be flexible thinkers? This includes planning. During a whole class presentation or in a saved audio or video file that you put on the class website, think aloud how you would initiate each step and highlight appropriate resources to use. That way, any students who could benefit from your think-aloud will have access to it during class and at home. Modeling is a powerful strategy to support students' understanding of your expectations, as well as their self-regulation (Schunk & Zimmerman, 2006).
- **SHARE EXAMPLES of completed assignments meeting specific criteria when introducing an assignment.** You can post an annotated online example using written and audio comments highlighting how evidence supports assignment criteria. Ask older students to review the assignment description and then work in teams to list the qualities of a "successful" submission. Teams can then compare their lists to the examples provided and debrief as a whole class about any possible barriers they may face and effective solutions.
- **PROVIDE STUDENTS WITH A TEMPLATE (or multiple templates) if you routinely use specific assignment formats.** Templates remove formatting concerns and make cognitive room for students to focus on the content of the assignment. Some students may choose to use the templates, while others may choose

## CASE IN POINT

When Ramona was in fourth grade, she completed a unit on famous explorers. Since there were multiple components, including a culminating project, her teacher worked with the class to break the assignment into pieces and do some backwards planning. Using bullet points, Mr. Medley listed each required component of the project and helped students to estimate the amount of time it would take them to complete each part. Students' estimations differed, based on their different skills. Using a calendar with the project's due date as the first entry, he taught students how to work backwards through the bulleted list, keeping the estimated time in mind. In the end, Ramona had a two-week plan that included a step-by-step process for work completion.

to do their own format. However, for students with EF, no more worrying about *how* to do the assignment allows the focus and thinking finally to be on learning the content!

- **SUPPORT STUDENTS making appropriate task priorities.** You can build check-ins within the due dates to monitor progress and assist students with troubleshooting. Rather than telling students next steps, ask them what they should do next and have them set up an action plan recorded in planners or notebooks. By asking instead of telling, students can practice cognitive flexibility and working memory.

- **BE SELECTIVE ABOUT HOW CHOICE IS INCORPORATED into assignments.** Students with EF challenges can be overwhelmed by too many choices or open-ended suggestions to "pick any topic you want!" Remember, students who struggle with EF skills actually like routine and predictability because they require less cognitive juggling. Younger students may benefit from a limited selection, because as little as two options can be enough for students who struggle to focus and make choices. Older students can navigate three to five options—base your choices on the students' attention levels and the specific assignment feature. For example, you may only want to offer choice for one assignment component (e.g., topic or format, but not both).

- **BUILD SELF-REFLECTION INTO ASSIGNMENTS by asking students to evaluate the quality of their work and final product.** Self-reflection checksheets can be customized to include images, which may help all students but will especially accommodate the needs of students with limited language skills or younger children. During the next assignment, use these checksheets to have students set personal goals around their work and task completion.

## BRINGING IT ALL TOGETHER

Students with EF challenges may struggle with cognitive flexibility, working memory, and inhibitory control skill sets in day-to-day activities and with varying academic tasks. Students may be impacted by each skill set differently, with some students demonstrating more strength in one skill set (e.g., working memory) than another (e.g., cognitive flexibility), while other students may find themselves impacted equally among all EF skill sets. With strategic and goal-directed UDL supports, teachers can target representation, engagement, and expression, while also encompassing cognitive flexibility, working memory, and inhibitory control. Regardless of the profile of a student with EF challenges, UDL can reduce barriers and provide supports for not only students with EF challenges, but for all students.

# BACKWARDS LONG-TERM PLANNING EXAMPLE

**Student Name:** *Ramona S.*

**Assignment Name:** *Famous Explorers (FE) Project*

**Due Date:** *January 19*

| Assignment Step (complete from the bottom up) | Estimated Time for Completion (as decided by student) | Informal Due Dates (complete from the bottom up) |
|---|---|---|
| 1. Submit paper and monument | 1 day (extra day built in) | January 18 |
| 2. Write final draft paper on FE | 1 day | January 17 |
| 3. Create monument for FE | 3 days | January 16 |
| 4. Write 1-page draft paper on FE | 2 days | January 13 |
| 5. Take notes on 3 sources | 2 days | January 11 |
| 6. Find 3 sources of information on FE | 1 day | January 9 |
| 7. Decide on FE, get teacher approval | 1 day | January 8 |

## TOP FIVE WEBSITES TO SUPPORT EXECUTIVE FUNCTIONING AND UDL

→ https://childmind.org/topics/concerns/executive-function/

→ https://developingchild.harvard.edu/science/key-concepts/executive-function/

→ https://www.eduplace.com/graphicorganizer/

→ http://memorise.org

→ https://www.understood.org/en/learning-attention-issues/child-learning-disabilities/executive-functioning-issues

## APPS WE LOVE

→ Evernote

→ Fit Brains Trainer

→ Google Calendar

→ Idea Sketch

→ Quizlet

## RECOMMENDED READINGS

Armstrong, T. (2010). *The power of neurodiversity: Unleashing the advantages of your differently wired brain.* Cambridge, MA: Da Capo Press.

Brown, T. E. (2008). *Executive functions: Describing six aspects of a complex syndrome.* Retrieved from http://www.chadd.org/AM/Template.cfm?Section=Especially_For_Adults&Template=/CM/ContentDisplay.cfm&ContentID=5802

Medina, J. (2014). *Brain rules: 12 principles for surviving and thriving at work, home, and school.* Seattle, WA: Pear Press.

Sousa, D. A. (2016). *How the brain learns.* Thousand Oaks, CA: Corwin.

## REFERENCES

Bryant, D., Goodwin, M., Bryant, B., & Higgins, K. (2003). Vocabulary instruction for students with learning disabilities: A review of the research. *Learning Disability Quarterly, 26*, 117–128.

Davidson, M. C., Amso, D., Anderson, L. C., & Diamond, A. (2006). Development of cognitive control and executive functions from 4–13 years: Evidence from manipulations of memory, inhibition, and task switching. *Neuropsychologia, 44*, 2037–2078.

Diamond, A. (2013). Executive functions. *Annual Review of Psychology, 64*, 135–168.

Ellis, E., & Howard, P. (2007). Graphic organizers: Power tools for teaching students with learning disabilities. *Current Practice Alerts, 13*, 1–4.

Joseph, L. M., & Eveleigh, E. L. (2011). A review of the effects of self-monitoring on reading performance of students with disabilities. *Journal of Special Education, 45*, 43–53.

Klingner, J., & Vaughn, S. (1998). Using collaborative strategic reading. *Teaching Exceptional Children, 30*, 32–37.

Lodewyk, K. R., Winne, P. H., & Jamieson-Noel, D. L. (2009). Implications of task structure on self-regulated learning and achievement. *Educational Psychology, 29*(1), 1–25.

Melby-Lervag, M., Redick, T. S., & Hulme, C. (2016). Working memory training does not improve performance on measures of intelligence or other measures of "far transfer": Evidence from a meta-analytic review. *Perspectives on Psychological Science, 11*(4), 512–534.

Meuwissen, A. S., & Zelazo, P. D. (2014). Hot and cold executive function: Foundations for learning and healthy development. *Zero to Three, 35*(2), 18–23.

Novak, K. (2016). *UDL now: A teacher's guide to applying Universal Design for Learning in today's classrooms.* Wakefield, MA: CAST Professional Publishing.

Rapp, W. H. (2014). *Universal Design for Learning in action: 100 ways to teach all learners.* Baltimore, MD: Paul H. Brookes.

Schunk, D. H., & Zimmerman, B. J. (2006). Influencing children's self-efficacy and self-regulation of reading and writing through modeling. *Reading and Writing Quarterly, 23*(1), 7–25.

Scruggs, T. E., Mastropieri, M. A., Berkeley, S. L., & Marshak, L. (2010). Mnemonic strategies: Evidence-based practice and practice-based evidence. *Intervention in School and Clinic, 46*(2), 79–86.

Smith, E. E., & Jonides, J. (1999). Storage and executive processes in the frontal lobes. *Science, 283*, 1657–1661.

Wright, L. W. (n.d.). *Eight fun games that can improve your child's executive functioning skills.* Retrieved from https://www.understood.org/en/school-learning/learning-at-home/games-skillbuilders/8-fun-games-that-can-improve-your-childs-executive-functioning-skills#slide-3

Zelazo, P. D., Blair, C. B., & Willoughby, M. T. (2016). *Executive function: Implications for education* (NCER 2017–2000). Washington, DC: National Center for Education Research, Institute of Education Sciences, U.S. Department of Education. Retrieved from https://ies.ed.gov/ncer/pubs/20172000/pdf/20172000.pdf

# 7

# *UDL and Positive Behavioral Interventions and Supports*

## *Making Classroom Management Positive*

### Brittany L. Hott
*Texas A&M—Commerce*

### Kathleen M. Randolph
*University of Colorado—Colorado Springs*

### Amelia Martin
*Texas A&M—Commerce*

## SETTING THE STAGE FOR UDL AND PBIS

Have you struggled with classroom management and meeting the needs of students with persistent behavioral difficulties? Did you know that student behavior is one of the most frequently cited challenges that teachers face? Do you hear about strategies, interventions, supports, and practices and wonder about the difference or where to start? How about all of the confusing acronyms? If so, you are *not* alone! This chapter is for you. We do not have magical powers, but we can demystify some of the jargon and share strategies that work. The ability to successfully manage a classroom and student behavior increases the likelihood of teacher retention. For students with behavioral difficulties, implementation of effective interventions increases academic success, the likelihood of high school completion, and positive postsecondary outcomes. Grab a cup of coffee and let's get this party started!

You should already know a bit about UDL by this point. So let's move on to Positive Behavioral Interventions and Supports (PBIS). PBIS offers an evidence-based alternative to reactive and punishment-type approaches to managing student behavior, resulting in safer schools and increased academic progress (Lane, Kalberg, & Menzies, 2009). Key elements of PBIS include: (a) high-quality instruction; (b) a comprehensive school or districtwide system of teaching and supporting behavior; (c) differentiated instruction for all learners, including students with disabilities; (d) progress monitoring; (e) early intervention for students experiencing behavioral difficulties; and (f) data-driven decision making (Sugai & Horner, 2009).

Now for the connection between UDL and PBIS. Student social, emotional, and behavioral needs can vary greatly. Having a tool kit of interventions and strategy choices to address these needs is the first step in supporting student success. The premise of UDL is to design an instructional framework with the needs of students in mind, rather than merely fitting the student to the instruction. PBIS reflects this inclusive approach as it is intended to support *every* student. For UDL and PBIS to be effective, it is necessary that teachers understand student needs, interventions that have worked, areas that need to be addressed, and effective data collection methods. Inclusion is a driving principle of both frameworks. Students should not only have access to the same environments as their peers, but also to the same educational benefits.

UDL and PBIS require collaboration, meaning that all school resources must work together for the system to run seamlessly. Because students' needs, preferences, and choices may differ from one area to another, students may require different supports in different settings. This reinforces the importance of teachers being aware of both student needs and preferences to implement UDL in their classrooms effectively. Don't discount student knowledge! Affording students the opportunity to communicate needs and select strategies often significantly decreases behavior.

Below we outline several strategies and interventions that can be implemented within PBIS and UDL frameworks. We offer tips for putting PBIS into practice by providing multiple means of representation, engagement, and expression while facilitating student voice and choice. Together, UDL and PBIS are designed meet the behavioral needs of *all* students upfront, decreasing the likelihood of behavioral infractions.

# PUTTING UDL AND PBIS INTO PRACTICE: REPRESENTATION

One way of providing students with multiple means of representation within PBIS and UDL frameworks arises when establishing and teaching routines and expectations (Myers, Freeman, Simonsen, & Sugai, 2017). The majority of students know rules exist, but may not necessarily know how to apply them in every context. How can we expect students to meet our expectations when they may not know what they look like in every possible setting throughout their school day?

Students encounter different expectations across settings throughout the school day, with different levels and requirements for applying those expectations in each setting. Schools can ease the transition between settings by having a standard set of schoolwide expectations, along with ways to teach and reinforce those expectations.

While academic instruction needs to be effective, engaging, and individualized (Stronge, Ward, & Grant, 2011), so does the behavior management system. If the academic setting isn't engaging for the student, how can we expect them to sit and listen? Students want to be involved and challenged by the class, and behavior issues occur when they are bored and off task. Pairing effective and engaging instruction with a PBIS framework for establishing routines and expectations while allowing for multiple means of representation provides a comprehensive support system for students both academically and behaviorally.

Classrooms rooted in PBIS include evidence-based practices (EBPs) for establishing and teaching routines and classroom expectations (Myers et al., 2017). Students, regardless of ability, should be able to demonstrate mastery of rules and procedures across settings (Loman, Strickland-Cohen, & Walker, 2018). To effectively infuse schoolwide PBIS within the UDL framework, Lewis and colleagues (2016) recommend using the following steps created by school-based behavior support teams:

- **CREATE AN OVERARCHING FRAMEWORK OF EXPECTATIONS for schoolwide expectations** (e.g., Be Respectful, Be Responsible, and Be Ready; Myers et al., 2017). Be sure they are worded positively as opposed to what students should *not* be doing.
- **PUBLICLY POST EXPECTATIONS across all school settings** (e.g., classrooms, cafeteria, gym, hallways). Have a variety of ways those expectations are represented, to include posters, digital displays, cartoons, and presentations at school events.
- **TEACH SCHOOLWIDE AND SETTING-SPECIFIC EXPECTATIONS at the beginning of the year in each classroom.** These instructions should continue throughout the school year to reinforce the expectations.

- **DEVELOP A SYSTEM TO REINFORCE STUDENTS** who engage with and meet behavioral expectations. The system should identify and respond to students who are, and who are not, meeting the expectations.
- **MEET TO REVIEW DATA** and create a system to support students who need additional behavioral supports to meet success. Be sure there are adults in the school who are focused on PBIS, able to make data-driven decisions, and can take positive actions to improve student success.

In addition to defining a system to teach and reinforce positive behavior in the school setting, schools can focus efforts in providing multiple means of representation for students of different ability levels throughout the content areas. Representation can be varied throughout the content areas in a variety of ways, to include:

- **WRITE STORIES ABOUT EXPECTATIONS** in English/Language arts classes. Tailor these to students' abilities and provide them with choices (e.g., using dictation software to orally create an essay, writing in a "blue book" or on loose leaf paper, typing an essay, drawing and labeling a series of pictures).
- **TRANSLATE EXPECTATIONS** in foreign language class. Encourage students to speak formally and informally in their new language.
- **DRAW EXPECTATIONS** in art class. Students can use comics to create different examples and nonexamples of ways students do and don't meet the expectations.
- **SEW EXPECTATIONS** in home economics class. Let students choose their fabrics, design, product (e.g., pillows, wall hangings, T-shirts), and sayings.

Additionally, expectations can be displayed in a variety of ways to address representation across skill and ability levels to accommodate students of all abilities, including the following:

- Auditorily address expectations with accompanying visuals.
- Provide pictures of what behavioral expectations should "look like" across different settings (Loman et al., 2018).
- Use age-appropriate vocabulary and pictorial representations of expectations across settings that can tap into students' current knowledge, as well as background knowledge.
- Identify patterns, critical features, big ideas, and relationships to maximize knowledge transfer and generalization across settings.
- Connect challenging students with the expectations to get them engaged and for them to buy into appropriate behavior

in the classroom. For example, teachers might use a student's favorite superhero character to illustrate classroom behavioral expectations.

## PUTTING UDL AND PBIS INTO PRACTICE: ENGAGEMENT

Both UDL and PBIS support engaging lesson content and a positive social climate for *all* students. When students are interested and invested in learning, behavioral infractions decrease because we avoid boredom and disengaged behavior! Although there is no magic fairy dust to sprinkle to ensure all students are engaged, there are many powerful strategies and interventions that improve engagement and behavior. It is impossible to cover all of the interventions, so we will share a few of our favorites, as well as some resources.

- **PROVIDE CHOICE!** One of the most powerful ways to increase engagement is to provide student choice. There are various approaches to choice making, which can be applied in all classrooms, regardless of grade. For example, provide several seating options to complete morning work (e.g., carpet area, bean bag, traditional desk). Allowing students to choose builds ownership and increases investment. When students engage in an activity that they wish to do, there is less disruption and students remain on task longer. That all sounds great, but what happens when a few students cause a disruption or, worse, refuse to complete assignments? Goal setting, self-monitoring, and collaborative learning to the rescue!

### 💡 STRATEGY SPOT
FLEXIBLE SEATING

Allot time for students to share their classroom seating preferences. Ask students to design their ideal classroom using room planning software (see http://www.planyourroom.com/) or butcher paper with drawings or pictures of seating options that can be pasted in desired areas. Need inspiration? Check out https://www.prodigygame.com/blog/flexible-seating-classroom-ideas/. Discuss options and collaboratively make room arrangements that meet the needs of all students. Flexible seating arrangements can be redone at any time. If it is not working, change it. If the design is working but students are bored, change it.

- **GOAL SETTING can be completed classwide, individually, or both.** Openly discussing challenges and setting measurable class goals are helpful. Extrinsic rewards may be needed to motivate younger students or students with more challenging behavioral difficulties. The ultimate goal is to phase out extrinsic rewards

## CASE IN POINT

Ms. Taleb's seventh graders frequently arrive late to class. When students prefer to linger in the lunchroom and chat in the hallway rather than get excited for algebra, goal setting can help change their behaviors. Ms. Taleb started the conversation by sharing that the class was missing five to eight minutes of algebra instruction daily because the class wandered in late. The class unanimously agreed they did not want to return at the end of the day to make up those five to eight minutes of instruction. Setting a realistic class goal (e.g., "By November, all members of the class will arrive before the tardy bell or with a pass due to extenuating circumstances"), the goal of getting to class on time shifted the responsibility from Ms. Taleb to the students and promoted some independence in their actions.

After identifying the classwide goal, Ms. Taleb noticed two students who frequently continued to be found in the hallways, bathrooms, and lunchroom well beyond the tardy bell. Rather than just calling them out or punishing them, Ms. Taleb shared a few self-monitoring strategies with the entire class, including steps for creating a self-monitoring chart. Students were asked to determine if they need to self-monitor and to select the best method. She reminded them that if the class was unable to meet the goal, they would need to determine how to get back their five to eight minutes of lost instruction.

Asher, one of the students who frequently arrived late to class, was encouraged by his peers to create a self-monitoring strategy. Asher chose to set his watch to beep five minutes before lunch to cue packing up. He then focused on checking-off his list: (a) go to the bathroom if needed, (b) check his locker to get class materials, (c) walk to class, and (d) sit in his seat with materials ready to go. Asher's watch is set to beep one minute before the tardy bell to facilitate the transition between talking with friends and getting set up for class. With the self-monitoring chart, Asher was able to get to class on time along with his classmates. The combination of positive peer pressure and supports, as well as goal setting and self-monitoring strategies, changed the entire tenor of the algebra class and allowed for fewer tardies and more instruction to occur.

as soon as possible to support students in becoming intrinsically motivated (Rafferty, 2010).

- **SELF-MONITORING interventions teach students to independently evaluate their behaviors.** Students often are unaware how challenging their behavior is to others. If a student has the skill to demonstrate the desired behavior, self-monitoring may be an appropriate intervention (Hott, Walker, & Brigham, 2014). The student, with support from a teacher or counselor, develops measurable goals and a system for measuring progress. Progress can be recorded a variety of ways, including paper/pencil, electronically, on a Post-it, or inside a student agenda. The student then reviews progress and sets more ambitious goals until the self-monitoring intervention can be phased out as the student masters the skill.

- **CHECK-IN/CHECK-OUT (CICO) can help support students who need interventions in addition to self-monitoring or in conjunction with self-monitoring** (McDaniel, Bruhn, & Mitchell, 2015). CICO requires that the student *check-in* with a mentor at the start of each day to pick up their data sheet and discuss behavior goals. The student receives scores from teachers, or self-scores, each class period for their behavior performance, which is then presented to the mentor at the end of the day for *check-out*. There is evidence that the consistent feedback from teachers and the mentor–mentee bond have a positive impact on both academic and behavioral outcomes (Hunter, Chenier, & Gresham, 2014). To incorporate choice and voice, discuss the CICO program as an option, provide a list of faculty and staff who are willing to serve as mentors, choice of CICO times, and choice of recording options.

## PUTTING UDL AND PBIS INTO PRACTICE: EXPRESSION

Like engagement and representation, providing multiple means of expression improves both academic and behavioral outcomes. Three interventions that foster expression, increase work completion, and decrease behavioral infractions are choice boards, response options, and self-reflection.

- **CHOICE BOARDS OR MENUS** include a list of activities or products that a student chooses to demonstrate mastery of concepts. Choice boards can be differentiated to meet the needs of

 **Tech Tips**

Find out more about choice boards by going to https://daretodifferentiate.wikispaces.com/Choice+Boards

> **STRATEGY SPOT**
> DIALOGUE FOLDERS

> Use dialogue folders to facilitate communication about social, emotional, and behavioral progress. Students select a file folder and customize it (e.g., draw pictures, include stickers, list goals). Teachers then provide a daily, weekly, or biweekly prompt and students respond using their preferred method such as drawing, writing a brief response, or using stickers. Just as students have a choice of response options, the teacher can then respond by writing a response with a sticker, list of resources, etc. The options are endless.

*all* learners, including students who are gifted and students who have disabilities. They can be as simple as a paper-and-pencil activity or created digitally. It is often helpful to include a choice block where students can propose an activity not listed in the matrix to demonstrate mastery.

- **RESPONSE OPTIONS allow students to choose how they will respond during lectures.** Students can choose to answer questions using paper/pencil, electronic response options such as a personal Clicker, or a combination of paper/pencil and electronic options. Consider use of response tools such as pre-printed response cards, whiteboards, or Clickers to quickly gauge an entire class's progress (Hott & Brigham, 2018).
- **SELF-REFLECTION allows students to communicate their behavioral progress and needs.** Providing students with options to share and reflect on their social, emotional, and behavioral progress promotes self-reflection. Students can share orally in one-on-one conferences with a teacher, counselor, or administrator; with a trusted peer or small group; participate in a class discussion; post blogs or vlogs; or any combination of self-reflection strategies.

## BRINGING IT ALL TOGETHER

Both PBIS and UDL frameworks foster student independence while promoting social, emotional, and behavioral progress. When students participate in the creation and implementation of classroom rules and procedures, are comfortable requesting support and offering ideas to address needs, and are provided with choices, they are more likely to be successful. Together, UDL and PBIS are a dynamic duo that support both academic and social growth. Want to learn more? Please check out the templates in Tables 7.1 and 7.2, as well as the apps and additional resources sections for more information.

**Table 7.1**   Tech Tips for Incorporating PBIS and UDL

| Low-Tech Strategies to Support Positive Student Behavior |
| --- |

**Tier 1—Universal for All Students**

- Schoolwide behavior systems—large, schoolwide rewards resembling dollars and specific to the school (e.g., Randolph Rewards or Birmingham Bucks), designed by students, and accessible to every student who earns the individual, predetermined criteria
- Token economies—students use incremental rewards leading to larger classwide rewards to purchase small items or special titles (class line leader, teacher's assistant)

**Tiers 2–3—Differentiated Based on Student Need**

- Sticker charts—students can earn stickers throughout the day for appropriate behavior
- Behavior tracking sheets, level forms, and checklists with yes/no checkboxes

| High-Tech Strategies to Support Positive Student Behavior |
| --- |

**Tier 1—Universal for All Students**

- Students create videos to model the classroom expectations they created—including examples and nonexamples
- Schoolwide reward dollar tracking using online checking account (i.e., spreadsheet)
- Online token economy
- Reward tracking apps—Class DoJo, RedCritter, Google Classroom

**Tiers 2–3—Differentiated Based on Student Need**

- Behavior tracking, level forms, and checklist sheets online—these can be shared with parents electronically, with appropriate permission and access
  - Google Forms, Microsoft Forms, LiveBinders
- Online schedule—pictures, visuals, or text
- Behavior tracking apps—Hero, ScoreIt, LiveSchool, Class, and Chore Tracker

**Table 7.2**    Sample Templates to Implement Strategies to Support Behavior

### Break Time Choice Board

| | | |
|---|---|---|
| Complete 5 Math challenge problems | 5 minutes in the Chill Corner | Research one animal's habitat |
| Locate 5 places on a map | Free choice! | 10 minutes active recess time |
| Break time! Do 5 jumping jacks | Draw a picture of the life cycle of a butterfly | Read for 10 minutes |

### Check-In, Check-Out

| Date | Check-In | Check-Out | Teacher Initials |
|---|---|---|---|
| | ☐ | ☐ | |
| | ☐ | ☐ | |
| | ☐ | ☐ | |
| | ☐ | ☐ | |
| | ☐ | ☐ | |
| | ☐ | ☐ | |
| | ☐ | ☐ | |
| | ☐ | ☐ | |

### Reward Board

# I'm Working for

(Chosen reinforcer)

# First I need to earn

☐ ☐ ☐ ☐ ☐ ☐
☐ ☐ ☐ ☐ ☐

### Student Reward Schedule

First    Second

If    Then

## TOP FIVE WEBSITES TO SUPPORT PBIS AND UDL

→ http://www.ci3t.org/

→ http://csefel.vanderbilt.edu/resources/training_modules.html

→ http://www.pbisworld.com/

→ www.pbis.org

→ http://successfulschools.org/

## APPS WE LOVE

→ Choiceboard Creator

→ Nearpod

→ Self-Monitor: Habit Changer

→ Smart Seat

→ Too Noisy

## RECOMMENDED READINGS

Baker, B., & Ryan, C. (2014). *The PBIS team handbook: Setting expectations and building positive behavior.* Minneapolis, MN: Free Spirit.

Harlacher, J. E., & Rodriguez, B. J. (2018). *An educator's guide to schoolwide Positive Behavioral Interventions and Supports: Integrating all three tiers.* Bloomington, IN: Marzano Research.

Simonsen, B., & Myers, D. (2015). *Classwide Positive Behavior Interventions and Supports: A guide to proactive classroom management.* New York, NY: Gilford.

# REFERENCES

Hott, B. L., & Brigham, F. J. (2018). Effects of response options on the mathematics performance of secondary students with emotional or behavioral disorders. *Exceptionality.* Advanced online publication. Retrieved from https://www.tandfonline.com/doi/full/10.1080/09362835.2018.1480950

Hott, B. L., Walker, J. D., & Brigham, F. J. (2014). Implementing self-management strategies in the secondary classroom. In A. Cohan & A. Honingsfeld (Eds.), *Breaking the mold of classroom management: What educators should know and do to enable student success* (pp.19–26). Lanham, MD: R&L Education.

Hunter, K. K., Chenier, J. S., & Gresham, F. M. (2014). Evaluation of check in/check out for students with internalizing behavior problems. *Journal of Emotional and Behavioral Disorders, 22,* 135–148.

Lane, K. L., Kalberg, J. R., & Menzies, H. M. (2009). *Developing school-wide programs to prevent and manage problem behaviors: A step-by-step approach.* New York, NY: Gilford.

Lewis, T. J., Barrett, S., Sugai, G., Horner, R. H., Mitchell, B. S., & Starkey, D. (2016). Training and professional development blueprint for positive behavioral interventions and supports. *National Technical Assistance Center on Positive Behavior Interventions and Support.* Retrieved from https://www.pbis.org/blueprint/pd-blueprint

Loman, S. L., Strickland-Cohen, M. K., & Walker, V. L. (2018). Promoting the accessibility of SWPBIS for students with severe disabilities. *Journal of Positive Behavior Interventions, 20*(2), 113–123.

McDaniel, S. C., Bruhn, A. L., & Mitchell, B. S. (2015). A tier 2 framework for behavior identification and intervention. *Beyond Behavior, 24*(1), 10–17.

Myers, D., Freeman, J., Simonsen, B., & Sugai, G. (2017). Classroom management with exceptional learners. *TEACHING Exceptional Children, 49,* 223–230.

Rafferty, L. A. (2010). Step-by-step: Teaching students to self-monitor. *TEACHING Exceptional Children, 43,* 50–58.

Stronge, J. H., Ward, T. J., & Grant, L. W. (2011). What makes good teachers good? A cross-case analysis of the connection between teacher effectiveness and student achievement. *Journal of Teacher Education, 62*(4), 339–355.

Sugai, G., & Horner, R. H. (2009). Responsiveness-to-intervention and school-wide positive behavior supports: Integration of multi-tiered system approaches. *Exceptionality, 17,* 223–237.

*8*

# *UDL and Adaptive Behavior*

*Addressing Conceptual, Social, and Practical Skills*

Caitlyn A. Bukaty
*University of Central Florida*

Lauren A. Delisio
*Rider University*

## SETTING THE STAGE FOR UDL AND ADAPTIVE BEHAVIOR

What is adaptive behavior? How does it impact success in the classroom? As a teacher, how can I use my knowledge of adaptive behavior to help my students learn and develop? These are great questions to ask about the foundational behaviors that may affect the way your students learn. In this chapter, we'll answer these questions and equip you with ideas and strategies to address any of your students' adaptive behavior needs and expand their learning opportunities using UDL principles.

Adaptive behaviors are the skills learned and performed in everyday life. They were first organized into a scale for the purpose of measurement by Doll (1935) under the premise that although social inadequacy was a primary characteristic of abnormal intellectual development, there was a lack of established standards to measure the construct. These skills demonstrate a student's independence and social maturity (Doll, 1935; Sparrow, 2011). Adaptive behaviors are categorized into three areas: (a) conceptual, (b) social, and (c) practical (American Psychiatric Association, 2013; Schalock et al., 2010). See Table 8.1 for a depiction of these areas and the skills and behaviors within them, including classroom-specific examples of adaptive skills for each area.

Challenges relating to adaptive behavior are common in many subsets of students. Deficits in adaptive behavior are a defining characteristic of intellectual disability (American Psychiatric Association, 2013; Schalock et al., 2010). Students with autism spectrum disorders (ASD) do not always face the cognitive challenges shown in students with intellectual disabilities, but they do display adaptive functioning skills below their intellectual functioning level (American Psychiatric Association, 2013). Furthermore, the widely used assessment of adaptive behavior functioning, the Vineland Adaptive Behavior Scales II, includes information on anticipated results for additional groups of students with disabilities including those with attention deficit disorders, emotional and behavioral disturbances, learning disabilities, visual impairments, and those who are Deaf or Hard of Hearing (Sparrow, 2011). Specific patterns of adaptive behavior emerged for these groups when research was conducted to validate the test (Sparrow, 2011).

Research related to adaptive behavior is mostly focused on students with disabilities (Raines, Gordon, Harrell-Williams, Diliberto, & Parke, 2017). However, emerging research on other student groups shows a broader need for support related to adaptive behavior. Raines et al. (2017) studied adaptive behavior in Latino students without disabilities. They found adaptive behavior ratings to be a predictor of academic achievement. Raines and colleagues (2017) advised that the impact of cultural diversity on adaptive behavior warrants measures to promote these skills, even for students without disabilities. At-risk students can also benefit from support for adaptive behavior, especially for adaptive social skills. Prince, Ho, and Hansen (2010) noted after reviewing current research that poor social skills were linked to many negative outcomes, whereas improved social skills led to positive outcomes. To address this realization, they studied the effects of an adaptive behavior and social competencies intervention that targeted at-risk elementary age students, finding reduced school problem behaviors and increased social competencies in students who received the intervention (Prince et al., 2010). Considering all the groups of students who may face challenges with adaptive behavior, many teachers are sure to have students in their classrooms who can benefit from extra support.

As you can imagine, the skills surrounding adaptive behavior play a role in every facet of students' lives. From school to home and everywhere in between, challenges with adaptive behavior can translate into challenges with daily living, learning, and socialization. For example, each school day is filled with both routine and special events. Routine

**Table 8.1**  Adaptive Behavior Areas, Skills, and Classroom-Specific Examples

| Adaptive Areas* | Component Behaviors and Skills* | Classroom-Specific Examples |
|---|---|---|
| Conceptual | • Language<br>• Reading and writing<br>• Number concepts<br>• Money concepts<br>• Time concepts | • Academic curriculum<br>• Mathematics<br>• English Language Arts<br>• Reading across the content areas (e.g., science, social studies, mathematics word problems) |
| Social | • Interpersonal skills<br>• Social responsibility<br>• Self-esteem<br>• Gullibility<br>• Naiveté (wariness)<br>• Following rules/laws<br>• Avoiding victimization<br>• Social problem solving | • Communicating with peers and adults<br>• Group work<br>• Interacting with peers during noninstructional time (recess, lunch, choice time)<br>• Navigating social situations<br>• Interpreting and following classroom rules<br>• Understanding the possible intentions of peers and adults |
| Practical | • Daily living activities<br>• Personal care activities<br>• Occupational skills<br>• Use of money<br>• Safety<br>• Health care<br>• Travel and transportation<br>• Schedules and routines<br>• Use of telephone | • Navigating the school building and grounds<br>• Following classroom routines<br>• Transitioning between activities<br>• Following the classroom schedule<br>• Paying for lunch<br>• Using the restroom and addressing other hygiene needs such as handwashing |

*(Schalock et al., 2010)

events might include participating in a learning group, transitioning to music class, or eating lunch in the cafeteria. A special event could be a fire drill, a schoolwide assembly to kick off a reading initiative, or a classroom visit from a guest speaker. As a teacher, you probably find some of these events more disruptive than others, but most educators would agree that all are simply part of life in most schools. However, participating in or responding to each of these events requires a student to draw on adaptive behaviors. If a student faces challenges in that area, seemingly normal parts of classroom life can interfere with learning and disrupt interactions with teachers and peers. When adaptive behaviors are strengthened, problematic behaviors, which may disrupt the entire classroom, have been shown to decrease (Fulton, Eapen, Crnčec, Walter, & Rogers, 2014).

As you can see in Table 8.1, adaptive behaviors are quite broad. A student's adaptive behavior skills are expected to expand as they age (Doll, 1935), as will the adaptive behaviors they need in their repertoire to navigate everyday life (Schalock et al., 2010). Incorporating UDL principles classwide can support any students struggling with adaptive behavior, leading to enhanced learning and participation in your classroom for all students.

Currently, there is a lack of research on applying UDL principles specifically to support of adaptive behavior. However, based on what we know about both UDL and adaptive behavior, we can conceptualize ways to apply UDL to classroom settings to support any students who need to overcome challenges related to adaptive behavior.

Consider again the examples we shared above. All the activities we described happen on a regular basis. While some students engage adaptive behavior to navigate these situations, learning, socializing, celebrating, and staying safe in just the ways the adults who orchestrated these events intended, other students may not do so successfully. Applying UDL principles in your classroom will provide students with choices they can access to support each area of adaptive behavior, allowing everyone to learn and participate in ways that best meet their needs while keeping your classroom running smoothly.

Keep in mind that there will always be students for whom more intense, individualized supports are needed. While student-specific interventions do not fall within the realm of UDL, building upon UDL-informed strategies from which a student appears to benefit can lead teachers and students to effective individualized supports.

Remember, UDL will help you support a broad range of students. Applying UDL principles classwide will give your students the opportunity to make choices that customize their learning experiences to their own needs and gain experience advocating for supports and strategies that help them learn best. In this chapter, we will describe strategies within each UDL principle.

## PUTTING UDL AND ADAPTIVE BEHAVIOR INTO PRACTICE: REPRESENTATION

Being a teacher makes you the tour guide of your students' educational experience. It's your job to show them the sights, offer relevant information and details at each stop on your tour, and help students make sense of each thing they learn and how smaller pieces of information fit into the bigger picture. Applying the principles within multiple means of representation will help you avoid a boring tour from which your students will want to escape at the very first opportunity. Instead, it will guide you to share information in ways that are interesting and useful to them.

*Conceptual skills* of adaptive behavior support students in learning and applying language, reading and writing, and mathematics concepts. Deficits become more pronounced as content evolves from concrete to more abstract ideas through grade levels (American Psychiatric Association, 2013). Academic challenges may pose some of the most immediately noticeable barriers to student success. Providing multiple means of representation, as shown in these examples, will make content available in ways that meet a range of student needs.

- **ACTIVATE OR BUILD BACKGROUND KNOWLEDGE ON KEY TOPICS.** For example, to determine the volume of a cylinder in geometry class, Seth must solve for a variable (an algebra concept). Without that background knowledge he may just skip the problem when working independently. Avoid this by providing background knowledge in an easily accessible format. Technology keeps background knowledge at students' fingertips.
- **DRAW ATTENTION TO PATTERNS, FEATURES, BIG IDEAS, AND RELATIONSHIPS that will help students comprehend material by coding with colors, shapes, or other identifiers that work for your students and content.** For example, when working with parts of speech, teach students that they can come up with strategies to help them remember rules. For example, they might choose to label verbs with a green circle "because green means 'go' and that circle can roll" and nouns with a blue square "because you can put a nametag on a person, place, or thing."
- **USE PICTURES TO ACCOMPANY TEXT where you can . . . the more authentic the better.** Linking a picture with important vocabulary will support decoding and promote understanding even across languages.
- **OFFER ON-SCREEN TEXT—then help students learn to transform it!** Digital text can be manipulated in many ways (e.g., font size, contrast, and background colors can all be adjusted to meet needs and preferences). Screen readers offer audio to address visual, decoding, and comprehension needs, and built-in website translators or Google Translate (https://translate.google.com/) promote understanding in multiple languages. Using printed text? The Google Translate app also has a camera feature that will translate words or phrases!

*Social skills* have important connections to successful learning. While you may not grade students on their social skills specifically, many academic activities draw on these skills for participation. Laugeson, Ellingsen, Sanderson, Tucci, and Bates (2014) referred to the classroom as "arguably the most natural social setting of all" (p. 2244). Following that premise, classroom teachers can not only see their students benefit academically by improving the social skills of adaptive behavior, but also have a great opportunity to help support students' social skills development in the classroom. Providing multiple means of representation related to social skills can support students and guide growth.

- **ESTABLISH GUIDELINES for peer and adult interactions.** Help students comprehend how the guidelines transfer across settings. Use a variety of representations such as written guidelines, stories, and skits to explore how social guidelines apply in different places (in class, in the hallway, in the cafeteria, on the bus) and situations (during learning groups, when an adult visits the classroom, when interacting with students from other classrooms during an assembly).
- **PROVIDE MULTIPLE OPPORTUNITIES to practice social skills.** Some students are going to come to class with an abundance of social skills, while others are going to be sorely lacking. Have a variety of opportunities for those who need more work to practice and learn, while others may be working on other areas of need. Help students self-reflect to determine if they need work on social skills or not—and if your opinion differs from the student, have a dialogue to see why he or she disagrees.

*Practical skills* include a broad range of daily living activities. Some are encompassed in academic curricula, but many are expected to develop incidentally as students mature. Students with adaptive behavior challenges may learn practical skills later, and only when provided with more support than their peers. Applying UDL guidelines, including providing multiple means of representation, can support students in overcoming practical skill deficits and developing the skills over time.

- **GUIDE YOUR STUDENTS in visualizing their plans.** Teach them how to develop classwide visual schedules to show students what to expect in an instructional period, day, or even a whole week. The do2Learn website offers free resources for building visual schedules (http://do2learn.com/picturecards/printcards/index.htm). Students can choose the schedules that work best for them.

In some instances, a student who finds it difficult to follow routines or make transitions may benefit from an individualized visual schedule. This type of support at the student level is an example of differentiated instruction.

- **SHOW STUDENTS HOW TO SUCCEED.** Many practical skill tasks take place in the classroom every day. Support your students in things like handwashing, cleaning up after activities, packing up to go home, and other daily routines by having task reminders available with pictures. What should the literature center look like before Sam moves on to the next activity? See the "Tech Tip" to incorporate extended reality triggers using QR codes or other images near where tasks take place.

**Tech Tips**

Link to important information using a teacher-generated QR code, or other extended reality tool such as *HP Reveal* (formerly known as Aurasma). Learn how these educators use HP Reveal: https://youtu.be/ uHIxYpBW7sc

- **TELLING TIME IS IMPORTANT for keeping classroom routines.** While analog clocks appear in most curricula and classrooms, interpreting them may pose a challenge. Providing a digital clock alongside analog offers students multiple options for telling time and keeping to classroom schedules. Students can make connections between the two displays, encouraging conceptual skills.

## PUTTING UDL AND ADAPTIVE BEHAVIOR INTO PRACTICE: ENGAGEMENT

As your students progress on their guided educational tour, it is a teacher's hope that they will be compelled to do more than look on from behind the ropes. As a teacher-turned-tour guide, you want your students to feel excited about what they're learning. Providing multiple means of engagement will support your students in interacting with learning content in ways that meet their educational needs.

*Conceptual skills* can be supported through multiple means of engagement by maximizing students' choice in how and what they learn.

- **GUIDE STUDENTS to choose their own learning adventure.** Sounds exciting but complex, doesn't it? It doesn't have to be! Projects on chosen topics or books are an annual favorite for many students. Shift that choice into everyday activities, when possible. During a lesson about primary and secondary sources, fourth grader Kylie chose her favorite food: mango! She conducted a web search and found two sources with lots of information: the National Mango Board website and a Wikipedia page about mangoes. Kylie identified the Mango Board website as the primary source in this case and used information from it to create her own infographic about mangoes and shared the information with a group of first graders who were learning about nutrition. Learning choices can be used to boost relevance and heighten student interest.
- **SUPPORT STUDENTS IN SETTING THEIR OWN LEARNING GOALS.** Ask them questions like: What do you wish to achieve? What do you hope to accomplish in the next thirty minutes? How

many word problems do you think you can solve independently before lunch? How many pages do you want your essay to be? When possible, provide students opportunities to choose a pace and targets aligned with their own understanding and needs.

- **OFFER A VARIETY OF TOOLS AND RESOURCES with which to learn.** For example, when practicing single-digit multiplication, Jamie can choose from manipulatives such as bingo chips, pop cubes, or Cuisenaire rods, or he can use scribble paper to write or draw his own supports. Jamie chose pop cubes, because that's how he learned addition and subtraction. This allows students to transfer the resources with which they are most comfortable to new contexts.

*Social skills* challenges that become barriers when students struggle with adaptive behavior can be supported and addressed through multiple means of engagement. Helping students access the "why" of social skills within the classroom environment will build community and encourage students to work together developing interpersonal skills to enhance the classroom environment.

- **HELP STUDENTS UNDERSTAND THE "WHY" behind social interactions.** Building upon the class social guidelines described under multiple means of representation, collaborate as a class to establish consensus on why those guidelines are important. Discussing the value of showing respect, accepting differences, and allowing others to have a learning environment free from distractions enhances the relevance of social guidelines.
- **STUDENTS CAN ENGAGE THROUGH SELF-REFLECTION.** About halfway through the second quarter of the school year, Lara noticed something about her sixth-grade students. They had come to her middle school from several different K–5 buildings, and it seemed now that they'd settled into a new building and new routines, they'd forgotten how important it is to support one another and stick together. Lara built in a time for weekly reflection every Thursday afternoon. Sometimes reflections were based on a scenario, a news story, or something happening in the school. Students chose how to participate: by writing, typing, or drawing their response, or responding in another way of their choosing. Lara didn't collect or assess student reflections, but she did build in time for students to share voluntarily. She encouraged her students to consider how they could apply their responses and those shared by peers into their daily interactions. Reflections became so popular with her students that Lara transferred the practice to academic activities, encouraging students to reflect on their learning. You can find additional classroom reflection tips in this blog post: https://www.nureva.com/blog/15-ways-to-spark-student-reflection-in-your-classroom.

*Practical skills* have many implications to classroom life. Support students in applying these skills by providing multiple means for internalizing and addressing expectations in the classroom.

- **HELP STUDENTS FOCUS ON A GOAL.** Every Tuesday and Thursday at 9:50 a.m., Greg's second-grade classroom seemed to turn into a second-grade free-for-all as his students transitioned to music class at 10 a.m. The confusion of everyone getting their supplies and heading out the door, amplified by the excitement of going to the popular class, often subsided only when Greg sternly called the students to order and reminded them of the music time they were wasting, as the students rarely arrived on time. Greg realized he could support his students and achieve a more successful transition by heightening the salience of the goal, arriving to a favorite class with the full time to participate. He sat down with his students to brainstorm and analyze the steps to be taken before music class (bathroom breaks, supply gathering, lining up quietly). Greg helped the students work together to establish how these tasks improved their music class experience (not needing to leave for the restroom, having everything needed to learn, enjoying music class for the whole time period). As a class, they reviewed these steps, made clarifying changes, and established the "March to Music" routine, with the clearly stated goal of arriving to music class on time, with everything they needed, and without the stern reminders that were a prominent feature of the previous transition. The students helped Greg translate the steps into a chart paper poster they could use for reference, discussing and rehearsing strategies to make the transition successful.

## STRATEGY SPOT
### ACT IT OUT!

After establishing rules or guidelines as a class, engage your students in developing and acting out a scenario related to each rule or key idea. Allow students to choose their roles: director, stage manager, author, actor, producer, and so on. Practicing the desired behavior and modeling it for peers will heighten the salience of how students are expected to conduct themselves in school. *Bonus Tip:* Record the scenarios. This will give you video and audio versions of written classroom rules or guidelines providing additional means of representation! *Second Bonus Tip:* Think this is too elementary for your group? You can do the same strategy with secondary students around other behaviors you are studying. For example, how might lawyers act in a courtroom? How are political debates conducted?

## PUTTING UDL AND ADAPTIVE BEHAVIOR INTO PRACTICE: EXPRESSION

During and after their educational guided tour, students demonstrate their learning to show what they've accomplished. They communicate their needs so teachers know how to help them learn. Finally, students share their feelings and experiences as a way to relate to others and build relationships. Students who face challenges with adaptive behavior may find any of these types of expression challenging. Providing multiple means of action and expression will allow your students to show understanding, progress, and accomplishments related to academics and other classroom experiences.

*Conceptual skills* can show how a student is progressing with academic curricula. Providing your class with varied expression opportunities will maximize opportunities for students to show what and how they've learned.

### CASE IN POINT

Jayne has been teaching eighth-grade mathematics for six years. For the most part, her students perform well, and she's always working to incorporate UDL into her lessons. Jayne provides multiple means of representation where she can and offers a variety of resources and manipulatives to support her students' engagement with the content. This year, her personal professional development goal focused on supporting her students to tune into their own progress in her course. Last year, Jayne piloted this idea by having students track and graph their achievement on a series of practice problems for the state assessment. This year she wanted to expand upon that. Jayne chose three items for students to monitor: (a) progress through the curriculum, (b) completion of independent work (in-class or take-home), and (c) unit test scores. Every student uses a progress monitoring folder. Inside is a checklist of each benchmark for the year; students check off what they've learned about throughout the week, which also helps students see what they miss when absent. Students track the percentage of complete, partially complete, and missing independent assignments by month using circle graphs. Finally, students use a line graph to record scores across unit tests. Jayne encourages students to use their folders to self-monitor, to use them when meeting with her, and to share them with parents and guardians. Because Marvin has a significant cognitive disability that results in a modified curriculum, he doesn't necessarily do the same work or tests as his peers. However, he is still able to track his own independent progress, even though his checklist and graphs look a bit different than his peers'.

UDL
v. DI

- **ALLOW STUDENTS TO CHOOSE RESPONSE METHODS that capitalize on their own strengths and interests when possible.** In addition to providing options to write, type, or draw responses, try leaving an open-ended option for students to use their creativity to devise a response option of their own. A student who raps her way through the circulatory system may not only commit that information to memory herself, but might just inspire an otherwise confused or disinterested classmate to do the same!

- **HELP STUDENTS PLAN AND STRATEGIZE for their own success.** Students who experience challenges with adaptive behavior may find academic tasks overwhelming. Introducing your class to strategies and technologies that allow them to organize tasks for achievement can help everyone stay on track. Encourage students to choose the strategies that work for them!

 **Tech Tips**

Check out the *Do!* app in the App Store. It has a simple interface that allows students to color-code and set dates for to-do list items on iOS devices.

*Social skills* may be highly evident in the way students express their thoughts and ideas at school. Regardless of the reason, a student's deficits in adaptive behavior may affect his or her expression; thus, providing multiple means of action and expression can support participation by the whole class.

## CASE IN POINT

Tara teaches a first-grade inclusive class of students with and without disabilities. At her school, kindergarten students eat lunch in the classroom, but first graders eat in the cafeteria at the same time as the second- and third-grade students. Tara knows the cafeteria can be overwhelming. To support her first-time lunchers, Tara developed a Social Story for the whole class to use before lunch—every day for the first few weeks of school, and periodically for as long as it's needed. The Social Story begins by establishing the cafeteria as a place to eat and socialize with peers sitting close by. The story describes expected behaviors and strategies to try if you're feeling overwhelmed (putting your head down, asking those around you not to do something that's bothering you, raising your hand for a monitor if you need help). Students can recite lines of the story after Tara and act out portions if they wish. The story is projected onto the classroom smart board with pictures and text for students to follow along. You can learn more about Social Stories at https://carolgraysocialstories.com/.

The Case in Point is an example of a Social Story that has been used to help a whole class develop strategies for successful participation in lunch. However, in many cases, an individual student will benefit from a Social Story developed for a specific situation and need that his or her peers may not need. That would be an example of differentiated instruction.

- **ALLOW STUDENTS CHOICES FOR HOW THEY COMMUNICATE with peers and adults when possible.** If a student has trouble expressing her thoughts or needs verbally, she can write them in a letter or an e-mail—or even send a quick text or Bitmoji.

**Tech Tips**

If students in your class speak different first languages, introduce everyone to the *Google Translate* app for social settings and group work. Even if students use it only occasionally in school, they've learned about a tool that can help them communicate with many people in all sorts of places.

*Practical skills* navigating the learning environment and expressing understanding and needs are important parts of school participation. Students with adaptive behavior challenges may benefit from more options for action and expression.

## BRINGING IT ALL TOGETHER

Challenges posed by deficits in adaptive behavior can create learning barriers for students. Many students in your classroom may experience adaptive behavior challenges in conceptual, social, and practical areas to different degrees. Incorporating UDL principles into your curriculum and classroom environment will offer students choices to learn and participate in classroom activities in ways that best meet their individual needs. When it comes to using UDL principles in your classroom to support adaptive behavior, it is an ongoing process. As you notice students gravitating toward elements that meet their adaptive behavior needs you may find it helpful to explore how similar offerings might enhance other tasks or activities. At the same time, you may need to revise discontinued practices or elements that students don't access or from which they don't seem to benefit. In addition to observation and reflection, having discussions with students about what helps them can help drive these decisions.

## STRATEGY SPOT
### MASTER THE DRILL

Safety first—master the emergency drill. Fire, earthquake, and other emergency drills (depending on where you live) are common during the first few months of the school year. In many cases, students understand what's going on, follow the school procedures, and participate successfully. However, if students in your class experience challenges with adaptive behavior, the disruption and complex procedures may lead to a challenging few minutes, and ultimately, a safety concern for the whole class. Begin practicing for emergency drills early and incorporate graduated levels of support, providing opportunities for students to build response skills. Explain what an emergency drill is in case students need that background knowledge. Model and practice the schoolwide routine with your students, including your assigned evacuation route. If possible, scaffold the experience by introducing elements before the building drills begin, explain the noise and flashing lights students should expect, and help them plan appropriate strategies to address unpleasant parts (e.g., covering your ears is okay, but it's important to keep your eyes open; try not to look directly at the flashing lights, instead look at the person in front of you, etc.). Begin your practice sessions with verbal or visual prompts and gradually reduce them as students gain independence. If the whole routine is too complex at first, vary the demand by having students go only as far as the classroom door initially. Build in ways to provide timely feedback, such as holding up a green card to reinforce the correct behavior, or an orange card if students' noise level would interfere with safety. When your students have mastered this routine, you can help them think about how it transfers to other emergency drills. No one comes to school expecting an emergency, but being prepared is very important.

## TOP FIVE WEBSITES TO SUPPORT ADAPTIVE BEHAVIOR

→ https://aurasma.zendesk.com/hc/en-us/articles/206292695-Are-you-a-teacher-Guidance-for-teachers-and-other-educators-getting-started-with-Aurasma

→ https://carolgraysocialstories.com/

→ http://do2learn.com/

→ https://www.qrstuff.com/

→ https://translate.google.com/

## APPS WE LOVE

→ Book Creator

→ Do!

→ Google Translate

→ HP Reveal App (formerly Aurasma)

→ Voice Memos (iOS) or Voice Recorder (Android)

# REFERENCES

American Psychiatric Association. (Ed.). (2013). *Diagnostic and statistical manual of mental disorders: DSM-5* (5th ed.). Arlington, VA: Author.

Doll, E. A. (1935). A genetic scale of social maturity. *American Journal of Orthopsychiatry, 5*(2), 180–190. doi:10.1111/j.1939-0025.1935.tb06339.x

Fulton, E., Eapen, V., Crnčec, R., Walter, A., & Rogers, S. (2014). Reducing maladaptive behaviors in preschool-aged children with autism spectrum disorder using the early start Denver model. *Frontiers in Pediatrics, 2*, 40. doi:10.3389/fped.2014.00040

Laugeson, E., Ellingsen, R., Sanderson, J., Tucci, L., & Bates, S. (2014). The ABC's of teaching social skills to adolescents with autism spectrum disorder in the classroom: The UCLA PEERS Program. *Journal of Autism and Developmental Disorders, 44*(9), 2244–2256. doi:10.1007/s10803-014-2108-8

Prince, K. C., Ho, E. A., & Hansen, S. B. (2010). Effects of a school based program to improve adaptive school behavior and social competencies among elementary school youth: The Living Skills Program. *Journal of Research in Character Education, 8*(2), 39–59.

Raines, T. C., Gordon, M., Harrell-Williams, L., Diliberto, R. A., & Parke, E. M. (2017). Adaptive skills and academic achievement in Latino students. *Journal of Applied School Psychology, 33*(4), 245–260.

Schalock, R. L., Borthwick-Duffy, S. A., Bradley, V. J., Buntinx, W. H., Coulter, D. L., Craig, E. M., . . . Yeager, M. H. (2010). *Intellectual disability: Definition, classification, and systems of supports* (11th ed.). Washington, DC: American Association on Intellectual and Developmental Disabilities.

Sparrow, S. S. (2011). Vineland Adaptive Behavior Scales. In J. S. Kreutzer, J. DeLuca, & B. Caplan (Eds.), *Encyclopedia of clinical neuropsychology* (pp. 2618–2621). New York, NY: Springer. doi:10.1007/978-0-387-79948-3_1602

# SECTION III

## *What Really Works With Instruction*

# 9

# *UDL and Co-Teaching*

## *Establishing the Perfect Union*

### Wendy W. Murawski
*California State University, Northridge*

### Leila Ansari Ricci
*California State University, Los Angeles*

## SETTING THE STAGE FOR UDL AND CO-TEACHING

Does the thought of universally designing lessons overwhelm you? Are you worried that you won't be able to identify all the different ways for students to access the curriculum, environment, and instruction? Consider adding another teacher to the mix! Co-teaching makes UDL that much easier. So what exactly is co-teaching, and how does it fit with UDL?

Co-teaching is often confused with collaboration or basic in-class support. However, just because two teachers are physically in the same space does not mean they are co-teaching. Done well, co-teaching occurs when two equal partners with differing primary areas of expertise jointly deliver instruction;

**Key Concept**

Co-teaching requires two or more educators to co-plan, co-instruct, and co-assess (Murawski, 2010).

that is, they co-plan, co-instruct, *and* co-assess a diverse group of students in the same, shared physical space (Murawski, 2010). Co-teaching is typically seen between a general educator and special educator, though others may use this approach as well. Co-teaching can occur with reading specialists, math coaches, speech teachers, English language specialists, another subject area teacher, a master or student teacher—the sky's the limit!

The research on co-teaching is vast, though scattered. There is strong support for the collaboration of teachers with diverse areas of expertise (Scruggs & Mastropieri, 2017), but Murawski and Goodwin (2014) ultimately defined the co-teaching research-to-practice base as involving "confusion, contradiction, and cautious optimism" (p. 293). Though evidence exists on co-teaching and its positive impact on academics, behavior, social skills, and self-esteem for both students with and without disabilities (e.g., Keeley, 2015; Sweigart & Landrum, 2015; Tschida, Smith, & Fogarty, 2015), there remains a constant call for additional data to support its use. Zigmond, Magiera, Simmons, and Volonino (2013) accurately summed up co-teaching research by stating, "The lack of empirical support for co-teaching is not surprising; co-teaching may be a service, but it is not a "treatment" that can be imposed with fidelity on an experimental group and withheld with equal fidelity from a control group" (p. 116). Thus, schools using co-teaching are implored to collect and share any data they have on co-teaching outcomes. Suggestions for data collection, analysis, and dissemination are offered by Murawski and Lochner (2018).

What are the benefits to co-teaching when you can just teach solo? Co-teaching is a service delivery model designed to facilitate the learning of students with diverse needs in inclusive settings (Friend, 2016). It lowers the student-to-teacher ratio and allows teachers to provide more individualized instruction (Murawski, 2006; Zigmond, Magiera, & Matta, 2003). Students' academic and social needs can be better met in co-taught classrooms versus non-co-taught classes for students with and without identified disabilities (Strogilos & Avramidis, 2016). Co-teaching is a perfect complement to UDL because it gives teachers more flexibility and resources—not to mention the great ideas of another teacher—to provide students with more options for multiple means of representation, engagement, and action and expression.

Have you ever walked into a formal presentation, artistic performance, or sports competition with no practice ahead of time and just nailed it? Probably not, right? You took the time to practice, to plan, and to rehearse, in order to *really* make sure you did your best. Co-teaching is no different; it requires shared co-planning ahead of time before the two of you step foot in front of your students (Murawski, 2010, 2012). You don't have to memorize lines or map out every second of your instruction together. You do, however, have to set aside planning time to discuss the objectives and goals of your lesson, what each of you will do, how you will assess your students' learning, and what adaptations you might need to make. (*Hint:* this fits in so well with UDL!)

What does co-teaching look like in a classroom? If co-teachers are using the three regrouping approaches to co-instruction, you may see them Station Teaching with small groups of students rotating among various stations focused on fractions; Parallel Teaching with two groups taking different sides of the Revolutionary War; or Alternative Teaching, in which a large group is reading silently under the supervision of one teacher, while the other teacher has a small group and is reading aloud to them. If the students remain as a large group, you may see co-teachers using the two whole-group approaches: Team Teaching to role-play a dialogue between characters in a novel or One Teach, One Support, as one teacher reviews homework while the other walks around stamping papers and documenting completion.

The last feature of co-teaching—co-assessing—ensures that both teachers are aware of their students' strengths and needs and are using this information to plan more effective, universally designed instruction. Teachers can co-assess their own actions or that of other co-teaching pairs. Naturally, co-teachers will also work collaboratively to ascertain the achievements and needs of their own students, using a variety of measures (Cornelius, 2014).

There is a natural fit between co-teaching and UDL. In fact, co-teaching has three major features (co-planning, co-instructing, and co-assessing), and so does UDL. In a nutshell, there is no point to co-teaching if teachers are merely replicating a solo-taught general education class, albeit with two adults. As Murawski and Spencer (2011) wrote, "The essential question for co-teaching is: How is what the two teachers are doing together *substantively different and better for students* than what one of them would do alone?" (p. 96).

It might be helpful to think about co-planning as the time you really put your minds together to think about how you can represent information and content for your students in multiple ways so all of them can "get it." Think about co-instructing as when you two are in high gear with multiple ways of engaging your students and getting them to interact with the content through the various co-teaching approaches. Think of co-assessing as the myriad ways you are utilizing both of your strengths as co-teachers to have students demonstrate that they have met the competencies in whatever way suits them best but still meets the overall objective of the lesson. Imagine all of this happening because you have a solid partner. Sounds pretty cool, no? We certainly think so!

## PUTTING UDL AND CO-TEACHING INTO PRACTICE: MULTIPLE MEANS OF REPRESENTATION

*Co-planning* helps set the stage for the co-instructing and co-assessing, brings in both educators' perspectives and expertise, and allows teachers to proactively consider students' needs, strengths, and learning profiles (Murawski, 2012). Co-teachers have different needs and strengths too, so consider universally designing the way in which you co-plan!

When universally designing co-planning between adults:

- **COMPLETE THE SHARE WORKSHEET (Murawski & Dieker, 2004) and review your results.** Discuss your personal preferences for co-planning and include a discussion of when, how often, to what degree, where, and how you prefer to plan.
- **BE OPEN TO CO-PLANNING both in real time and asynchronously.** You might plan together on Mondays but then post and respond online at different times during the week.
- **RESPECT DIFFERENCES in how often and to what degree each of you contributes in co-planning.** One of you might need to be very specific in planning, while the other is more of a generalist. As long as you've discussed it, both have input, and are agreeable, you're set. You will also find that the more you respect one another's planning differences, the more you will open your mind to multiple means of representation, engagement, and action and expression for students as well.
- **USE TECHNOLOGY** (e.g., Google docs, Slideshare, email, text) to co-plan . . . or choose instead to write your plans in Dieker's co-teaching lesson plan book (Dieker, 2016). Both of you don't plan the same way? That's cool too. Find out what works for each of you and create a compromise.

## CASE IN POINT

Baubb and Anne review their objective for next week's unit: students will identify systems of equations, apply the three types, and analyze which type will be easiest to use in solving a given problem. To represent the material in different ways, the co-teachers agree to use One Teach One Support for the first ten minutes to review systems of equations in general, then break into stations. Each station provides practice in using a different approach (substitution, graphing, elimination) to the same system of equation. Overwhelmed by the idea of creating or offering too many choices in their first foray into UDL, Baubb and Anne decide to ensure each station provides different methods of representation. Baubb uses dry erase boards in his substitution station, Anne employs manipulatives in her elimination station, and students put on headphones and select a short video from a provided list of choices on using the graphing approach and then apply with graph paper in the independent station. The class wraps up with Anne and Baubb using Team Teaching to facilitate a class debrief and a Ticket-out-the-Door activity, wherein students solve a systems of equations problem using their preferred approach.

*Co-instructing* uses different regrouping structures to fully engage students. Just as all students do not care to learn in the same way, neither do all teachers like to teach in the same way. Thus, UDL is helpful not just to students but to their instructors as well! When representing material to students in different ways, co-teachers can use Parallel, Station, or Alternative to teach in ways most comfortable for them. If Carolyn is a general educator who wishes she could have more face time with individual students, working with smaller groups might appeal to her. Consider examples of how regrouping approaches will help you represent the material:

- **SET UP "STATIONS" AROUND THE ROOM RELATED TO YOUR OBJECTIVE.** Create a Tic-Tac-Toe board and have students determine the three activities they want to accomplish of the eight stations offered to them. Since each path goes through the middle, that should be an activity everyone is required to do (e.g., unit test, note-taking, teacher lecture). At a predetermined time, sound a bell and have students rotate to their next station.
- **TAKE TWO SIDES ON ONE ISSUE.** Use Parallel Teaching so that one teacher facilitates one side and the other facilitates an opposing view. Let students choose which viewpoint they prefer. Use video, literature, discussion, and so on to help students understand a point of view and then have students on each side debate one another, using their preferred method of choice.
- **INTRODUCE MATERIAL TO STUDENTS IN THEIR PRIMARY LANGUAGE using Alternative Teaching, wherein there is a large and small group.** If one teacher speaks a different language, he or she can take a small group of English language learners and introduce the material orally. Other options include using captioning, Google Translate, other language apps, peers, parent volunteers, and materials in other languages.

*Co-assessing*, in reality, should be a part of all aspects of UDL. Co-teachers should use different ways to co-assess their own co-teaching experiences. For example, they may decide to do weekly "check-ins," or view their SHARE worksheet quarterly, or independently label each co-taught lesson plan with a ☺, ☺, or ☹, so they can see how they each felt the lesson went. Using the co-teaching core competencies (Murawski & Lochner, 2017), they can determine which competencies they would like to improve.

Trying to determine how to co-assess multiple means of representation? Try these strategies:

- **DOCUMENT THE DIFFERENT WAYS IN WHICH YOU REPRESENTED THE INFORMATION.** Look for trends. Are you lecturing too frequently? Are you relying on the same combination of website, videos, or role-play? Have you asked students for their feedback on the ways you represent material?

- **COLLECT DATA ON STUDENTS' CHOICES.** When you offer Parallel Teaching and students choose sides, are students selecting due to content, activity, peers, or instructor? Are students making good choices that facilitate their increased academic, social, and behavioral success? Do they need additional support and scaffolding in choice-making?
- **DEVELOP A UDL MINDSET and check for it frequently.** How often are you providing choice to students, and in what forms? Is this beginning to feel like one day a week is the "fun activity day," as opposed to truly embedding UDL throughout the class?
- **CRITICALLY ANALYZE WAYS in which information is being represented.** Are all students accessing the content and instruction? Is there still a need for additional differentiation for a particular student, and if so, has that been provided?

## PUTTING UDL AND CO-TEACHING INTO PRACTICE: MULTIPLE MEANS OF ENGAGEMENT

The National Research Council (2004) wrote, "Learning and succeeding in school requires active engagement. . . . Academic motivation decreases steadily from the early grades of elementary school into high school. Furthermore, adolescents are too old and too independent to follow teachers' demands out of obedience, and many are too young, inexperienced, or uninformed to fully appreciate the value of succeeding in school" (pp. 1–2). Over a decade later, this conundrum holds true. The objective of having multiple means of engagement is to recognize that students are motivated by, and therefore engaged by, a wide array of topics. There is no "one size fits all."

*Co-planning* for engagement requires co-teachers to work collaboratively to identify what motivates each student. This can be in the form of topics (e.g., skateboards, soccer), technology use (e.g., phones, Chromebooks), instruction (e.g., videos, small groups), individuals (e.g., specific peers, adults), or environment (e.g., sitting on floor, library). Strategies for co-planning for engagement include:

- **GIVE OUT INTEREST INVENTORIES early in the year and have students update them regularly.** Find out what motivates each of your students.
- **DISCUSS MATERIALS MANAGEMENT WITH ONE ANOTHER.** One co-teacher might be in charge of bringing

in technological devices/apps/ websites, while the other will bring in manipulatives.

- **CREATE OPPORTUNITIES FOR GENIUS HOUR in the school week.** Genius Hour allows all kids to use their own creativity and personal areas of interest to create something exceptional.

**Tech Tips**

Find out more about Genius Hour by going to www.geniushour.com or watching the video at https://www.youtube.com/ watch?v=NMFQUtHsWhc

- **ASK STUDENTS HOW THEY PREFER TO STAY ENGAGED.** If they mention something you don't have access to (e.g., apps, comics, information on dinosaurs), ask them to bring in materials that you can embed in lessons. Less work for you two!
- **USE ALL ADULTS WELL.** Discuss the best use of your instructional assistants or parent volunteers. There are way too many missed opportunities in classes in which adults are merely standing to the side, waiting to be told what to do! Find out the strengths of these adults and use them to your shared advantage.

## CASE IN POINT

Co-teachers Juan and Vik decided to use the "Vocab in a Hat" strategy so that their kids were more motivated to participate in their vocabulary lesson. While Juan introduced ten new words on the board, Vik had ten random students pull out a card from a hat. Each card had a new vocab word on it. Using team teaching, Juan and Vik explained that those students with a card were now responsible for defining and explaining the word so that their classmates would understand it (their peers would take a turn at this in future weeks). They could do so in any way they saw fit, as long as it was school-appropriate and wouldn't take more than two minutes. The co-teachers increased the stakes by saying that if 90 percent of the class got a word right on the weekly quiz, the student who taught that word would get bonus points. The next day, Juan and Vik were thrilled as their students used PowerPoint, pictures, video, role-plays, and other techniques to "teach" their peers their word, using examples that varied from sports to theater to literature. This was UDL at its best!

*Co-instructing* means there are multiple qualified adults in the room. While engaging students on an individual level is difficult when teaching a class alone, partners are encouraged to use different approaches to divide and conquer.

- **USE STATION, PARALLEL, AND ALTERNATIVE TEACHING** multiple times a week. Research is clear that smaller groups can result in more student engagement (Baker, Farrie, & Sciarra, 2016; Mathis, 2016). Challenge yourselves to combine the approaches as well. For example, while students are rotating through stations, one teacher could select a few students each time to work with on IEP goals and objectives through the use of Specially Designed Instruction (SDI), thereby infusing Alternative Teaching into Station Teaching.
- **MODEL PARTNER ASSIGNMENTS THROUGH TEAM TEACHING.** For example, when doing journal prompts, model how one partner comes up with a prompt and the other dictates her answer to her peer. Students can choose their prompt and who takes which role. Additional choice can be given in how they do their journal: handwriting, Siri, typing, or videos, and on the subject or content of their journal.
- **PROVIDE DIFFERENTIATION AND SPECIALLY DESIGNED INSTRUCTION.** In the "Case in Point," Juan and Vik might proactively select a more concrete word for Ruth, a student with Down syndrome, or Bento, an English language learner, and then provide additional support in helping them define the word. By doing so, they are *differentiating* to support those students. Ruth and Bento can still choose their own methods for teaching their words to their peers, but the co-teachers are setting them up for success.

UDL v. DI

*Co-assessing* for engagement can involve documenting who is engaged and when to determine trends for what works, as well as finding ways to assess students while keeping them engaged.

## STRATEGY SPOT
### MAGIC TABLECLOTH

Use the magic tablecloth (Murawski, 2009) to engage learners and provide assessment data! Tape a plastic tablecloth to the wall and spray it lightly with adhesive spray. Have students write their own test problems based on today's lesson on an index card. As the class wraps up, they show their problem to a co-teacher, who checks it off in the grade book; then they slap the card face-down on the tablecloth as they leave. Those problems can stay up until the next day, when students enter and have to randomly select someone else's problem to take down and try!

- **MIX UP YOUR ASSESSMENT STRATEGIES.** Cornelius (2014) offers excellent practical strategies for doing so, to include an anecdotal seating chart, daily scorecard, and objectives grid.
- **ASK MORE QUESTIONS!** Questions are an excellent way to engage students *and* ascertain their learning. One of the "listen for" aspects of the co-teaching core competencies (Murawski & Lochner, 2017) states: *Co-teachers ask questions at a variety of levels to meet all students' needs (basic recall to higher-order thinking).* Don't limit yourself to whole-group questions, though. Ask questions on cards, through texts, through group chats, through games, and one-on-one.
- **LET TECHNOLOGY ENGAGE STUDENTS AND PROVIDE ASSESSMENT DATA.** There are numerous options for the classroom: Kahoot!, clickers, Poll Everywhere, and Mentimeter are just a few.

## PUTTING UDL AND CO-TEACHING INTO PRACTICE: MULTIPLE MEANS OF ACTION AND EXPRESSION

For years, students in special education classes have been dictating answers, doing hands-on work, and showing what they've learned in different ways due to their disability. UDL emphasizes that it is *not only* students with disabilities who need to present their learning in different ways, and be given the choice as to which methods work best for them, but *all* students. As long as co-teachers are clear on their objectives, they can be creative in how they allow students to demonstrate mastery of the content.

*Co-planning* for action and expression does not have to be tedious. Many of the tried-and-true options already described, such as Tic-Tac-Toe and Choice boards, can be implemented to measure students' learning. The fact that co-teachers have diverse interests and skills actually makes co-planning options easier, as both teachers together are more likely to generate a variety of options to match student preferences and needs. Strategies for co-planning for action and expression include:

- **DON'T RECREATE THE WHEEL.** Ask teachers who teach the same grade or subject how they have assessed a learning objective. Check your district's internal website for other teachers in your district who teach the same content to find out what they do. Then, create a menu board that allows students to select different options to show they have met the objective.
- **ASK THE KIDS.** After explaining the objective of a unit/lesson to students, have students share with you how they would like to be assessed at the end. For those who need support to get the juices flowing, use Alternative Teaching and provide some suggestions

of options (e.g., presentation, journal, series of tweets, podcast, interview, worksheet, test/quiz, research, short story, create an app) to the smaller group.

> **Tech Tips**
>
> Find out more about ways for students to share their learning
> *through vlogs:*
> www.vlognation.com
> *through comics:*
> www.makebeliefscomix.com
> *through Voice Thread:*
> www.voicethread.com
> *through Padlet:*
> www.padlet.com

- **SEARCH THE WEB!** One of you can look for assessments and activities that other teachers have posted related to your objective, while the other can look up websites that allow students to display work in unique ways (e.g., vlogs, comics, Voice Thread, Padlet). Check out Pinterest and other websites with educational ideas to get your creative juices flowing.

*Co-instructing* around multiple means of action and expression allows co-teachers to help students with challenges in metacognition and executive functioning. Many students do not recognize how they learn best, how to chunk content, how to leverage their own strengths to minimize their deficits, or how to manage their learning and their resources.

- **BE VULNERABLE.** Co-teachers can share personal stories and examples of how they have different competencies and how they use those competencies to leverage their areas of need. Students' self-concept and confidence improve when they learn that even teachers may not "know it all" and may need instruction repeated or presented in different ways.

- **USE CUBING.** Cubing is an instructional strategy wherein students are asked to consider a question from different perspectives or to answer questions at different levels. Wormeli (2006) suggests that teachers integrate Bloom's Taxonomy to help with differentiation for some students or to create different cubes for different students. For an excellent resource on cubing, check out: https://study.com/academy/lesson/using-the-cubing-strategy-to-differentiate-instruction.html
- **COMMUNICATE WITH VOXER.** When co-teachers break into groups and use a different setting (e.g., library, another classroom), the use of Voxer (an app that acts like a Walkie Talkie) can be very helpful for teachers and engaging to students. Students can work separately and then use Voxer to check their answers with a partner prior to having their learning assessed.
- **EXPLICITLY TEACH APPS AND SKILLS.** Help teach organizational, time management, planning, and working memory skills through Station Teaching. Students bring their own smartphones

(or share) and try out a different supportive app at each station for three minutes. App stations might include: 30/30 (planning), Quizlet (working memory), YouNote! (note-taking), Google Calendar (organization), and In-Class (time management). Have options at each station so students can choose what works for them—or even teach their peers apps that they like and use successfully!

**Making Connections**

See Chapter 6 for more on UDL and Executive Functioning.

- **MANAGE YOUR CLASSROOM and help students take ownership of their behaviors** with apps like ClassDoJo, Too Noisy, Socrative, and TeacherKit. Using One Teach One Support allows instruction to continue as one of the co-teachers collects classroom behavior data.

*Co-assessing* the different ways students use action and expression to demonstrate mastery of an objective does not have to be difficult. A plethora of technological options exist to help co-teachers easily ascertain how students are doing academically, behaviorally, and socially.

- **CREATE STATIONS THAT EXPLORE DIFFERENT SOCIAL MEDIA OPTIONS and have students interact around your content.** Twitter, Instagram, Yellowdig, Edmodo, SnapChat, and Facebook are just a few sites that could be used for sharing pictures, favorite quotes, opinions, and song lyrics.
- **PROVIDE DIFFERENT DISCUSSION OPTIONS.** Using Parallel Teaching, one teacher could facilitate a small-group discussion around a topic in real time, while the other could facilitate Flipgrid, in which students create video responses to ignite a dialogue. Each teacher would collect data on students' contributions.
- **LET THEM BLOG.** Blogs are a popular way for students to share information and for co-teachers to assess student growth over time. Blogger.com is a popular website, but students can be encouraged to share information in multiple formats (e.g., Canva, Goanimate, MakeAMeme, Piktochart, Podcast, Popplet, PowToon, Prezi, Smore, Voice Thread, Vlog). Using One Teach One Support, one teacher can circulate and provide support for students able to work independently while the other teacher works with a small group of students who need technological or academic support.
- **GIVE STUDENTS A QR CODE for a Padlet or Symbaloo you both created on a particular subject.** Let students know they must search for artifacts that answer a given question to demonstrate an understanding of the content. Students can post

articles, songs, pictures of their own work, images found online, screenshots, audio messages, and more. Using an agreed-upon rubric, teachers can co-assess students' mastery of the objectives and assign grades accordingly.

- **DON'T FORGET TO CO-ASSESS YOUR OWN MASTERY of the co-teaching core competencies!** Using the CTIME (Collaborative Teaching Improvement Model of Excellence; Murawski & Lochner, 2018) process, administrators can observe co-teachers in action and assess their skills on the co-teaching core competencies. Co-teaching teams can support one another by selecting a competency on which to improve and doing microteaching sessions, which can be filmed or watched live by other co-teaching teams in order to give effective feedback, or by completing self-assessments.

## BRINGING IT ALL TOGETHER

Co-teaching requires co-planning, co-instructing, and co-assessing. UDL requires multiple means of representation, engagement, and action and expression. By working collaboratively, educators can share the load, come up with more ideas, and actively engage more students in meaningful learning. Having different areas of expertise benefits students by enabling those with and without disabilities to have appropriate options available in the general education classroom; those teachers who have embraced a UDL mindset will actually need to implement *fewer* accommodations and modifications to enable all students to access the general education content and instruction. The more teachers collaborate to employ multiple means in the inclusive classroom, the more successful all students will be!

## TOP FIVE WEBSITES TO SUPPORT CO-TEACHING AND UDL

→ www.2TeachLLC.com

→ www.cec.sped.org

→ https://marylandlearninglinks.org/co-teaching/

→ www.coteachsolutions.com

→ www.marilynfriend.com

## APPS WE LOVE

→ Class DoJo

→ Edmodo

→ Evernote

→ Explain Everything

→ Google Classroom

## RECOMMENDED READINGS

Conderman, G. & Hedin, L. (2012). Purposeful assessment practices for co-teachers. Teaching Exceptional Children, 44(4), 18–27.

Co-Teaching: Making it work. (Dec 2015/Jan 2016) Educational Leadership, vol.73, no.4 Retrieved from: http://www.ascd.org/publications/educational-leadership/dec15/vol73/num04/toc.aspx

Murawski, W.W. & Hughes, C. E. (2010). Response to intervention, collaboration and co-teaching: A logical combination for successful systemic change. Preventing School Failure, 53(4), 267–277.

# REFERENCES

Baker, B. D., Farrie, D., & Sciarra, D. G. (2016). *Mind the gap: 20 years of progress and retrenchment in school funding and achievement gaps*. ETS Research Report Series. doi:10.1002/ets2.12098

Cornelius, K. (2014). Formative assessment made easy: Templates for collecting daily data in inclusive classrooms. *Teaching Exceptional Children*, 47(2), 112–118. doi:10.1177/004005991453204

Dieker, L. A. (2016). *The co-planner: Two professionals + one plan for co-teaching*. Oviedo, FL: Knowledge by Design.

Friend, M. (2016). Welcome to co-teaching 2.0. *Educational Leadership*, 73(4), 16–22.

Keeley, R. G. (2015). Measurements of student and teacher perceptions of co-teaching models. *Journal of Special Education Apprenticeship*, 4(1), 1–15.

Mathis, W. J. (2016). *Research-based options for educational policy-making: The effectiveness of class size reduction*. National Education Policy Center, University of Colorado. Retrieved from http://nepc.colorado.edu/publication/research-based-options

Murawski, W. W. (2006). Student outcomes in co-taught secondary English classes: How can we improve? *Reading and Writing Quarterly*, 22(3), 227–247.

Murawski, W. W. (2009). *Collaborative teaching in secondary schools*. Thousand Oaks, CA: Corwin.

Murawski, W. W. (2010). *Collaborative teaching in elementary schools*. Thousand Oaks, CA: Corwin.

Murawski, W. W. (2012). 10 tips for co-planning more efficiently. *Teaching Exceptional Children*, 44(4), 8–15.

Murawski, W. W., & Dieker, L. A. (2004). Tips and strategies for co-teaching at the secondary level. *Teaching Exceptional Children*, 36(5), 52–58.

Murawski, W. W., & Goodwin, V. A. (2014). Effective inclusive schools and the co-teaching conundrum. In J. McLeskey, N. L. Waldron, F. Spooner, & B. Algozzine (Eds.), *Handbook of research and practice for inclusive schools* (pp. 289–305). New York, NY: Routledge.

Murawski, W. W., & Lochner, W. W. (2017). *Co-teaching core competency framework*. Retrieved from www.coteachsolutions.com

Murawski, W. W., & Lochner, W. (2018). *Beyond co-teaching basics: A data-driven, no-fail model of continuous improvement*. Alexandria, VA: ASCD.

Murawski, W. W., & Spencer, S. (2011). *Collaborate, communicate, and differentiate! How to increase student learning in today's diverse schools*. Thousand Oaks, CA: Corwin.

National Research Council, & Institute of Medicine. (2004). *Engaging schools: Fostering high school students' motivation to learn*. Washington, DC: National Academies Press.

Scruggs, T. E., & Mastropieri, M. A. (2017). Making inclusion work with co-teaching. *Teaching Exceptional Children*, 49(4), 284–293.

Strogilos, V., & Avramidis, E. (2016). Teaching experiences of students with special educational needs in co-taught and non-co-taught classes. *Journal of Research in Special Educational Needs*, 16(1), 24–33.

Sweigart, C. A., & Landrum, T. J. (2015). The impact of number of adults on instruction: Implications for co-teaching. *Preventing School Failure*, 59(1), 22–29.

Tschida, C. M., Smith, J. J., & Fogarty, E. A. (2015). "It just works better": Introducing the 2:1 model of co-teaching in teacher preparation. *The Rural Educator, 36*(2), 11–26.

Wormeli, R. (2006). Accountability: Teaching through assessment and feedback, not grading. *American Secondary Education, 34*(3), 14–27.

Zigmond, N., Magiera, K., & Matta, D. (2003, April). *Co-teaching in secondary schools: Is the instructional experience enhanced for students with disabilities?* Paper presented at the annual conference of the Council for Exceptional Children, Seattle, WA.

Zigmond, N., Magiera, K., Simmons, R., & Volonino, V. (2013). Strategies for improving student outcomes in co-taught general education classrooms. In D. J. Chard, B. G. Cook, & M. Tandersley (Eds.), *Research-based practices for improving outcomes in academics*. Boston, MA: Pearson.

# 10

UDL and Assistive Technology

*Utilizing Technology Beyond Mere Accessibility*

Lauren A. Delisio
*Rider University*

Caitlyn A. Bukaty
*University of Central Florida*

## SETTING THE STAGE FOR UDL AND ASSISTIVE TECHNOLOGY

When you hear the term *assistive technology* (AT), what do you think of? If you are like most people, you probably think of highly advanced and expensive tools, such as eye gaze technology, speech generating devices (SGDs), robotic shopping carts, or motorized wheelchairs. However, AT is more than just high-tech devices, and AT supports can help everyone, not just individuals with disabilities. For example, if you wear eyeglasses, you use AT. If you read using the Kindle app or listen to recorded books on the Audible app, you use AT. If you use an Apple watch or a Fitbit to track your steps or monitor your heart rate, you guessed it, you use AT! In this chapter, we will help you explore AT that can be implemented classwide to incorporate the principles of Universal Design for Learning (UDL).

According to the special education law, the Individuals with Disabilities Education Act (IDEA), "AT device means any item, piece of equipment, or product system, whether acquired commercially off the shelf, modified, or customized, that is used to increase, maintain, or improve the functional capabilities of a child with a disability" (IDEA, 2004, Part A, Definitions, 300.5). Therefore, when you put on your eyeglasses, you are improving your own functional capabilities—your ability to see clearly—which will, in turn, improve your ability to read, write, drive, watch a video, etc. You might use Audible to "read" books while driving; without audio books, you would not be able to read and drive at the same time—or you shouldn't! Many individuals wear heart-rate monitors to monitor their health; it might be medically necessary for some individuals with heart conditions, while others may access the same technology to enhance their exercise routine and improve their well-being.

Assistive technology supports exist on a continuum (Dell, Newton, & Petroff, 2016). *Low or no-tech tools* include items such as pencil grips, slant boards, and highlighting tape. Items classified as *mid-tech tools* might include personal dictionaries and grammar checking software. *High-tech tools* are typically devices, such as speech-generating communication devices like Proloquo2Go (the iPad augmentative and alternative communication [AAC] application).

According to Dell and colleagues (2016), low-tech AT includes tools and devices that are more affordable (e.g., pencil grips, commonly used for students with fine motor difficulties, cost approximately $2 each), do not require extensive training, and do not include electronic components. These tools can be implemented fairly quickly and easily, and many can be teacher-made. Mid-tech AT includes tools and devices that may have some electronic or digital features, may require some training to use, and typically cost more than low-tech AT devices (e.g., digital recorders, calculators, electronic dictionaries, portable note-takers, and audio books; Dell et al., 2016). Finally, high-tech AT encompasses a wide array of complex, often expensive devices with digital or electronic components. Typically, these devices require extensive training to use. However, although they are expensive, high-tech AT devices can offer a powerful level of flexibility and customization that low and mid-tech AT devices cannot; this includes the use of computers and laptops, iPads, applications, software, and many AAC devices, such as the Tobii Dynavox (Dell et al., 2016).

Assistive technology supports, when successfully and appropriately implemented, have been found to improve the skills of students with a variety of special needs across a range of both academic and nonacademic areas, including academic endeavors, and behavioral, social, and communication skills (Virnes, Marna, & Vellonen, 2015), as well as across all ages, from early intervention to postsecondary transition (Houchins, 2009). For example, students with intellectual disabilities have demonstrated an increase in their independence through the use of auditory recorders (Bouck, Satsangi, & Muhl, 2013), augmentative and alternative communication (AAC; Fisher & Shogren, 2012), and visual schedules (Douglas & Uphold, 2014).

Regardless of the type of AT support implemented (low-, mid-, or high-tech), the use of AT can provide students with a means of accessing the general education curriculum as well as social activities, thus promoting their inclusion in general education settings (Bruce et al., 2013; Dyal, Carpenter, & Wright, 2009). Use of AT can help students with disabilities become more independent students and employees (Haydon et al., 2012; Sauer, Parks, & Heyn, 2010). The importance of AT in the lives of individuals with *and without* disabilities can best be summed up with this quote from Mary Radebaugh, who was an employee with the IBM Disability Support Center: "For people without disabilities, technology makes things easier. For people with disabilities, technology makes things possible."

Assistive technology can have a positive impact on academic abilities, social skills, and independence for students with disabilities, as well as improve accessibility. Therefore, IDEA requires that child study teams consider a student's need for AT devices and services as part of the evaluation process (20 U.S.C. § 1414(d)(3)(B)(v)). If no AT services or devices are deemed necessary, the team must provide a rationale in the IEP, explaining why the student does not require AT in school. The role of AT is just that important, and it can be easily integrated into the framework of a universally designed classroom.

## THE CONVERGENCE OF AT AND UDL

At first glance, it may seem that AT and UDL are different from both a theoretical and practical standpoint, given that the use of AT is a customized, individualized approach to accessibility, while UDL is characterized by a more global approach to meeting the needs of a wide variety of diverse learners (Rose, Hasselbring, Stahl, & Zabala, 2005). However, in reality the two are very similar concepts, in that both promote *accessibility* in the classroom. In some applications, AT might be student specific, such as the use of an AAC device, which may not speak directly to broad classroom UDL application, while other uses of AT, such as providing an entire class of students with a choice of graphic organizers to use during a writing lesson, coincide perfectly with UDL implementation.

When students with disabilities are supported with AT or AAC that is mandated in their IEPs, such as the use of a personal AAC device, programmed specifically for that individual, the learning is then *differentiated* for that one individual student. However, AT supports that are offered to an entire class or large groups of students as options for representing content in multiple ways, engaging students in multiple ways, giving students multiple options to demonstrate their knowledge and understanding (i.e., action and expression), and as a means of promoting universal accessibility, are universally designed.

UDL v. DI

Furthermore, "accessible curricular content increases the efficacy of AT" (Rose et al., 2005, p. 514). Therefore, if AT supports are designed in concordance with UDL guidelines, they will meet the needs of more individuals with even more diverse needs and abilities. Although the application of UDL principles and guidelines will not completely eliminate the need for individualized AT devices and tools, the more accessible the curricula, media, software, and printed materials become, the less it will be necessary to utilize individualized AT devices and services. According to Hitchcock and Stahl (2003), "In school environments today, assistive technologies, universal design, and UDL must co-exist, since no single solution provides all of the accessibility and supports necessary for learning" (p. 49).

This relationship between UDL and AT is also supported in the legislation. According to the Assistive Technology Act of 1998, "The use of universal design principles reduces the need for many specific kinds of assistive technology devices and assistive technology services by building in accommodations for individuals with disabilities before rather than after production. The use of universal design principles also increases the likelihood that products (including services) will be compatible with existing assistive technologies" (Sec.2(a)10), TE).

Finally, as the concept of UDL becomes more widely understood and accepted as an educational and social norm, the hope is that more people will understand that AT is not just for people with disabilities. Rather than being solely associated with disability, universally designed technologies are used as a means of providing accessible options for *all* people, across a continuum of ability and need. "For example, speech recognition technology is applied in voice-activated cell phones, airline reservation systems, banking systems, and sometimes installed in automobiles" (Hitchcock & Stahl, 2003, p. 48). That was in 2003; in 2019, voice-activation is practically ubiquitous.

So how does one utilize AT supports in a universally designed classroom? Simply put, by combining the three UDL guidelines with no-tech, low-tech, mid-tech, and high-tech AT supports that typically might have been thought of as individualized supports, and offering these supports to any students who might benefit from their use.

## PUTTING UDL AND ASSISTIVE TECHNOLOGY INTO PRACTICE: REPRESENTATION

Representing classroom content in multiple ways through the range of AT supports can make curricular material in the content areas more accessible to *all* students with diverse learning needs. The use of AT supports, spanning the range of no tech to high tech, can support the delivery of content in multiple ways and offer students options for how they receive and comprehend complex curricular material, such as the adapted books described below. Furthermore, AT supports can aid students with behavioral, social, and/or communication deficits by offering multimodal presentations of abstract concepts.

### No-Tech or Low-Tech AT

No-tech or low-tech AT supports can offer multiple means of representation across academic content areas and can be created quickly and inexpensively, or purchased at a fairly low cost:

- **HIGHLIGHTING TAPE** can be used across content areas to help students with many learning needs. The transparent tape is placed on text (or mathematical equations or word problems) to draw attention to smaller selections, making it easier for students to focus, read, and not become overwhelmed by large sections of text.
- **MAGNIFIERS** can be used to improve access to text by increasing font size.
- **SLANT BOARDS** provide an ergonomically correct position for writing, helping students with physical or visual impairments find an easier-to-reach work surface, and allowing easier visual tracking during reading for many students.

### Mid- to High-Tech AT

Efficient and fluent reading skills support learning across content areas. Many students may struggle with some or all of the areas of reading instruction, including vocabulary, fluency, decoding, comprehension, phonemic awareness, and phonics. These examples of multiple representation can be implemented to support students in overcoming those barriers:

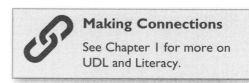

**Making Connections**

See Chapter 1 for more on UDL and Literacy.

- **IMPLEMENT ACCESSIBLE TEXT by providing students with a choice of text formats,** including traditional paper books, as well as text with enlarged print, speech to text, and audio books. Variety helps engage all learners.
- **EMBED GLOSSARIES AND DICTIONARIES into text to support access to background knowledge.**
- **USE PROGRAMS THAT HIGHLIGHT TEXT AS IT IS BEING READ ALOUD to support students with fluency, vocabulary, or decoding.** They can also be more engaging for students who struggle with attention or energy. The Kindle app with Whisper-Sync is a good example of this.

- **INTRODUCE ADAPTED BOOKS** that provide options for perception through the multimodal presentation of the text as well as options for language through the use of illustrations, interactive graphics, vocabulary supports, and multilingual texts, to name a few.

## CASE IN POINT

In one inclusive fourth-grade classroom, co-teachers Lisa Boggs and Christine Zaworski, affectionately known as "Ms. B. & Ms. Z," noticed that one of their students, Angela, who has a learning disability in reading, wanted to read grade-level texts alongside some of her peers during their independent reading time in reading workshop. However, her independent reading level was two grade levels below, and Angela struggled with fluency, decoding, and comprehension. Angela was very aware of and sensitive to the fact that she was not on the same reading level as many of her peers, and Ms. B and Ms. Z wanted to help Angela boost her confidence in reading, as well as to provide her with a means of accessing grade-level content. They noticed that Angela's listening comprehension of grade-level texts was strong, as she was always the first to respond with thoughtful commentary and insight about the text any time they asked a question during a read-aloud. Given Angela's strengths and needs, the co-teachers decided to make sure adapted books were available as an option to students. For Angela specifically, audiobooks with built-in supports would provide her with means of representation that would work with her learning strengths. Angela could follow along with the text visually, while it was being read aloud, and while the text was being highlighted on the screen. Ms. B and Ms. Z knew that if Angela was successful with adapted books, they could then offer this same AT support for students (including Angela) across all content areas, including grade-level texts in social studies and science. The co-teachers introduced students to adapted books through the website *Epic!* (www.getepic.com). *Epic!* is free for teachers; has a wide variety of popular books across all grade levels and genres; is available in multiple formats; and includes resources for teachers, like quizzes. After a few weeks of accessing some of the same texts as her peers, Angela was feeling more confident, and was able to demonstrate her strong listening comprehension by responding to verbal comprehension quizzes that her co-teachers created through the website.

Additional adapted book resources and examples include the following free or membership-based options:

- **LEARNING ALLY** (http://www.learningally.org/)—Over 80,000 audio books for Grades K–12; paid membership required.
- **TUMBLEBOOKS** (http://www.tumblebooks.com/)—Audio book options for all grade levels; paid membership required.
- **STORYLINE ONLINE** (http://www.storylineonline.net/)—K–5 picture books read by celebrities; free resource.
- **PROJECT GUTENBERG** (http://www.gutenberg.org/)—Over 57,000 ebooks (digital text, not audiobooks); free resource.
- **BOOKSHARE** (https://www.bookshare.org/cms/)—Over 600,000 adapted books in a variety of formats; free resource.
- **YOU CAN CREATE YOUR OWN ADAPTED BOOK** (in Microsoft PowerPoint or Word), which will meet a variety of student needs (e.g., visual impairment, intellectual disabilities, sensory needs, working memory, auditory processing disorder, physical and fine motor skill deficits, or students who are reading below grade level). Check out Pinterest for some ideas on how to create your own adapted books!

## PUTTING UDL AND ASSISTIVE TECHNOLOGY INTO PRACTICE: ENGAGEMENT

Assistive technology can be developed and applied in the classroom to help students with academic, behavioral, social, and/or communication needs remain engaged during lessons and activities throughout the school day, self-regulate, and persist in tasks and assignments.

### No-Tech or Low-Tech AT

Visual supports are a form of no-tech or low-tech AT that can be teacher-made or adapted from existing resources, and have been found to be an evidence-based practice for students with autism spectrum disorder (ASD; National Professional Development Center on Autism Spectrum Disorders, 2010). The use of visual supports aligns with UDL guidelines for multiple means of engagement by providing options for sustaining effort and persistence, and providing options for self-regulation. Visual supports can be used for both academic as well as behavioral and social endeavors.

- **VISUAL ACTIVITY SCHEDULES**, defined as "sets of pictures used to depict a sequence of events" (Pierce, Spriggs, Gast, &

Luscre, 2013, p. 253), are a form of visual supports that have proven effective in assisting students with ASD to remain on task, as well as to reduce problem behaviors and tantrums during transitions (Lequia, Machalicek, & Rispoli, 2012). Thus, making them available to any students who choose to use them can be beneficial to many and critical for some. You can make a schedule for the whole class or individualized daily schedules for students, broken up into smaller chunks of the day, with clocks, to help with transitions.

- **TIMERS** can improve on task behaviors and help students transition to the next activity or class. There are some great online timers, such as the ones found at https://www.online-stopwatch.com/classroom-timers/.

- **FLEXIBLE SEATING OPTIONS** offer your entire class the opportunity to find where they're most comfortable in the learning environment. Seating options promote independence and permit students to move throughout the day, which can potentially improve time on task.

## CASE IN POINT

In Ms. Stone's kindergarten classroom, there are very few desks. It seems a bit odd to newcomers at first glance! During lessons, the children sit on the carpet or on chairs, or they stand. Before sending them off to work independently after each lesson, Ms. Stone consistently reminds her students to "choose a place to work where you're going to get your *best* work done." Offering students this choice—but still providing some consistent guidance—promotes student independence at a young age. Flexible seating options can be especially beneficial for students with attention and sensory needs, as they are able to move freely when necessary, and choose spaces in the room that are comfortable (e.g., proper lighting, noise control, etc.).

During independent work, the students can be found sitting in laundry baskets (they fit perfectly!) with their clipboards for writing, sitting with cushions up against the wall, kneeling or sitting with their legs crossed at low tables, or standing up while working. Other choices include: T-chairs, medicine balls, and couches. When their choice of seating isn't working anymore—sometimes Ms. Stone will notice, but most of the time the students will say, "I need to move" or "I need a new place to work"—they still have a number of seating options.

## Mid- to High-Tech AT

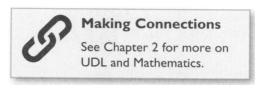

**Making Connections**

See Chapter 2 for more on UDL and Mathematics.

In the content area of mathematics, the needs of all students are varied and diverse (Vaughn & Bos, 2015). However, the needs of students with disabilities are even *more* critical—only 19 percent of fourth-grade students with disabilities nationwide are performing at the proficient or advanced level, as compared with 53 percent of students without disabilities (U.S. Department of Education, 2018). As students with disabilities progress into the middle school grades, the achievement gap widens even further, with only 11 percent of eighth-grade students with disabilities performing at the proficient or advanced level, as compared with 49 percent of students without disabilities (U.S. Department of Education, 2018).

To address these varied, diverse, and highly critical needs in mathematics classes, mid-tech and high-tech AT tools allow teachers to vary the resources available to students and minimize threats and distractions students may experience when presented with a problem or unfamiliar concept.

- **VIRTUAL MANIPULATIVES** offer electronic, online versions of traditional hands-on manipulatives across Grades K–12, such as fraction bars, base-10 blocks, algebra tiles, and fractals, and maintain student engagement by optimizing the relevance, value, and authenticity of the learning experience. They can be found for free at the National Library of Virtual Manipulatives (http://nlvm.usu.edu/en/nav/vlibrary.html).
- **PHOTOMATH** (https://photomath.net/en/) is a mobile app that utilizes the camera on a cell phone or tablet to recognize mathematical equations; once the equation has been scanned in and recognized, the PhotoMath app displays the step-by-step solution onscreen.
- **MATHPAD** (http://zurapps.com/all/index.php/mathpad/mathpad/) allows users to create mathematical documents including mathematical expressions, geometrical shapes, and graphs. A math keyboard is provided and users can change the font size or color of the mathematical expressions.
- **GRASPABLE MATH** (https://graspablemath.com/) is a Google Chrome extension for mathematics that is highly visual and kinesthetic and specific to algebraic equations.
- **KHAN ACADEMY** (https://www.khanacademy.org/) is a free online library of instructional videos and content. You can find videos that directly relate to specific content and make them available to your students to watch to reinforce a concept, use in small groups, or incorporate into whole-class lessons

# PUTTING UDL AND ASSISTIVE TECHNOLOGY INTO PRACTICE: EXPRESSION

Teachers frequently ask students to demonstrate their understanding of content or to express their thoughts and ideas through written work. However, successful and fluent writing requires a series of complex and simultaneous cognitive processes (Graham, Harris, & Santangelo, 2015), and students with disabilities often have difficulty with *all* of the processes, including handwriting, spelling, grammar, and the nonlinear writing process (i.e., pre-writing, drafting, revising, editing, etc.). Furthermore, as students progress into the upper grades, especially in high school, they may struggle to take effective notes in class, because note-taking is a skill that requires strong listening comprehension and handwriting skills, along with the ability to differentiate between relevant and irrelevant content during a lecture.

**Tech Tips**

Want to turn your students into poets or even songwriters? There are a number of writing AT apps specific to writing poetry that are worth checking out:
Poet's Pad for iPad ($9.99)
PortaPoet ($1.99)
Rhymer's Block (free!)
Word Palette (free!)

In any of these situations, optimizing access to UDL-friendly tools and AT can offer students multiple ways to express their knowledge and understanding of content.

## No-Tech or Low-Tech AT

- **GRAPHIC ORGANIZERS** can improve learning for students across grade levels and content (e.g., Dexter & Hughes, 2011; Kaldenberg, Watt, & Therrien, 2015). You can offer the printable, no-tech, paper versions to your students—try to have several available from which students may choose—to help them demonstrate their understanding of a book, science or social studies concepts and how they are related, or to allow them to express the steps to a mathematical equation.
- **PENCIL GRIPS** can be purchased virtually anywhere (e.g., on Amazon) and cost approximately $2 a piece. They can help students with fine motor issues to grasp their pencil correctly. Other students may select to use them just because they are fun.
- **RAISED LINE PAPER** offers students with fine motor, visual, and/or visual-spatial difficulties both a tactile and visual approach to letter and sentence formation. There are other paper choices available, such as those with wider margins, more lines, fewer lines, and so forth. You can purchase it from a specialty school supply website and may even be able to find it on general online retail sites.

Mid- to High-Tech AT

- **NOTE-TAKING APPS**, such as SoundNote (https://soundnote .com/) and Noteability (https://itunes.apple.com/us/app/ notability/id360593530?mt=8), have recording and playback capabilities in addition to note-taking and sketching options. If students spend all their time trying to form legible letters (and spell words correctly), this can impact their working memory, thus leaving little room for generating and composing content. Try writing a paragraph with your nondominant hand—you will quickly learn how difficult it is to focus on *what* you're writing, because all of your brain power is being used up to focus on *how* you're writing!
- **SPEECH-TO-TEXT APPS AND SOFTWARE** are practical, inexpensive (sometimes even free!), and can be implemented for students with a variety of difficulties such as fine motor skill deficits that translate into handwriting issues, working memory issues, other physical disabilities, or difficulties with information transfer. The Google Chrome extension, Voice Note, is a free speech-to-text tool that can easily be offered to all students as an option during writing lessons and activities. Using headphones with a microphone, your students can easily speak their ideas into a Chromebook, iPad, or desktop computer, reducing the stress associated with transferring their thoughts and ideas onto paper.
- **ELECTRONIC GRAPHIC ORGANIZERS, CONCEPT MAPS, AND MIND MAPS**, like those found at Popplet (http:// popplet.com/), Kidspiration (for Grades K–5); found at

### STRATEGY SPOT
MENUS

Instead of a traditional book report as a means of assessing student comprehension of a text, provide your entire class with a menu of options to demonstrate their understanding. Menus, also referred to as tiered activities (Tomlinson, 1999), engage learners by offering them a choice and provide valuable assessment data. The menu can include creating a website (www .wix.com), writing a blog (www.wordpress.com), creating an interactive Glogster multimedia poster (http://edu.glogster.com/), creating a quiz on *Kahoot!*, Quizlet, or Socrative, making a video and uploading it to your own channel on YouTube, or writing and performing a song!

http://www.inspiration.com/Kidspiration, and Inspiration (for Grades 6–Adult); found at http://www.inspiration.com/Inspiration, can offer support to any students who need it.

- **DESIGN APPLICATIONS AND WEBSITES,** such as Canva (www.canva.com) and Assembly Art and Design (http://assemblyapp.co/), provide students with fun and unique options they can use to demonstrate their content knowledge and/or understanding of a concept, especially in content areas like social studies and science.

Tiered activities are often considered a differentiated instruction strategy, but by offering this menu to the entire class, you have now turned it into a universally designed assessment.

If you are working on a particular IEP objective with a student, you may guide him to select particular options, or you may offer an option not available to other students such as working with you on Specially Designed Instruction. In this situation, you have then provided differentiation. When possible, offering a menu of options applicable to all students is the most desirable—and universally designed—approach!

**UDL v. DI**

## BRINGING IT ALL TOGETHER

Providing all of your students with a variety of AT options doesn't have to be complicated or expensive. You can support a diverse array of strengths and needs with no-, low-, mid- and high-tech tools that span the curriculum as well as the social, emotional, and behavioral needs of students with and without disabilities across all grade levels. These tools can be handouts such as graphic organizers, teacher-made supports, inexpensive items that can easily be purchased online, mobile apps, free websites, software, the list goes on and on! Offering all of your students access to a range of AT tools that support multiple means of engagement, representation, and action/expression helps to create a universally designed classroom environment.

## TOP FIVE WEBSITES TO SUPPORT ASSISTIVE TECHNOLOGY

→ http://assistivetech.net/

→ http://www.gpat.org/Georgia-Project-for-Assistive-Technology/Pages/default.aspx

→ https://www.iidc.indiana.edu/pages/using-visual-schedules-a-guide-for-parents

→ http://www.inclusive.co.uk/

→ http://www.pbisworld.com/tier-2/individual-visual-schedules/

## APPS WE LOVE

→ Canva

→ First Then Visual Schedule

→ Noteability

→ Photomath

→ Word Palette

## REFERENCES

Assistive Technology Act of 1998, 29 U.S.C. § 3001 et seq (1998).

Bouck, E. C., Satsangi, R., & Muhl, A. (2013). Using audio recorders to promote independence in grocery shopping for students with intellectual disability. *Journal of Special Education Technology, 28*(4), 15–26.

Bruce, D., DiCesare, D. M., Kaczorowski, T., Hashey, A., Boyd, E., Mixon, T., & Sullivan, M. (2013). Multimodal composing in special education: A review of the literature. *Journal of Special Education Technology, 28,* 25–42.

Dell, A. G., Newton, D. A., & Petroff, J. G. (2016). *Assistive technology in the classroom* (3rd ed.). Upper Saddle River, NJ: Pearson.

Dexter, D. D., & Hughes, C. A. (2011). Graphic organizers and students with learning disabilities: A meta-analysis. *Learning Disability Quarterly, 34*(1), 51–72.

Douglas, K. K., & Uphold, N. M. (2014). iPad or iPod Touch: Evaluating self-created electronic photographic activity schedules and student preferences. *Journal of Special Education Technology, 29*(3), 1–14.

Dyal, A., Carpenter, L. B., & Wright, J. V. (2009). Assistive technology: What every school leader should know. *Education, 129*(3), 556–560.

Fisher, K. W., & Shogren, K. K. (2012). Integrating augmentative and alternative communication and peer support for students with disabilities: A social-ecological perspective. *Journal of Special Education Technology, 27*(2), 23–39.

Graham, S., Harris, K. R., & Santangelo, T. (2015). Research-based writing practices and the Common Core: Meta-analysis and meta-synthesis. *Elementary School Journal, 115*(4), 498–522.

Haydon, T., Hawkins, R., Denune, H., Kimener, L., McCoy, D., & Basham, J. (2012). A comparison of iPads and worksheets on math skills of high school students with emotional disturbance. *Behavioral Disorders, 37*(4), 232–243.

Hitchcock, C., & Stahl, S. (2003). Assistive technology, universal design, Universal Design for Learning: Improved learning opportunities. *Journal of Special Education Technology, 18*(4), 45–52.

Houchins, D. E. (2009). Assistive technology barriers and facilitators during secondary and post-secondary transition. *Career Development for Exceptional Individuals, 24,* 73–88.

Individuals with Disabilities Education Improvement Act of 2004, 20 U.S.C. § 1400 et seq (2004).

Kaldenberg, E. R., Watt, S. J., & Therrien, W. J. (2015). Reading instruction in science for students with learning disabilities: A meta-analysis. *Learning Disability Quarterly, 38*(3), 160–173. doi:10.1177/0731948714550204

Lequia, J., Machalicek, W., & Rispoli, M. J. (2012). Effects of activity schedules on challenging behavior exhibited in children with autism spectrum disorders: A systematic review. *Research in Autism Spectrum Disorders, 6*(1), 480–492. doi:10.1016/j.rasd.2011.07.008

National Professional Development Center on Autism Spectrum Disorders. (2010). *Visual supports: Evidence base.* Retrieved from http://autismpdc.fpg.unc.edu/content/visual-supports

Pierce, J. M., Spriggs, A. D., Gast, D. L., & Luscre, D. (2013). Effects of visual activity schedules on independent classroom transitions for students with autism.

*International Journal of Disability, Development and Education, 60*(3), 253–269. doi :10.1080/1034912X.2013.812191

Rose, D. H., Hasselbring, T. S., Stahl, S., & Zabala, J. (2005). Assistive technology and Universal Design for Learning: Two sides of the same coin. In D. Edyburn, K. Higgins, & R. Boone (Eds.), *Handbook of special education technology research and practice* (pp. 507–518). Oviedo, FL: Knowledge by Design.

Sauer, A. L., Parks, A., & Heyn, P. C. (2010). Assistive technology effects on the employment outcomes for people with cognitive disabilities: A systematic review. *Disability and Rehabilitation: Assistive Technology, 5*(6), 377. doi:10.3109/1748310100374636

Tomlinson, C. A. (1999). *The differentiated classroom: Responding to the needs of all learners.* Alexandria, VA: ASCD.

U.S. Department of Education, National Center for Education Statistics. (2018). *National Assessment of Educational Progress (NAEP), 1992–2017 Mathematics Assessments.*

Vaughn, S., & Bos, C. (2015). *Strategies for teaching students with learning and behavior problems.* Upper Saddle River, NJ: Pearson.

Virnes, J., Marna, E., & Vellonen, V. (2015). Review of research on children with autism spectrum disorder and the use of technology. *Journal of Special Education Technology, 30*, 13–27.

# 11

# *UDL and Implementation Fidelity*

## *Providing Consistency Within Flexibility*

Kimberly M. Johnson

Kyena E. Cornelius

*Minnesota State University, Mankato*

## SETTING THE STAGE FOR UDL AND IMPLEMENTATION FIDELITY

Do you want to implement principles of Universal Design for Learning (UDL) into your instruction and learning environment but worry that you might not do it quite right? Well, don't worry! This chapter will explore the matter of implementation fidelity as it relates to UDL and put your mind at ease. Implementation fidelity (also referred to as *treatment fidelity*) is essential to ensure that practices

**Key Concept**

*Implementation fidelity* specifies the extent to which an intervention is implemented or practiced as it was originally designed (Lane, Bocian, MacMillan, & Gresham, 2004; O'Donnell, 2008).

and interventions in education have successful outcomes. We measure implementation fidelity so that we can monitor the impact of the practice or intervention. However, questions often arise about the flexible nature of UDL and implementation fidelity; the two ideas (flexibility and fidelity) seem to be at odds with each other. We could not agree and disagree more.

First, it is important to understand what is meant by the term *implementation fidelity*. Simply stated, it means implementing a practice the way it was originally designed. If an intervention is not implemented the way it was intended, we would not know if the intervention is responsible for the positive outcome or if some other element was a factor.

Implementation fidelity is one quality indicator that must be measured when reviewing empirical research to determine the evidence base of a practice or intervention. The field of education, however, has not agreed on an "acceptable level" of fidelity, and therefore only requires that researchers report that fidelity was, in fact, measured (Cook et al., 2015). This could be because even the most respected researchers understand that teachers must balance fidelity with flexibility and school context (Cook, Tankersley, & Harjusola-Webb, 2008; Harn, Parisi, & Stoolmiller, 2013). Just because *you* want to implement the intervention as it was intended doesn't mean there won't be a fire drill, absent students, a mild crisis, or missing materials!

The first step in measuring implementation fidelity of an intervention is to operationally define it. That means that what you are doing is defined in such a way that someone else could do it in the same way. A very clear understanding of the intervention is critical in order to replicate it and eventually make a claim that a specific intervention resulted in a specific outcome. Evidence-based practices are established when interventions can be clearly connected with student outcomes in multiple studies (Cook et al., 2015).

Although researchers acknowledge the benefits of UDL based on the principle of proactively applying sound instructional design (Coyne, Kame'enui, & Carnine, 2011; Pisha & Coyne, 2001), they have not reached consensus on an operational definition of UDL or how to determine whether UDL is happening in a classroom (Edyburn, 2010). It would be impossible to define UDL implementation by listing elements that must be present during a lesson, because there are too many possibilities to name. By definition, UDL requires many choices and lots of flexibility and individualization! However, we *can* define UDL implementation by what it *is not*. A lesson that does *not* provide multiple means of engagement, representation, and action and expression *cannot* acknowledge learner variability and thus *could not* be considered a UDL lesson.

Therefore, at the most basic level, implementation fidelity in UDL is ensuring that each principle is proactively and intentionally addressed.

- **THINK ABOUT HOW CONTENT WILL BE REPRESENTED/ PRESENTED when planning a UDL lesson.** Students need to properly perceive and understand all vocabulary and have language clarified, as well as make sense of the content by relating it to what they already know. Because students' learning strengths, barriers, and preferences vary widely, one way of presenting content is not sufficient. Multiple means must be incorporated in order to meet the needs of all students.

- **PLAN A UDL LESSON THAT ENSURES THAT STUDENTS WILL GET "HOOKED," that they will stay committed, and that they can manage their learning environment.** Because students' interests and enthusiasm for learning tasks vary, one instructional strategy or approach to providing support will not work for all students. Multiple means must be incorporated in order to authentically engage and properly support all students.
- **PREPARE OPTIONS FOR HOW STUDENTS WILL ENGAGE WITH THE CONTENT AND EXPRESS WHAT THEY HAVE LEARNED when planning a UDL lesson.** Because students' preferences for learning activities vary, one activity (however fun it may be) will not align with the preferences of all learners. Multiple learning activities are required in order for students to think about their learning in a personal way.

By intentionally thinking of and planning for these principles you can be assured you are implementing UDL with some degree of fidelity.

Recall that we began the chapter by pointing out the seemingly incompatible ideas of implementation fidelity and flexibility in UDL. On the one hand, we know the basic idea of implementation fidelity is to follow certain steps to remain as true to the original design of the intervention as possible, and we want to do that. On the other hand, UDL calls for teachers to be flexible as they plan ahead for learner variability and adjust curriculum and learning environments in order to reduce barriers. Knowing both of these are true, a teacher might ask, "Are there steps that I can follow so I know I'm implementing UDL with fidelity?," and "If I follow steps, am I still being *flexible*?"

It is common that a predetermined checklist is used to monitor fidelity. However, a simple checklist would introduce a *barrier* to UDL implementation by constraining teachers' flexibility, creativity, and decision making, as well as stifle student voice and choice making—all of which are needed to address learner variability and create UDL classrooms. Although a published tool to examine K–12 UDL implementation fidelity does not currently exist, UDL researchers have identified basic reporting criteria (Rao et al., 2018). A list of considerations has been established that should be addressed in order to make a claim that UDL is present in a research study. These considerations can be adapted into a list of questions teachers can ask themselves as they design the learning environment and plan instruction.

## KEY QUESTIONS TO GUIDE UDL IMPLEMENTATION

How will I:

1. Identify a specific learning goal that is flexible enough to allow for learner variability?

2. Provide multiple options for assessments?
3. Design instruction to address learner variability?
   ○ Consider students' strengths, interests, preferences, and barriers related to learning.
   ○ Consider curriculum and learning environment barriers.
4. Apply the UDL guidelines and checkpoints?

Below, we describe a lesson plan and compare elements of a "UDL" and a "Not UDL" lesson. One life science standard is for students to understand cell structures. Looking further at that standard, we can develop a lesson plan to have students identify and describe cell parts and functions.

## UDL/NOT UDL EXAMPLE LESSON PLAN

| UDL | Not UDL |
|---|---|
| **Goal:** | **Goal:** |
| • Students will correctly identify each cell part and describe its function. | • Students will write the name of each cell part and its correct function. |
| **Assessment:** | **Assessment:** |
| Students will have the following options: | • Given a worksheet, students will fill in the blanks by writing names of cell parts and their functions. |
| • Write cell part names and descriptions of functions on blank diagram. | |
| • Point to and verbally name each cell part and describe its function (on the 3D cell model). | |
| • Other options if approved by teacher. | |
| **Learning Activities:** | **Learning Activities:** |
| *Facilitate individual executive-functioning skills regarding attending to lectures.* | |
| • Lecture (PowerPoint with pictures, video clips) | • Lecture (PowerPoint with words) |
| *Facilitate individual self-regulation skills regarding behavior for partner activities.* | |
| • 3D models examined and discussed (partners) | • Cell models created with cookies and decorations |

| UDL | Not UDL |
|---|---|
| *Facilitate individual choice-making and executive-functioning skills/self-regulation skills regarding choice activities.* <br>• Individual, partner, small-group activity: <br>  ○ Product: cell parts named and cell part functions described <br>  ○ Options: cookie model, poster, 3D model, song, video, interactive web-based program on cells, other (get teacher approval) | |
| *Materials available: cookies, icing, decorations, poster boards, writing utensils, computers and iPads with needed software/apps | *Materials available: cookies, icing, decorations* |
| *Physical space: tables, desks, computer stations, open spaces | *Physical space: students sit in their assigned seats* |

After reviewing the UDL and Not UDL lesson plans above, consider the following questions that guide the implementation of UDL.

### Did the Teacher Identify a Flexible, but Specific, Learning Goal?

All lessons must have a goal in order for the teacher to define what he or she wants students to understand or be able to do at the end of the lesson. Both the UDL lesson plan and the Not UDL lesson plan include a goal. Both goals allow for the same result: students will name cell parts and functions. In the UDL lesson example, the goal to *correctly identify each cell part and describe its function* is written to be flexible so students will have choices for how the goal is to be achieved. In the Not UDL lesson, the goal is for students to *fill in the blanks of a worksheet by writing the name of each cell part and the correct function.*

Because this goal specifies the method for reaching mastery (writing answers on a worksheet), students do not have choice; therefore, this does not represent UDL implementation fidelity. That goal also requires a particular task (writing) that does not relate to the overall goal of naming the cell parts but that would serve as a real barrier for students who struggle with writing but could otherwise meet the lesson objective.

STRATEGY SPOT

FLEXIBLE GOAL WRITING

In order to write a flexible learning goal, remove words that specify exactly *how* the goal must be met.

*Not flexible:* Given an essay prompt, students will write a three-paragraph essay that includes an opening, body, and closing.

*Flexible:* Given an essay prompt, students will compose a three-paragraph essay that includes an opening, body, and closing.

In the flexible example, the student can write, type, use voice-to-text software, or even audio record their work. In any of these options, the student will be able to demonstrate their ability to construct an essay with the required parts, but in a way that meets their needs and preferences.

### Did the Teacher Identify Options for Assessments?

All lessons must also have aligned assessments in order for teachers to evaluate whether the students have learned what they wanted them to learn. Both the UDL lesson plan and the Not UDL lesson plan have included assessments. In the UDL lesson example, the assessment allows for students to have options for demonstrating their learning. They can write cell part names and descriptions of functions on a blank diagram, they can work with a teacher and point to cell parts on a 3D model and verbally name each part and describe its function, or they can come up with a different plan for showing the teacher that they have learned the material.

In the options provided here, the students have the opportunity to show they have met the goal of the lesson (to name cell parts and functions) in a way that works best for them. In the Not UDL lesson, all students are required to complete the same assessment (worksheet) in the same way. This does not allow for students to leverage their strengths and/or work around their barriers, and therefore this does not represent UDL implementation fidelity.

### Did the Teacher Design Instruction to Address Learner Variability?

In addition to a goal and a plan for assessment, all lesson plans include learning tasks and activities. These methods of instruction vary depending on the content and the most effective way to teach it. They can include a wide variety of teacher-directed or student-directed activities. In a UDL lesson, the teacher plans for learner variability by first considering students' strengths, interests, and preferences and then planning learning tasks and activities that will allow students to leverage them. The teacher also considers students' barriers to learning and plans learning tasks and activities that will allow students to work around their barriers and still meet the learning goal. This is not to say that teachers should design learning tasks and activities that allow students to avoid practicing skills in which they are less proficient (e.g., reading fluency). Rather, it means that teachers should think carefully about the goal of the lesson and plan learning tasks and activities that allow students to meet the goal in multiple ways.

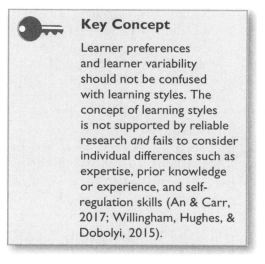

**Key Concept**

Learner preferences and learner variability should not be confused with learning styles. The concept of learning styles is not supported by reliable research *and* fails to consider individual differences such as expertise, prior knowledge or experience, and self-regulation skills (An & Carr, 2017; Willingham, Hughes, & Dobolyi, 2015).

In the UDL lesson example, the plan for learning tasks and activities may have been designed to meet the needs of learners who prefer to interact with the content using technology (e.g., interactive web-based program) and learners who prefer to engage with the content in artistic activities (e.g., songs, videos, posters). Each of these options allows for learning on a deeper level. The Not UDL lesson activity of creating a cookie model also allows students to interact with the content on a deeper level in a fun way. Just like the activity options available on the UDL lesson plan, the learners will have to think about each cell part and its function and determine how best to represent it on the cookie. The problem with the Not UDL lesson is that it does not allow for any other options. The cookie model activity might be engaging for some learners, but others might find it very distracting because they would rather eat the candy than design a cell model. A student with autism spectrum disorder or obsessive compulsive disorder might be distracted by the activity because they do not like to be messy with icing and candy pieces. Because this option creates a barrier to student choice, it does not represent UDL implementation fidelity.

When planning a UDL lesson, the teacher also considers barriers caused by the curriculum or learning environment and addresses those barriers in light of what is known about individual learners in the classroom. Sometimes even a carefully selected and well-designed curriculum introduces a barrier for some learners. Consider, for example, a curriculum that requires the teacher to present the content only in verbal format. This would create a barrier for students who find it difficult to attend to verbal information without additional elements to hold their attention.

Likewise, just as adults have preferences for working environments (consider the recent trend of sit/stand workstations), students have preferences for learning environments (e.g., some may prefer to sit at a desk, while others like to stand at a table to work or even sit on the floor). Addressing curriculum-related or environment-related barriers should not be confused with differentiating instruction. The difference is that in UDL, options are provided to all students proactively and the teacher facilitates students' choice making as they become expert learners. In differentiated instruction, the teacher determines alternative options for content, process, and product based on his or her perception of student needs and assigns students to groups or work accordingly (Hall, Strangman, & Meyer, 2003).

**UDL v. DI**

### Did the Teacher Apply the UDL Guidelines and Checkpoints?

By considering key questions related to flexible learning goals, multiple assessment options, learner variability, and UDL guidelines and checkpoints, teachers will know that their plans for designing instruction and learning environments address essential aspects of UDL. Thus, they can be certain they are implementing UDL with fidelity.

## PUTTING UDL AND IMPLEMENTATION FIDELITY INTO PRACTICE: REPRESENTATION

In the UDL lesson plan example above, the teacher plans to begin with a lecture because students will need basic information related to cell parts and their functions before they engage in learning activities on their own. The teacher planned to include pictures and video clips in the lecture in order to address the principle of multiple means of representation (e.g., the teacher lectures about the nucleus of the cell and its function and then also shows a picture of a cell and points out the location of the nucleus and what this means for its function). The teacher could have chosen any number of methods to present the information about cell parts and functions, and that part of the lesson would be considered a UDL lesson because the intentional use of *multiple* methods of representation allows for all students to take in the information. Conversely, the Not UDL lesson plan only provides *one* method of presentation, which would certainly introduce barriers for some students.

- **MAKE A "BARRIERS AND SOLUTIONS" LIST where you gather several ideas related to barriers that are revealed.** Revisit the list when you encounter a barrier to see how you have addressed it previously.

- **MAKE OPTIONS AVAILABLE FOR STUDENTS TO SELF-CUSTOMIZE HOW THEY ACCESS CONTENT** (e.g., digital text where font sizes and page contrast can be adjusted, audio textbooks, voice to text software).
- **MAKE OPTIONS AVAILABLE FOR STUDENTS TO SELF-CUSTOMIZE TO INCREASE UNDERSTANDING** (e.g., hyperlinks to vocabulary definitions in documents, posters to clarify symbols).
- **FACILITATE STUDENTS' SELF-CUSTOMIZATION OF PERSONAL CONNECTIONS BETWEEN EXISTING KNOWLEDGE AND LIFE EXPERIENCES TO NEW CONTENT** (e.g., link new and previously mastered skills and concepts through graphic organizers).
- **TEACH STUDENTS HOW TO CUSTOMIZE THE WAY THEY ACCESS CONTENT** (e.g., demonstrate steps, provide visual supports in the form of posters or videos, use various graphic organizer options).

## PUTTING UDL AND IMPLEMENTATION FIDELITY INTO PRACTICE: ENGAGEMENT

Consider the pictures and video clips included in the lecture. They provide multiple means of engagement (as well as additional methods of representation). Students who tend to lose interest during lectures may be drawn back in when a video clip plays. Similarly, the partner activity provides another means of engagement because students have the opportunity to touch and move the cell parts while talking about it.

In addition to addressing multiple means of engagement through varied activities and grouping options, *engagement* is addressed by providing options for supporting students' self-regulation skills. In the UDL lesson plan example, the teacher has planned to facilitate students' self-regulation skills at key points during the lesson by providing options such as reminders/prompts, checklists, and opportunities for reflection on personal learning goals. This portion of the lesson would be considered a UDL lesson because the intentional use of *multiple* methods of engagement allows for all students to be interested while their self-regulation is supported. Conversely, the Not UDL lesson plan only provides *one* method of engagement and does not support self-regulation, which would introduce barriers for some students.

 **Tech Tips**

Use websites such as Flipgrid for students to collaborate with each other. Flipgrid empowers student voice and helps students respect the voice of others.

- **COMPILE A COLLECTION OF IDEAS RELATED TO RECRUITING AND MAINTAINING STUDENT INTEREST AND ENGAGEMENT.** If you add a couple strategies to the list each year, you'll have many to choose from in no time—especially if you collaborate with colleagues!
- **USE CHOICE MENUS OR TIC-TAC-TOE BOARDS** to spark initial interest while still maintaining boundaries that enable you to support multiple engagement options.
- **ALLOW FOR CHOICE IN OTHER AREAS** such as seating (desk or table) or grouping (individual, partner, small group) when options are not possible in one area (e.g., students must handwrite a paragraph because the learning objective is handwriting).
- **FACILITATE STUDENTS' REFLECTIONS ON THEIR PERSONAL ENGAGEMENT** with strategies such as think-pair-share.

## PUTTING UDL AND IMPLEMENTATION FIDELITY INTO PRACTICE: ACTION AND EXPRESSION

To deepen student learning of the content, the UDL lesson plan provides multiple means of action and expression by allowing students to choose how they interact with the content (e.g., cookie model, poster, 3D model, song, video, interactive web-based program on cells). This final learning activity will vary from one student to another as students choose from options that align with their strengths and interests, and minimize their barriers. Students will not all complete the same learning activity in the same way at the same time, so after initial instruction and the partner activity, the teacher plans to support students' executive-functioning skills by facilitating choice-making skills and attention to on-task behavior.

This part of the lesson would be considered a UDL lesson because the intentional use of *multiple* methods of action and expression allows for all students to interact with the content and demonstrate learning in ways that meet their needs. Conversely, the Not UDL lesson plan only provides *one* method for interacting with the content, which would present barriers for some students. Additionally, in the Not UDL lesson, skills related to executive functioning may not be addressed because the learning activities are generally teacher-directed and do not promote student independence.

- **MAKE ALL LEARNING ACTIVITY OPTIONS AVAILABLE TO ALL STUDENTS.** A major benefit of UDL is that students can choose what works for them. Try not to limit them by putting them in selected options based on what *you* think they'll like best.
- **MAKE ALL ASSESSMENT OPTIONS AVAILABLE TO ALL STUDENTS.** Always look back to your objective. The point is

that they demonstrate mastery of that objective, not that they demonstrated their mastery in a particular way.

- **WORK WITH STUDENTS TO CUSTOMIZE THEIR LEARNING EXPERIENCES AND ASSESSMENTS** (e.g., individual learning goal, individual work pace, individual plan of action).
- **MAKE SUPPORTS AVAILABLE TO ALL STUDENTS** (e.g., checklists, posts with steps). In the past, these have only been made available to students with special needs. We know now that these are excellent supports for many students and do not take away from their learning.
- **SUPPORT ALL STUDENTS** in monitoring and evaluating their learning progress.
- **USE RUBRICS** for grading products.

**STRATEGY SPOT**
GRADING WITH RUBRICS

A rubric is a great way to grade a variety of assessment options. Your clear learning goal defines the rubric criteria, and each assessment option can be evaluated against that criteria. Rubrics also help communicate to students what the objective is and then enable them to become more creative in determining how to meet that clear objective.

## BRINGING IT ALL TOGETHER

Let's get back to the question we first asked: is the flexibility that is inherent to UDL at odds with the need for implementation fidelity in educational practices? Yes, if we try to pin UDL down to a precise checklist of items to be included in a lesson; and no, if we embrace the personalized, individualized nature of UDL and the creativity of teachers. We can bring implementation fidelity and the flexibility of UDL together by addressing the key questions outlined in this chapter.

Universal Design for Learning classrooms are not traditional, stereotypical, 1950s classrooms. Isn't that great!?! We're teaching 21st century learners who have never known a world without technology, where the answer to any question is in the palm of their hand. The idea of teaching every concept in every content area the same way to every student does not fit today's generation, which celebrates and values individuality. As a UDL teacher, you must know your students and understand your content so that you can plan a lesson that is motivating, meaningful, and allows students to customize their learning activities to meet their individual needs.

## TOP FIVE WEBSITES TO SUPPORT UDL AND IMPLEMENTATION FIDELITY

→ https://www.chalk.com/planboard/

→ http://www.enchantedlearning.com/graphicorganizers

→ https://flipgrid.com/

→ https://padlet.com

→ https://sim.drupal.ku.edu/sim-curricula

## APPS WE LOVE

→ Done

→ Inspiration Maps

→ Journaly

→ Rubric Scorer

→ SimpleMind+

## RECOMMENDED READINGS

UDL-IRN (Development of Reporting Criteria): https://udl-irn.org/udl-reporting-criteria/

# REFERENCES

An, D., & Carr, M. (2017). Learning styles theory fails to explain learning and achievement: Recommendations for alternative approaches. *Personality and Individual Differences, 116*, 410–416. doi:10.1016/j.paid.2017.04.050

Cook, B. G., Buysse, V., Klingner, J., Landrum, T. J., McWilliam, R. A., Tankersley, M., & Test, D. W. (2015). CEC's standards for classifying the evidence base of practices in special education. *Remedial and Special Education, 36*(4), 220–234. doi:10.1177/0741932514557271

Cook, B. G., Tankersley, M., & Harjusola-Webb, S. (2008). Evidence-based special education and professional wisdom: Putting it all together. *Intervention in School and Clinic, 44*(2), 105–111.

Coyne, M., Kame'enui, E., & Carnine, D. (2011). Effective teaching strategies that accommodate diverse learners (4th ed.). Upper Saddle River, NJ: Pearson Education.

Edyburn, D. (2010). Would you recognize Universal Design for Learning if you saw it? Ten propositions for new directions for the second decade of UDL. *Learning Disability Quarterly, 33*, 33–41.

Hall, T., Strangman, N., & Meyer, A. (2003). *Differentiated instruction and implications for UDL implementation.* Wakefield, MA: National Center on Accessing the General Curriculum. Retrieved from http://aem.cast.org/about/publications/2003/ncac-differentiated-instruction-udl.html#.WzVqINgzq-s

Harn, B., Parisi, D., & Stoolmiller, M. (2013). Balancing fidelity with flexibility and fit: What do we really know about fidelity of implementation in schools? *Exceptional Children, 79*(2), 181–193.

Lane, K. L., Bocian, K. M., MacMillan, D. L., & Gresham, F. M. (2004). Treatment integrity: An essential--but often forgotten--component of school-based interventions. *Preventing School Failure, 48*(3), 36–43. doi:10.3200/PSFL.48.3.36–43

O'Donnell, C. L. (2008). Defining, conceptualizing, and measuring fidelity of implementation and its relationship to outcomes in K–12 curriculum intervention research. *Review of Educational Research, 78*(1), 33–84.

Pisha, B., & Coyne, P. (2001). Smart from the start: The promise of Universal Design for Learning. *Remedial and Special Education, 22*(4), 197–203.

Rao, K., Smith, S. J., Edyburn, D., Grima-Farrell, C., Van Horn, G., & Yalom-Chamowitz, S. (2018). UDL reporting criteria. Developed by a working group of the Universal Design for Learning Implementation and Research (UDL-IRN) Research Committee. Retrieved from https://udl-irn.org/udl-reporting-criteria/

Willingham, D. T., Hughes, E. M., & Dobolyi, D. G. (2015). The scientific status of learning styles theories. *Teaching of Psychology, 42*(3), 266–271. doi:10.1177/0098628315589505

# SECTION IV

## *What Really Works With Special Populations*

# 12

# *UDL for Advancement*

## *Unblocking the Traffic Jam*

### Claire E. Hughes
*College of Coastal Georgia*

## SETTING THE STAGE FOR UDL AND ADVANCEMENT

Have you ever been in a traffic jam? Sat there, frustrated that you can't go anywhere? Ever worried that you're going to run out of gas while your engine idles? Sure, people in the movie *La La Land* broke into song and dance when they were stuck in a traffic jam, but that's a movie, and most of us haven't had that experience when we've been stuck on the interstate.

Our educational system is in a traffic jam. Only, instead of traffic engineers, education has curriculum designers. There are some students who cannot get on the road to learning, and there are others who sit on the highway of learning, unable to move forward. As Katie Novak wrote in the Introduction to this book, the goal of UDL is to "make learning accessible for all students." Making learning accessible for all students means that not only do you have to think about barriers to entrance or participation, but also the barriers to learning that keep a child from moving forward. UDL emphasizes that *all* children should be learning and moving forward from where they currently are in the learning process.

Though UDL is designed with all children's needs in mind, it is often emphasized for its support of students with disabilities. However, there is another group of students whose needs often go unmet in traditional classrooms: advanced and gifted students. The National Center on Universal Design for Learning (CAST, 2012) concluded, "One of the groups that has not been effectively reached within the general education classroom is learners with gifts and talents" (para. 3). UDL won't merely support identified gifted learners; it is necessary for those learners who need advanced opportunities, identified or not. Even students who are ahead of their peers in a particular learning area need to have educational opportunities to move forward from where they are.

At first glance, it might seem difficult to have sympathy for students who appear to have met the age-based, grade-based standards for a particular subject and who learn easily. After all, if they learn the traditional content easily, why should the curriculum be redesigned with their needs in mind? While it is understood that talent and an ability to learn are found across every racial category and socioeconomic level (National Association for Gifted Children, 2018), the reality is that only those children who have been provided opportunities to learn will learn. You can't learn Shakespeare unless you have access to Shakespeare. You can't learn algebra unless you have been exposed to algebra. And if you're eight years old, capable of learning Shakespeare or algebra and no one gives you an opportunity to learn these things, the sad reality is that you won't learn them.

Who benefits from advanced educational opportunities? Certainly, identified gifted students. However, there are also the unidentified gifted students who didn't get labeled because of underachievement or because, for a variety of reasons, they have chosen not to participate. Certainly, children from poverty or a nonmainstream background may sit in the traffic jam of grade-level expectations, and may have to depend on the school for any advanced opportunities. In addition, children with disabilities often have hidden talents that are overlooked in the focus on accommodating their areas of challenge. "Twice-exceptional," or "2e," students are students who have *both* a disability *and* a significant ability (Baldwin, Baum, Pereles, & Hughes, 2015). For twice-exceptional students, the disability has to be mediated and accommodated, but the ability also has to be identified and developed. These two simultaneous processes can be accomplished by eliminating barriers through UDL. Advanced opportunities and curriculum options will allow students the chance to engage in material and lessons that are designed to be interesting, advanced, and integrated in ways that can free up their learning.

## ADVANCEMENT AND UDL: REPRESENTATION

Increased access is needed to curriculum that is (a) advanced, (b) enriched, (c) based around the students' area of interest, and/or (d) integrated. While these aspects of curriculum are not unique to advanced learners, they are *necessary* for advanced learners. Expanded curriculum can be provided as an option to all students, but not all students will select these options. Those students who learn new material quickly and excel in these opportunities can be screened or identified as having talents—not prior to curriculum intervention, but during and afterwards. This method of using curriculum as a means of identification is a cornerstone for the Response-to-Intervention (RTI) practice of identifying gifted learners (Coleman & Hughes, 2009). How can teachers provide multiple means of representation that will address those students for whom the traditional curriculum, pacing, or content are not advanced enough?

- **GO UP THE STANDARDS.** Advanced curriculum opportunities are necessary options to meet the needs of advanced learners. When the curriculum is linear in nature, such as some mathematical concepts, vocabulary development, and reading skills, a teacher can use the educational standards to determine what the next level of expected behavior could be. Studies are very clear that students who are provided advanced content opportunities, whether through whole-grade acceleration or single-subject advancement, do significantly better on academic and social-emotional measures than their peers who have been held back (Assouline, Coleangelo, VanTassel-Baska, & Lupkowski-Shoplik, 2015).
- **PROVIDE A RANGE OF PRE-ASSESSMENTS.** One of the best ways to determine how high the material you need to offer should be is to do pre-testing that is off-level. Many advanced students will "top out" the grade-level pre-test, which means there is no room for growth. You may have to go and find a test from another grade, or use an overall diagnostic test that determines what skills a child has.
- **TRY TO FIND THAT MAGIC INSTRUCTIONAL SPACE all children need that falls between their ability to do things independently and their frustration at not being able to understand it at all.** Recognize that some children will have a higher instructional level than other children. Teach where the child is, not where he or she "should" be for his or her age or grade level. Every child has the "right to learn something new every day" (Siegle, 2009), even those students who are already above grade level. Teachers will need to have access to a full range of content and assessments. That is a key part of UDL.
- **ENRICH IN DEPTH, BREADTH, AND COMPLEXITY.** Want to provide options for extending a particular area of content? Simply bringing in more difficult reading material may not be the answer. Not all content is linear, and a great deal of content can be enriched and broadened just by the way it is presented.

Have opportunities for students to look at how content is used in real life, explore aspects of content that the teacher doesn't often have time to get to, and participate in academic competitions. Each of these strategies allows for students to be enriched at a higher level of complexity, depth, or breadth.

- **EMPHASIZE AREAS OF INTEREST.** All students will find class content more engaging if their personal areas of interest are included in the multiple means of representation. Advanced learners *must* have content that is targeted at their area of strength, not just to keep them motivated, but to move them forward in that area. Sounds like all kids, doesn't it?

- **PROVIDE OPPORTUNITIES AND POSSIBILITIES.** Development of a child's ability in a particular area of real strength or ability often means exposing them to a variety of possibilities and then following their directions of interest and strength. Interests become strengths and strengths become careers. After all, who knows how many talented future marine biologists there may be who live in the desert?

- **ACCEPT VARIABILITY IN ABILITY.** It is important to recognize that talented students are not advanced at everything. Just because a child is doing advanced algebra in third grade does not necessarily mean they will have similar skills in reading or science. That is one of the reasons why the principles of UDL emphasize multiple means of representation, engagement, and expression for all students!

- **INTEGRATE THE SUBJECTS.** What do you do as the teacher if an advanced child is passionately interested in bugs and you teach math? Or you teach social studies and you have a math-crazy kid in your classroom? One strategy for integration is to look for *overlaps in the content*—reading about historical events, for example, is an opportunity to connect reading comprehension skills to social studies. There is a whole genre of books that use math concepts as part of the plot line. Teaching "The History of Zero" to fourth graders is an integration of math and history!

- **LOOK FOR COMMON CONCEPTS as another strategy for integrating subjects.** Teachers are often familiar with finding topics in common, such as "bears," and using bear figures to learn counting, reading stories about bears, and learning about the habitats of bears. However, the use of concepts is one that allows students to truly see connections between content areas and provide deeper connections to their own lives and future learning by applying and testing generalizations to new content and new situations (Taba, 1962; VanTassel-Baska & Little, 2016).

**CASE IN POINT**

Ms. Ariel is a second-grade teacher who uses "change" as her central concept for the second nine weeks of school (VanTassel-Baska & Little, 2016). Students have discussed how change is related to time, may be perceived as positive or negative, and may be natural or caused by people. As Ms. Ariel's students study rocks, they think about how rocks change over time (slowly and naturally); and Javier, a student who is passionate about geology and an advanced reader, shares with the class how various types of rocks change differently based on knowledge gained from his reading of a middle school textbook. In reading, students reflect on how characters change and how their actions play a role in the plot line. Chwee is asked by Ms. Ariel how the characters' changes in the class reading compare and contrast to the independent reading she is doing. In math, students discuss changes in temperature in their classroom and how changing a sign can change what happens to a group of numbers. Hasim acknowledges that change also occurs when numbers with different signs are multiplied. At the end of the nine weeks, students are looking at examples of change in the world around them and comparing these changes to what they have learned.

## PUTTING ADVANCEMENT AND UDL INTO PRACTICE: ENGAGEMENT

"You are a junior archeologist at a research museum and discover that construction work has been halted on a new school because historic artifacts were discovered" (College of William and Mary, 2007, p. 1). Thus begins a social studies unit for third graders in which students learn about archeology, how history is explored, and how knowledge of both informs decisions in the real world.

- **USE PROBLEM/PROJECT BASED LEARNING (PBL).** PBL allows advanced students to engage with content they may already "know," but permits them to see where the content can be used in the real world. "Why do we have to know this stuff?" is not a question that is asked in a PBL situation! In the Engagement network of UDL, the focus is on the thinking

**Making Connections**

See Chapter 3 for more on UDL with Project-Based Learning.

skills that allow a student to self-regulate, sustain effort and persistence, and recruit interest. PBL is one example of a curriculum strategy that develops the skills of inquiry, research, creativity, and critical thinking—all through a high level of engagement that develops self-regulation, effort, and persistence. Talk about 21st century skills in action!

- **USE INQUIRY LEARNING.** PBL is an example of inquiry learning, which is an "instructional model that centers learning on solving a particular problem or answering a central question" (Heick, 2017, para 1). Inquiry learning is essentially the opposite of direct instruction, where information is provided in a clear, scaffolded approach. There is some evidence that inquiry learning works "only when learners have sufficiently high prior knowledge to provide internal guidance" (Kirschner, Sweller, & Clark, 2010, p. 75). In other words, inquiry learning should be used to advance the curriculum experience for those students who already have a background knowledge in the content! It should absolutely be in the UDL strategy repertoire for advancing learners.

- **ENCOURAGE INDEPENDENT RESEARCH.** One way teachers can create opportunities for inquiry-based learning is to encourage the use of independent research by students. Too often, students are assigned a "research paper" and the steps of the research process are provided to them, or they go to the Internet and summarize what they find there. In independent research, students are encouraged to pick a problem or a topic of their own interest. This provides choice to all students and allows more advanced students to be challenged at an appropriate level.

Think of research as a "Plan-Do-Review" (Humble ISD, 2017) process:

1. **Plan**—What is it that you're asking? What do you want to know?
2. **Do**—What do others say about this? Are some sources better than others? Are there any sources that disagree with each other?
3. **Review**—What did you learn? How do you want to show this to others?

One teacher stated, "I am neither the Sage on the Stage, nor the Guide on the Side. I am the Meddler in the Middle," indicating that she saw hers as a very active role, challenging students and getting them to reevaluate their learning and to sustain their thinking through challenges.

- **TEACH CRITICAL THINKING!** One of the defining characteristics of advanced education is the applied use of critical thinking. Most school systems will have a model of Bloom's Taxonomy (Anderson, Bloom, & Krathwohl, 2000) that leads students from one level to another, moving up. Often, these are called

"Higher-Order Thinking Skills," or HOTS. The real problem with this model is that a student cannot move from one level to the next until he or she has mastered the lower level. Some kids can get stuck at the bottom levels because they encounter these basic road-blocks. Planning while using Bloom's taxonomy can definitely sometimes feel like a stop-and-go one-way traffic light that creates a serious backup. Besides, how do you move some students up the level while others need more time and support at a lower level? Enter UDL!

- **ASK QUESTIONS.** Other models of critical thinking are non-linear, thereby allowing teachers to dip in and out of questions. There are many questioning strategies: Fat/Skinny questions; Divergent/Convergent questions; Who, What, When, Why, How, and Where Questions . . . there are many ways to ask a question! However, it is important to plan questions, because without planning, teachers and students tend to get stuck in lower-level, basic, closed-ended questions that lead to students merely being consumers and users, rather than producers of knowledge.

### STRATEGY SPOT
PAUL'S ELEMENTS OF THOUGHT

In this "roundabout" method, teachers can plan a set of questions to enter and exit where they like. Paul's Socratic Questioning (Paul & Elder, 2014) is a way of looking at material and thinking about it in six different ways that deepen students' understanding and build persistence because they aren't blocked from the "upper" levels. This approach more closely fits with the UDL premise of having multiple means of engagement for *all* learners.

- Questions of *clarification*: What do you mean by that? Can you give me an example?

- Questions that probe *assumptions*: What does the author assume about the reader? What do you assume is already known about this problem?

- Questions that examine *reason and evidence*: What information are you given? What information is this based upon? What evidence is missing?

- Questions that examine *implications and consequences*: What might be the consequences of this point of view? What conclusions are you jumping to? If this is true, what else must be true?

- Questions about *viewpoints or perspectives*: What would be another way of saying that? How do your viewpoints differ from the author's? Does the author include other "voices"?

- Questions about the *purpose*: What is the purpose of this? What else could it be used for? How might it be used?

- **TEACH CREATIVE THINKING.** In addition to teaching *critical* thinking, it is important to teach *creative* thinking. Not unique to advanced learners, but a necessary part of advancing the curriculum, creativity and critical thinking are two of the skills at the top of the list needed by employers (Trilling, Fadel, & Partnership for 21st Century Skills, 2009). Critical thinking and creative thinking have a unique relationship in that creativity can be supported by, or destroyed by, critical thinking (Facione, 2013). We want students to create, and then improve their creations through critical thinking.

But *how* can creativity be built in? The 4P Model (Rhodes, 1987) recognizes that creativity happens in four categories:

1. **Person** who creates
2. **Place** where creativity happens
3. **Product** that is requested
4. **Process** that is encouraged

Teachers can recognize creative tendencies in children by looking for it and being encouraging when they see it. "That's such a creative answer!" is much more nurturing than "No, wrong answer." Teachers can arrange their classrooms in ways that encourage creativity: highlighting student work, providing materials to be creative with, and being creative yourself! You can encourage products that require creative thinking to construct, and you can teach children how to be creative (Goodale & Hughes, 2018).

### STRATEGY SPOT
SCAMPER

SCAMPER is an example of a creative process that can be built into a lesson, and it provides students options about how to engage with the material—perfect for opportunities for advancement! SCAMPER (Eberle, 1996) is a process by which teachers can look at a product (a written work, a thing, a process) and ask students to change it by seeing what they can:

- **S**ubstitute
- **C**ombine
- **A**dapt
- **M**odify

- **P**ut to another use
- **E**liminate
- **R**everse

Changing the components of an original can create something else that is new and different. For example, the movie *Oceans 8* substituted women for men from *Oceans 11*, while *West Side Story* is an adaptation of *Romeo and Juliet*! See more at https://www.mindtools.com/pages/article/newCT_02.htm.

UDL is a process through which teachers design lessons that allow all students to engage with the curriculum. It is important that teachers give students opportunities to engage with content at higher, deeper, and more complex levels that allow them to advance beyond the standard age-grade level imposed on them. Doing so will allow them to develop self-regulation, sustain effort in the curriculum, and develop their interest. By giving students a reason and a way to do so, teachers can open up the curricular road to students. And who doesn't want a green light?!

## ADVANCEMENT AND UDL: EXPRESSION

It's easy to say "Plan advanced opportunities" or "Provide enrichment options" as part of the UDL menu, but how does a teacher do this when there are so many other children's needs and state requirements and limited resources, and . . . the list goes on and on? The last aspect of UDL advancement is deciding *how* students will demonstrate their knowledge and understanding. This is a wonderful opportunity for relatively easy enrichment opportunities. These options can include: tiered assignments, flexible grouping, use of a co-teacher, involvement of older students and adults, and the use of assessments that are off-level and high-level.

- **TIER UP.** Tomlinson (2014) notes that teaching for students at different levels can be accomplished by thinking about the content in terms of "Tiers." While teachers often think about taking the central concept and teaching its essential components in ways that are accessible for struggling students, it is also important to think tiering it *up* as well. Not knowing how to appropriately challenge and assess academically gifted students in a UDL environment might have made you "tear up" in the past, but dry your eyes! "Tiering up" efficiently only really involves two simple tools that will allow you to remove barriers to those who need more challenge; these tools allow you to (a) raise the level of the work and (b) increase the complexity and depth of the work.

1. Have a copy of the *standards from the grades or levels* above the one you are teaching and an alignment chart so you can see what skill or concept comes next after the grade-level one on which you are working; and
2. Keep a copy of a *critical thinking or creative thinking model* that allows the child to change the verb of the grade-level activity to a more challenging level. Offer choices to students so they can express their understanding of the content with more rigor and challenge.

*Tip:* Some unenlightened administrators may focus on why you are not teaching grade-level standards. There are two things you need to have: (a) pre-test data demonstrating that the students you are working with already have the grade-level content and (b) alignment of the advanced content or above-grade-level standard you are providing with the grade-level standards. For example, if you have a student who is reading an advanced novel and is working on above-grade-level concepts, be prepared to show how the new standard is aligned with the grade-level standard. Understanding vertical alignment of the standards is one of the greatest ways to justify differentiation.

It is important to note that putting students in advanced groups or using above-grade-level content are not the only ways to provide advanced content. Some teachers use Tic-Tac-Toe cards, where students can self-select activities listed in each block; some choices are very high-level, while others are more low-level and essential. Others can use Think Dots and Cubing activities, where ideas are placed on cards or a die that can be rolled. However, no matter how they are provided, students will be doing activities that are different than others in the class.

## CASE IN POINT

### Example of Tiered Learning Objectives*

Ms. Rix recognized that she had students at a variety of levels in her class. In trying to universally design her lesson, she created tiered learning objectives:

a. ABOVE GRADE LEVEL: Some students will provide description by referring to parts of stories from text, using terms such as *chapter* and *scene*, analyzing how each successive part builds on earlier sections.

b. GRADE LEVEL: Most students will provide description of the overall structure of a story, including how the beginning introduces, how the middle provides major events/challenges, and how the ending concludes the action.

c. BELOW GRADE LEVEL: All students will provide description of the characters, settings, and major events in the story.

*Note how all objectives enable students to have options in how they meet the objective of "provide description."

**STRATEGY SPOT**
THINK DOTS

Think Dots (University of Virginia, 2002) are a way to encourage student choice and activities. For each readiness level, you will need a set of six laminated cards with 1–6 dots on each card. The cards can be hole-punched and fastened together. For the higher-readiness level for children who are working on advanced material, each dot aligns with a Bloom's higher-level taxonomy. You will also need a die to roll.

For example, a ninth-grade unit on Setting could include:

| | | |
|---|---|---|
| Compare the setting of this book to the setting of the book we just read.<br><br> | Create a PowerPoint that looks at four different settings and how they might impact the actions of a story. *Example:* What kinds of stories take place in small towns? Dark and stormy nights? Why?<br><br> | Write a story that takes place on a dark and stormy night. Use an instance from your history book.<br><br> |
| Analyze how the setting of the book reflected and supported the emotions and actions within the story.<br><br> | Describe how cultural values and geography impact settings for different stories. Using a map of the world, identify four geographic features that might impact the setting of a story.<br><br>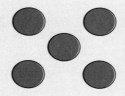 | Using the setting of a story, create a single-sentence submission for the Bulwer-Lytton Fiction Contest (http://www.bulwer-lytton.com/).<br><br> |

- **USE FLEXIBLE GROUPING WITH CHOICES OF ACTIVI-TIES.** Flexible grouping remains one of the easiest and most effective ways to build in opportunities to work with students who are advanced. Too many advanced students are often used as the "helpers" in the classroom and rarely get an opportunity to work ahead with other strong students. Not all strong students are good teachers, and if they are forced to teach their peers, they often end up doing the work for the group. Remember that the key to "flexible grouping" is the "flexible" part! Both homogenous and heterogeneous groupings can play a part in the universally designed classroom.
- **PROVIDE CONTENT OPTIONS.** In her seminal work, Rogers (2002) found that both academically and socially-emotionally gifted students do better in homogenous classrooms and in cluster groups when the content itself has been altered for their learning level. There are few differences when the curriculum itself has not been changed. Thus, just putting the "smart kids" or the "strong readers" together is not going to result in improvement (not to mention the fact that it flies in the face of inclusive practices); ultimately, teachers need to provide options in content and curriculum: exactly what UDL promotes!
- **PRE-TEST, PRE-TEST, PRE-TEST.** One of the easiest ways to determine your groups is to do some formative assessments to ascertain where they are. If a group of students has already mastered the material, or is very close, they don't need a lot of instruction in that content. However, if they have already mastered the material, what do you teach them? Also, if they have been learning off-level, how do you show improvement? Your assessment practices are going to have to include pre-tests that include material and concepts from upper grades as well as grade-level concepts.
- **ASSESS WHERE THEY ARE.** Rubrics are very helpful in the universally designed classroom, but don't forget to have an area for "above-grade-level expectations" that describes what the next level would look like. The best source for above-grade-level expectations is from the next year's standards that scaffold right above your current grade. Some teachers may say "it's not fair" to grade above grade level. What is not fair about it? You are merely removing the barrier of the artificially created "grade-level" expectations so that students have room to grow. The grading itself can reflect grade-level expectations, but the rubric should allow room for beyond grade-level expectations.
- **PROVIDE COLLABORATIVE OPTIONS.** Let's say you have some advanced students grouped together based on assessment data. You have strong and clear learning objectives, and some wonderful advanced content and ways to engage them. Where do you find the time to work with them? Great question! In the past, teachers were encouraged to send their gifted children off

to do "independent" work, but that process is not recommended any longer. Not only is it highly unmotivating and essentially removes the teacher from the learning process, it also is stigmatizing, boring, and exclusive. Instead, consider various options for small-group work, collaborative grouping, technological options, as well as collaborating with a co-teacher.

- **WORK WITH A CO-TEACHER.** Co-teachers are often in classrooms that have students with special needs, but by adapting the classroom to work with small groups with two or more teachers, advanced students can have their needs met too—one of the very significant benefits to co-teaching! If you have a small group of advanced students, the tiered instruction method (Hughes & Weichel, 2001) or alternative teaching approach (Murawski, 2010)—where one of you can work with the large group and the other can work with the smaller advanced group—is one option that lends itself easily to working with a small group. Tiered teaching is not just for students with special needs! Similarly, in the use of rotation or station teaching, when the advanced group cycles to a station, that activity can be different than the activities that were designed for other learners.

**Making Connections**

See Chapter 9 for more on Co-Teaching.

## CASE IN POINT

Mr. Nikolaus is a fifth-grade teacher with a class of thirty students. He did a pre-test of his students before he taught a science unit on the parts of cells and found that four of them passed the pre-test with an 80 percent before the topic had even been taught. Furthermore, he knew that Xavier, one of the four students, was very interested in animals and had talked about becoming a veterinarian someday. In addition to having other UDL strategies for providing access to the content through varied means for all of his students, Mr. Nikolaus designed a unit in which there were advanced centers for students to choose to learn about cloning of animals through cell replication by watching a documentary on cloning, a center where students could create a jingle to remember the parts of the cell, and a center where students could study career opportunities in cell biology. Mr. Nikolaus offered the four more advanced students an opportunity to do independent research on *"Should stem cells be used for medical research?"*—an option that became available to other students as they mastered the content throughout the unit. Mr. Nikolaus also integrated the content by including *A Wind in the Door*, a book by Madeleine L'Engle about children who travel inside mitochondria, in the choices offered on the reading list for his Language Arts class.

## BRINGING IT ALL TOGETHER

The UDL framework is designed to meet the needs of all learners in a classroom by designing lessons that provide multiple means of representation, engagement, and expression. It is important to recognize the needs of those learners who are learning faster, broader, and in more complex ways than other students. Removing barriers to learning also includes designing for advanced opportunities so that all students can have their needs met, regardless of labels and identification criteria. In the highway of learning, we want to give every student the opportunity to reach their top speed. Therefore, teachers, start your engines!

## TOP FIVE WEBSITES TO SUPPORT UDL FOR ADVANCEMENT

➜ https://k12.kendallhunt.com/site-search?search_api_views_fulltext=william+and+mary

➜ https://kudoswall.com/index.php/easyblog/entry/50-competitions-your-child-can-participate-in

➜ www.nagc.org

➜ www.prufrockpress.com

➜ www.rfwp.com

## APPS WE LOVE

➜ Code Academy: Hour of Code

➜ GarageBand

➜ Google Earth

➜ Harry Potter: Hogwarts Mystery

➜ Khan Academy

# REFERENCES

Anderson, L., Bloom, B., & Krathwohl, D. (2000). *A taxonomy for learning, teaching, and assessing*. London, England: Longman.

Assouline, S. G., Coleangelo, N., VanTassel-Baska, J., & Lupkowski-Shoplik, A. (2015). *A nation empowered*. Iowa City, IA: Acceleration Institute.

Baldwin, L., Baum, S., Pereles, D., & Hughes, C. (2015). Twice-exceptional learners: The journey toward a shared vision. *Gifted Child Today, 38*(4), 206–214.

CAST. (2012). *Gifted and talented FAQs*. Retrieved from http://www.udlcenter.org/advocacy/faq_guides/gifted_talented

Coleman, M. R., & Hughes, C. E. (2009). Meeting the needs of gifted students within an RTI framework. *Gifted Child Today, 32*(3), 14–17.

College of William and Mary. (2007). *What a find: Analyzing natural and cultural systems*. Dubuque, IA: Kendall Hunt.

Eberle, R. (1996). *SCAMPER: Games for imagination development*. Austin, TX: Prufrock Press.

Facione, P. A. (2013). *Critical thinking: What is it and why it counts*. Retrieved from https://www.nyack.edu/files/CT_What_Why_2013.pdf

Goodale, T. A., & Hughes, C. E. (2018). Deconstructing the constructed: Reforming science materials to develop creativity. *School Science Review, 99*(368), 45–52.

Heick, T. (2017). *Four phases of inquiry-based learning: A guide for teachers*. Retrieved from https://www.teachthought.com/pedagogy/4-phases-inquiry-based-learning-guide-teachers/

Hughes, C. E., & Weichel, W. W. (2001). Lessons from another field: Applying coteaching strategies to gifted education. *Gifted Child Quarterly, 45*(3), 195–204.

Humble Independent School District (ISD). (2017). *Research project guide: A handbook for teachers and students*. Retrieved from https://www.humbleisd.net/cms/lib2/tx01001414/centricity/domain/29/researchguideelem.pdf

Kirschner, P. A., Sweller, J., & Clark, R. E. (2010). Why minimal guidance during instruction does not work: An analysis of the failure of constructivist, discovery, problem-based, experiential and inquiry-based learning. *Educational Psychologist, 41*(2), 75–86.

Murawski, W. W. (2010). *Collaborative teaching in elementary schools: Making the coteaching marriage work!* Thousand Oaks, CA: Corwin.

National Association for Gifted Children. (2018). *What is giftedness?* Retrieved from http://www.nagc.org/resources-publications/resources/what-giftedness

Paul, R., & Elder, L. (2014) *Critical thinking: Tools for taking charge of professional and personal life*. Upper Saddle River, NJ: Pearson.

Rhodes, M. (1987). An analysis of creativity. In S. G. Isaksen (Ed.), *Frontiers of creativity research: Beyond the basics* (pp. 216–222). Buffalo, NY: Bearly. (Original work published 1961)

Rogers, K. (2002). Grouping the gifted and talented. *Roeper Review, 24*(4), 103–107.

Siegle, D. (2009). *Gifted children's Bill of Rights*. Retrieved from https://www.nagc.org/resources-publications/resources-parents/gifted-childrens-bill-rights

Taba, H. (1962). *Curriculum development: Theory and practice*. New York, NY: Harcourt, Brace & World.

Tomlinson, C. A. (2014). *The differentiated classroom: Responding to the needs of all learners* (2nd ed.). Alexandria, VA: Association for Supervision and Curriculum Development.

Trilling, B., Fadel, C., & Partnership for 21st Century Skills. (2009). *21st century skills: Learning for life in our times.* San Francisco, CA: Jossey-Bass.

University of Virginia. (2002). *Cubing and think dots.* Retrieved from http://curry .virginia.edu/uploads/resourceLibrary/nagc_cubing__think_dots.pdf

VanTassel-Baska, J. & Little, C.A. (2016). *Content-based curriculum for gifted learners* (3rd ed.). Waco, TX: Prufrock Press.

# 13

## UDL and Early Childhood

### Giving Young Children Choices Too

Zhen Chai
*California State University, Northridge*

Ching-I Chen
*Kent State University*

## SETTING THE STAGE FOR UDL AND EARLY CHILDHOOD

Do you feel overwhelmed by the increasing diversity of your early childhood classroom? For the past twenty years, the demographic of early childhood education classrooms in the United States has significantly changed. The Individuals with Disabilities Education Act (IDEA, 2004) supports the inclusion of young children with disabilities in the educational settings of their typically developing peers. Furthermore, the demographic shift in population leads to an increasing number of young children from diverse cultural and linguistic backgrounds and economic status attending in typical early childhood settings (Cochran, 2007; West, Denton, & Germino-Hausken, 2000). These children differ dramatically in their early experiences, which may contribute to the different developmental repertoire of each child. Plus, there is a 30 million word gap between those who are from low socioeconomic homes and those who are affluent due to the differences in resources and exposure to quality communication exchanges (Hart & Risley, 2003). This situation poses greater challenges for teachers to reduce the gaps and promote learning and development in all children. Given these challenges, what should teachers do?

**Key Concept**

High-quality early childhood inclusion (ECI) programs provide "access, participation, and supports" (DEC & NAEYC, 2009).

To help teachers address the increasing diverse needs of young children, the National Association for the Education of Young Children (NAEYC, 2009) recommends that teachers use developmentally appropriate practices (DAP) as the fundamental guideline to serve young children, which means that teachers should understand the characteristics of child development, know each child well, and make learning experiences culturally meaningful and relevant to them. The NAEYC and the Division for Early Childhood of the Council for Exceptional Children (DEC) also jointly define the key features of high-quality early childhood inclusion (ECI) programs as "access, participation, and supports" (DEC & NAEYC, 2009). These key features require teachers to remove the physical and structural barriers to promote engagement of young children with disabilities, provide accommodations and adaptions to support learning, and further develop their skills to provide high-quality ECI. UDL is a framework that allows educators to create an environment and design activities that maximize active participation and meaningful inclusion of all children in the classroom (Horn, Kang, Classen, & Palmer, 2016; Stockall, Dennis, & Miller, 2012). The three primary principles of UDL align well with the recommendations of NAEYC and DEC in promoting high-quality early childhood education for *all* children.

There is limited but promising research documenting the impact of UDL in early childhood education. Coyne, Pisha, Dalton, Zeph, and Smith (2012) compared a technology-based literacy curriculum that incorporated UDL principles to the traditional literacy instruction with sixteen students with intellectual disabilities from kindergarten to second grade. The students who received reading instruction using the UDL curriculum made significantly higher gains in reading comprehension than those who received traditional instruction.

UDL does not only support academic learning but also social skills, like friendship skills, problem solving, anger management, and emotional literacy. Lieber, Horn, Palmer, and Fleming (2008) developed a curriculum that aligned with UDL principles to address both the academic and social skills of fifty-eight preschool children with disabilities in general education classrooms. Among these fifty-eight children were English language learners, children from diverse language and cultural backgrounds, and children from low socioeconomic homes. The results indicated that these children demonstrated significant gains in literacy, math, and social skills in a school year.

The UDL framework can easily be applied to routine, teacher-directed, and child-directed activities in early childhood settings. UDL allows educators to design a supportive learning environment that allows all children to have access to activities and materials, to be socially accepted as a member of the community, and to have choices to demonstrate what they have learned (Conn-Powers, Cross, Traub, & Hutter-Pishgahi, 2006). Below, we will further explain how each of the UDL principles is applied in early childhood settings. Also see Table 13.1 for guiding questions in applying each UDL principle.

**Table 13.1**   Universal Design for Learning Guiding Questions

**Instructions:** This form helps teachers ensure that they have addressed Universal Design for Learning (UDL) key elements and component parts as they develop activity plans. Indicate "yes" or "no" for each question. If you indicate "yes," then describe how. If you indicate "no," then describe how you plan to address the item. The "hows" are then placed into the Activity Plan to show how UDL will be addressed.

| Guiding questions for means of representation | | |
| --- | --- | --- |
| **Consider these aspects** | **Ask these questions** | **Yes/No— How?** |
| Formats for communication | Have I considered all appropriate options for presenting materials and content in different formats, including visual, auditory, and tactile forms? | |
| | Have I provided for the simultaneous presentation in more than one format? | |
| Complexity of communication | Have I identified the key concept and made plans for providing scaffolding to address multiple levels of complexity? | |
| | Have I reviewed my instructions, questions, and expectations and planned for providing simultaneous options for children's understanding? | |
| Guiding questions for means of engagement | | |
| Recruiting children's engagement | Have I identified multiple types of activities and materials that children in my class are currently drawn to and systematically incorporated several into my activity plan? *Note:* Consider the influence of gender, temperament, life experiences, and family culture as you generate ideas. | |
| | Have I identified opportunities for child choice and systematically incorporated several options into my activity plan? | |

| | | |
|---|---|---|
| | Have I identified and planned for multiple opportunities for incorporating novelty and connecting to known or prior experiences so that there is a good balance of both? | |
| Sustaining children's attention | Have I considered the difficulty/complexity level of the activity, concept, or materials and planned for flexibility in providing for a range of challenging, but not frustrating, complexity levels throughout the activity? | |
| | Have I planned for the provision of multiple types of and opportunities for feedback, encouragement, and scaffolding for the children throughout the activity? | |
| | Have I ensured that activity plans across the children's day and/or work represent multiple learning contexts, including large groups, small groups, and independent time? | |
| *Guiding questions for means of expression* | | |
| Acceptable formats for making responses | Have I identified multiple, acceptable format options for children to appropriately respond, including<br>• Verbal<br>• Physical (e.g., pointing, nodding or shaking head, gesturing, acting out the response)<br>• Nonverbal, symbolic, adult-produced (e.g., pictures, drawings, symbols, writing)<br>• Nonverbal, symbolic, child-produced (e.g., pictures, drawings, symbols, writing) | |
| Acceptable levels of complexity of responding | Have I identified multiple, acceptable levels of complexity for children to appropriately respond, including<br>• Nonverbal<br>• Single responses<br>• Multiple component responses | |
| | Have I identified multiple, acceptable levels of scaffolding or independence in children's responses, including<br>• Following adult prompt or partial cue<br>• Following adult or peer model<br>• Responding chorally<br>• Responding independently<br>• Self-initiating behavior or communication | |

# PUTTING UDL AND EARLY CHILDHOOD INTO PRACTICE: REPRESENTATION

Young children are active learners, and they learn through demonstrations and hands-on experiences (Piaget, 1968). As a result, most young children do not learn well when they passively receive auditory or visual information. Teachers should use a variety of strategies to guide young children's access to lesson content. Horn, Kang, Classen, and Palmer (2016) further divided multiple means of representation into multiple forms for communication and multiple levels of complexity to help teachers understand how to present content and scaffold for young children.

## Providing Multiple Forms of Communication

Cognitive theorists (e.g., Mayer, 2005) believe that working memory has two separate channels to process visual and auditory information, and the amount of information that a person can process in each channel is limited. When information is too complicated or too much is presented at one time, a person may not have enough cognitive capacity to process the information. As a result, people typically learn better when information is presented using mixed modes (Mousavi, Low, & Sweller, 1995; Sombatteera & Kalyuga, 2012).

A multisensory strategy uses two or more senses simultaneously, which may include visual, auditory, tactile-kinesthetic, and articulatory-motor (Moats & Farrell, 2005). Multisensory teaching was recommended by experts even before the 20th century (Moats & Farrell, 2005). It is believed that memory is reinforced when learning occurs through multiple senses. Young children have different preferences for learning, and they learn in more than one way. Some may be auditory learners, some may need to learn through visuals, some may learn by touching and feeling the materials, and still others are a combination thereof. In early childhood settings, teachers should prepare to present information in multiple ways, give young children different options to access information, and always pair auditory information with visuals like pictures, felt board, signs or gestures, or real objects during instruction or when giving a direction. Try out some of these examples:

- **PROVIDE A SENSORY BIN when reading a story.** Allow all children the option to manipulate materials. For example, provide the straw, sticks, and bricks, and let young children feel them and play with them when reading a story like *Three Little Pigs*. Not every child has had the experience of interacting with these materials before, so don't assume that all children understand that a house made of straw or sticks is not as strong as a house made of bricks. Show children how easily a straw or a stick can break and let them try.

- USE THE CHOICE OF DIFFERENT PROPS to help young children understand the sequence of a story. When reading *Goldilocks and the Three Bears*, the teacher could let children choose to use a felt board, stuffed animals, or finger puppets to demonstrate what happens first, next, and in the end.
- PAIR VERBAL EXPLANATION WITH THE PRODUCTS children will make or the materials and tools they will use in the activity. When introducing the next activity, many young children will not understand if the teacher merely explains the activity verbally. Give children the options to see and touch the products/materials first.
- USE PICTURES AND/OR GESTURES ALONG WITH THE VERBAL DIRECTIONS when reviewing classroom rules to ensure that young students understand the expectations. Young children may have a different understanding of what "keep hands to yourself" or "use gentle touches" means.
- PROVIDE AN OPTION OF USING A SHORT VIDEO to introduce young children to exactly what they need to do during an activity like making playdough. Also offer a picture schedule or a real object schedule to remind them of the steps to follow when making the playdough, instead of just telling them to mix all the ingredients into the bowl.

### STRATEGY SPOT
INVOLVE ALL SENSES

Always plan to present your information using a multisensory approach. Pair your verbal description with pictures, signs, gestures, or real objects, so students will have the option of receiving information in whatever format they learn best.

## Providing Multiple Levels of Complexity

Even if the teacher has presented the content using multiple forms of communication, some children still may not comprehend. Young children come to school with a variety of prior learning experiences. In early childhood settings, it means that teachers need to use different strategies to present difficult concepts to ensure all children—no matter their previous learning experience—can understand them. Some strategies include defining vocabulary, breaking communication into discrete components, and pairing verbal description with modeling (Horn, Kang, Classen, & Palmer, 2016). Try these options:

- DEFINE VOCABULARY. When reading a story or doing an activity, you will notice there are some words that young children just don't encounter on a daily basis, and without knowing the meaning of these words, it will be very hard for them to understand the content. For example, young children who have a washer and dryer at home may not know what a laundromat is. The teacher will need to verbally define what it is or ask peers if they know what it is and can describe it, show them a picture or video of a laundromat, or even plan a visit to a laundromat in the community.
- BREAK COMMUNICATION INTO DISCRETE COMPONENTS. Instead of giving young children all the materials to ask them to make a jack-o'-lantern, the teacher should break the task into small steps for those who need it. First, students can choose a pumpkin. Second, they can make the eyes for the jack-o'-lantern. Teachers should give children choices regarding how to draw the eyes. They can use markers, glue the wiggle eyes on the pumpkin, and so forth.
- PAIR VERBAL DESCRIPTION WITH MODELING. When teaching young children about recycling, you can model how to sort trash into different recycling bins. For example, say that the first step of sorting is to choose an item for the trash as you take a bottle out. Then explain that the second step is to ask yourself, "What materials is it made of?" and ask yourself loudly, "What is this bottle made of? Is it made of glass or aluminum?" Children may help you figure out what material it is, and then you will model putting the bottle into the corresponding trash bin.

## CASE IN POINT

When reading *Pete the Cat: I Love My White Shoes*, Ms. Miller asked her students to "tell me what you see in the picture." Eric raised his hand and answered verbally, "I see Pete the Cat." Ashley, who was very shy, pointed to the shoes on the page as Ms. Miller showed the picture in front of her. Brandon, who was not yet talking, signed "bird," and Michael, with the assistance of a paraprofessional, used his picture exchange system to show Ms. Miller a picture of "strawberry." All the children were able to actively participate in the learning activity via various ways of responding.

## PUTTING UDL AND EARLY CHILDHOOD INTO PRACTICE: ENGAGEMENT

In early childhood settings, the provision of multiple means of engagement is essential for all children to meaningfully attend classroom routines and activities that involve their interests. Stockall and colleagues (2012) defined multiple means of engagement in early childhood settings as "ensur[ing] that various opportunities exist for arousing the attention, curiosity, and motivation of children, addressing a wide range of interests, preferences, and learning styles. Levels of scaffolding, repetition, and appropriate challenges then maintain engagement to ensure successful learning" (p. 12). Horn, Kang, Classen, and Palmer (2016) then condensed engagement into a two-aspect concept, including *recruiting children's interests* and *sustaining children's attention*.

### Recruiting Children's Interests

When designing activities, it is important for teachers to consider the following question: "Why would children want to participate in the planned activities, engage with the materials, and interact with adults and peers?" (Horn, Kang, Classen, & Palmer, 2016, p. 79). Depending on the child's temperament, life experiences, and exposure to the surroundings, they may be interested in different things and activities. By capitalizing on children's interests and motivation when designing activities, teachers can make learning in daily lives more natural, active, and authentic. Likewise, teachers can follow children's lead to identify teachable moments and provide choices so that they have the opportunity to make decisions for themselves (Johnson, Rahn, & Bricker, 2014). Additionally, when introducing a new concept, teachers can build on children's previous experiences and balance the amount of new and familiar information presented. This will keep their interests and avoid overwhelming them. Try these suggestions:

- **PROVIDE CHOICES to ensure that children are involved with the activities, materials, and individuals of their preference during classroom routines and activities.** For example, during free play, provide choices by saying, "Would you like to play with blocks or cars?" to a child when showing a piece of block and a car, and ask them to select which one they would like to play with.

- **LET THEM LEAD.** When a group of children decide to open a grocery store in the dramatic play area, it is a great opportunity for the teacher to follow the children's interests and use the grocery store as the context to teach them related vocabulary, math skills, and social skills such as turn taking.

**Tech Tips**

- Learn more about how to follow children's lead by going to https://eclkc.ohs .acf.hhs.gov/video/following-childrens-lead.

- Go to http:// headstartinclusion.org/ classroom-visuals for resources on classroom visuals and supports.

- **CONNECT HOME AND SCHOOL.** When teaching children the alphabet letter of the week (for example, the letter *B*), after introducing the letter, invite children to bring an item from home that starts with the letter *B* to make meaningful connection to their life.

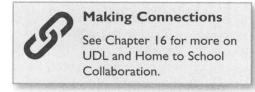

**Making Connections**

See Chapter 16 for more on UDL and Home to School Collaboration.

### Sustaining Children's Attention

To ensure that children stay engaged throughout a task or an activity, teachers should focus on sustaining children's effort and persistence. Haley-Mize and Reeves (2013) pointed out the use of *affective hooks*, which means that varying levels of support and challenge should be provided within the task or activity so that the task or activity is closely connected to prior knowledge and experience while remaining challenging. The teacher should be mindful regarding the difficulty and complexity level of a task or an activity; the task or activity should stay challenging to the child so that with adequate guidance, they can easily become successful. Furthermore, the organization of activities should be taken into consideration. Be aware of young children's attention span and the arrangement of different types of activities, (e.g., balancing active and quiet activities throughout the day to maintain children's attention and engagement; Horn, Kang, Classen, & Palmer, 2016). Consider these options:

- **TRY ALTERNATING BETWEEN ACTIVE MOVEMENT AND QUIET PARTICIPATION.** For example, during circle time, start with greetings, followed by talking about the weather and/or the calendar, and then invite children to enjoy music and movement before reading a book.
- **PROVIDE DIFFERENT LEVELS OF SCAFFOLDING when children are working on a challenging task to sustain their interest in the activity.** For example, when coloring an elephant that is divided into several different numbered zones with different colors, you can model for some children by coloring all the #1 zones in blue and encourage them to follow as you model or to choose their own color and type of coloring utensil. For others, you might just point to the places where they need to color and always praise their effort.
- **CONSIDER THE LENGTH OF EACH CLASSROOM ACTIVITY.** Generally, the suggested length of each activity is between ten to fifteen minutes for young children; thus, during center time, the teacher should keep an eye on the time and initiate the rotation of activities when time is up.

In the art center, Mr. Johnson asked children to draw their favorite animals because the theme of the unit was pets and wild animals. He prepared markers, colored pencils, watercolor paints and brushes, crayons, scissors, pictures of different animals, and animal coloring pages for the students to use. Children were encouraged to use any item or way they wanted to show their favorite animals. Some children chose to draw their favorite animals independently as they talked about the animals they had seen during their field trip to the zoo last week, while some used the pictures of the animals that Mr. Johnson provided as a model. A few children asked Mr. Johnson to draw their favorite animals first so they could follow along, some chose the coloring page and colored their favorite animals, and some cut out the pictures of the animals and glued them on the paper. One child decided to create and draw his own favorite animal, the cabramur—an amalgamation of a cat, zebra, and ring-tailed lemur! All children enjoyed creating a picture about their favorite animals.

## PUTTING UDL AND EARLY CHILDHOOD INTO PRACTICE: EXPRESSION

It is important to allow children to demonstrate what they have learned and express their ideas in different ways. Use of multiple means of expression takes the individual differences of children in all aspects of development into account and addresses the strengths, needs, and preferences of each child (Horn, Kang, Classen, & Palmer, 2016; Stockall et al., 2012). Providing multiple means of expression creates opportunities for all children to practice interpreting and synthesizing the information they gather from their learning environment, as well as articulate their thoughts in meaningful formats. Additionally, teachers can examine the effectiveness of their instruction and reflect on whether adjustments should be made. To embed multiple means of expression into early childhood classroom learning, Horn, Kang, Classen, and Palmer (2016) indicated that two key aspects of multiple means of expression should be carefully considered, including *accepting multiple formats for making responses* and *accepting multiple levels of complexity of responding.*

## Accepting Multiple Formats for Making Responses

As mentioned above, each child has individual strengths, preferences, ways of learning, and needs. When designing learning environment and activities, teachers should be responsive to the individual variations of each child and make adaptations to instruction so that each child is able to show what he or she has learned (NAEYC, 2009). In early childhood settings, young children could respond and make inquiries using verbal, gestural, or written responses and/or assistive technology.

**Making Connections**

See Chapter 10 for more on UDL and Assistive Technology.

## Accepting Multiple Levels of Complexity of Responding

Besides providing varying formats of responding, it is also essential to consider the levels of complexity and length when children respond. Depending on the level of development of each child, some children may be able to independently respond with complex skills, and some children may need prompting or support from teachers to demonstrate what they know. Take the developmental variations among children in your classroom into account so that the preschool classroom activities maximize the learning effects, and promote the individual development and learning of each child (NAEYC, 2009).

Even if the teacher has utilized UDL in planning and instruction from the outset, some young children may still have difficulty with fully participating in the early childhood curriculum. When this happens, teachers need to consider using differentiated instruction (DI) to support these children. Horn, Kang, Classen, and Lieber (2016) recommended eight curriculum modifications: environmental support (e.g., place individual mats with their names on them on the floor to indicate where to sit during circle time), materials adaptation (e.g., put popsicle sticks on book pages to make them easy to turn), simplification (e.g., let the child trace the dots when writing her name), child preferences (e.g., let the child hold his favorite toy during transition), special equipment (e.g., use loop scissors), adult support (e.g., give the child an individualized warning before transition), peer support (e.g., let a friend hold the child's hand while walking to the next activity), and invisible support (e.g., plan low-demand activities after a long weekend). These DI strategies together with UDL will ensure that the majority of young children actively and meaningfully participate in early childhood settings and have access to general education curriculum.

**Tech Tips**

Learn more about how to scaffold children's learning by going to https://eclkc.ohs .acf.hhs.gov/video/scaffolding-childrens-learning to watch the video and read the tips for teachers.

UDL v. DI

## STRATEGY SPOT
### OPEN RESPONSE OPTIONS

To plan multiple acceptable ways for children to respond, teachers should know each child in the group well. This can be achieved via the use of authentic assessments, which means observing children's performance in familiar environments, usually with peers or adults they know well. For example, teachers may use the Assessment, Evaluation, and Programming System (AEPS; Bricker, 2002), an authentic, curriculum-based assessment that examines functional and developmental skills in various domains as a guide to observe children's performance and seek parents' input. With the information gathered, teachers will be able to understand children's interests, preferences, strengths, and needs, and can then plan the possible different formats of responding during activities.

## BRINGING IT ALL TOGETHER

"The desired results of inclusive experiences for children with and without disabilities and their families include a sense of belonging and membership, positive social relationships and friendships, and development and learning to reach their full potential" (DEC & NAEYC, 2009; p. 2). UDL promotes high-quality ECI for *all* children, regardless of their abilities or previous experiences. By providing multiple forms for communication and multiple levels of complexity, teachers give young children options to safely access activities and materials. To keep young children engaged, teachers should consider using their preference and follow their lead as teachers recruit their interests and sustain their attention. Teachers should also provide young children the opportunities to demonstrate what they have learned using *multiple formats* and with *multiple levels of complexity*. Intentional planning to use these elements in every aspect of instruction from the very beginning will ensure successful incorporation of UDL in early childhood settings (Conn-Powers et al., 2006), which will eventually lead to optimal learning and development outcomes for all children.

## TOP FIVE WEBSITES TO SUPPORT UDL IN EARLY CHILDHOOD EDUCATION

→ http://bookbuilder.cast.org/

→ https://eclkc.ohs.acf.hhs.gov

→ http://ectacenter.org/decrp/

→ https://www.naeyc.org

→ https://blog.brookespublishing.com/

## APPS WE LOVE

→ Draw and Tell

→ Epic!

→ Park Math HD

→ Proloquo2Go

→ Signed Stories

## RECOMMENDED READINGS

Grisham-Brown, J., & Hemmeter, M. L. (2017). *Blended practices for teaching young children in inclusive settings* (2nd ed.). Baltimore, MD: Paul H. Brookes.

Horn, E. M., Palmer, S. B., Butera, G. D., & Lieber, J. A. (2016). *Six steps to an inclusive preschool curriculum: A UDL-based framework for children's school success*. Baltimore, MD: Paul H. Brookes.

# REFERENCES

Bricker, D. (2002). *Assessment, Evaluation, and Programming System (AEPS®) for infants and children* (2nd ed.). Baltimore, MD: Paul H. Brookes.

Cochran, M. (2007). *Finding our way: The future of American early care and education.* Washington, DC: Zero to Three.

Conn-Powers, M., Cross, A. F., Traub, E. K., & Hutter-Pishgahi, L. (2006). The universal design of early education: Moving forward for all children. Beyond the Journal: Young Children on the Web. Retrieved from http://journal.naeyc .org/btj/200609/ConnPowersBTJ.pdf

Coyne, P., Pisha, B., Dalton, B., Zeph, L., & Smith, N. (2012). Literacy by design: A Universal Design for Learning approach for students with significant intellectual disabilities. *Remedial and Special Education, 33,* 162–172.

Division for Early Childhood & National Association for the Education for Young Children. (2009). Early childhood inclusion: A joint position statement of the Division for Early Childhood (DEC) and the National Association for the Education of Young Children (NAEYC). Chapel Hill, NC: Author.

Haley-Mize, S., & Reeves, S. (2013). Universal Design for Learning and emergent-literacy development: Instructional practices for young learners. *The Delta Kappa Gamma Bulletin, 79*(2), 70–78.

Hart, B., & Risley, T. R. (2003). The early catastrophe: The 30 million word gap by age 3. *American Educator, 27,* 4–9. Retrieved from http://www.aft.org/pdfs/ americaneducator/spring2003/TheEarlyCatastrophe.pdf

Horn, E., Kang, J., Classen, A., & Lieber, J. A. (2016). Foundations of differentiation and individualization. In E. Horn, S. Palmer, G. Butera, & J. Lieber (Eds.), *Six steps to an inclusive preschool curriculum: A UDL-based framework for children's school success* (pp. 91–110). Baltimore, MD: Paul H. Brookes.

Horn, E., Kang, J., Classen, A., & Palmer, S. (2016). Understanding the foundational component of Universal Design for Learning. In E. Horn, S. Palmer, G. Butera, & J. Lieber (Eds.), *Six steps to an inclusive preschool curriculum: A UDL-based framework for children's school success* (pp. 75–90). Baltimore, MD: Paul H. Brookes.

Individuals with Disabilities Education Act, 20 U.S.C. § 1400 (2004).

Johnson, J., Rahn, N., & Bricker, D. (2014). *An activity-based approach to early intervention* (4th ed.). Baltimore, MD: Paul H. Brookes.

Lieber, J., Horn, E., Palmer, S., & Fleming, K. (2008). Access to the general education curriculum for preschoolers with disabilities: Children's school success. *Exceptionality, 16,* 18–32.

Mayer, R. E. (2005). Cognitive theory of multimedia learning. In R. E. Mayer (Ed.), *The Cambridge handbook of multimedia learning* (pp. 31–48). New York, NY: Cambridge University Press.

Moats, L. C., & Farrell, M. L. (2005). Multisensory structured language education. In J. R. Birsh (Ed.), *Multisensory teaching of basic language skills* (pp. 23–41). Baltimore, MD: Paul H. Brookes.

Mousavi, S. Y., Low, R., & Sweller, J. (1995). Reducing cognitive load by mixing auditory and visual presentation modes. *Journal of Educational Psychology, 87,* 319–334.

NAEYC. (2009). *Position statement: Developmentally appropriate practice in early childhood programs serving children from birth through age eight*. Retrieved from https://www.naeyc.org/resources/topics/dap/position-statement

Piaget, J. (1968). *Six psychological studies*. New York, NY: Vintage Books.

Sombatteera, S., & Kalyuga, S. (2012). When dual sensory mode with limited text presentation enhance learning. *Procedia–Social and Behavioral Sciences, 69,* 2022–2026.

Stockall, N. S., Dennis, L., & Miller, M. (2012). Right from the start: Universal design for preschool. *TEACHING Exceptional Children, 45,* 10–17.

West, J., Denton, K., & Germino-Hausken, E. (2000). *America's kindergartners: Findings from the Early Childhood Longitudinal Study, Kindergarten Class of 1998–99, Fall 1998*. NCES 2000–070. Washington, DC: U.S. Department of Education, National Center for Education Statistics.

# 14

## UDL and Students With Emotional/Behavioral Disorders

### *Promoting Self-Managers*

Kimberly M. Johnson

Kyena E. Cornelius

*Minnesota State University, Mankato*

## SETTING THE STAGE FOR UDL AND STUDENTS WITH EMOTIONAL/BEHAVIORAL DISORDERS

What teacher wouldn't delight in thinking about an engaging classroom where students are contentedly working on learning tasks and activities they find interesting and worthwhile? When teachers learn about UDL, they often immediately embrace the concept (Edyburn, 2010). Many teachers can even imagine planning a variety of learning activities so students have options for how they engage with the new content. Of course, it will take some additional planning time up front, but it will be well worth the effort. Unfortunately, enthusiasm for UDL is sometimes halted as teachers begin thinking about managing classroom behavior, especially that of students with emotional/behavior disorders (EBD). You

**Key Concept**

**Emotional and behavioral disorders** (EBD) includes both *externalizing behaviors* (behaviors directed outward, usually toward other people; e.g., physical aggression) and *internalizing behaviors* (behaviors directed inward; e.g., social withdrawal).

might wonder, "How can I (along with my behavior support team) design or adapt individualized behavioral interventions for students with emotional behavioral disorders to suit a UDL learning environment where students have options and autonomy?" Don't worry. We've got your back. A method for designing or adapting individualized behavioral interventions for students with (and without) EBD will be shared in this chapter.

Students with EBD demonstrate inappropriate behavior, experience academic difficulties, and consistently have trouble with interpersonal relationships (Kauffman & Landrum, 2013). Inappropriate behaviors fall into two categories: externalizing and internalizing. Externalizing behaviors include acting-out behaviors, such as talking out during instruction, refusing to follow directions, using profanity, arguing with peers and teachers, damaging property, and fighting. Internalizing behaviors are less noticeable and are often overlooked. They include not engaging with classmates, poor participation in learning activities, complaining of illness, and self-injury.

Whether externalizing or internalizing, these behaviors keep students from learning because they cause them to miss important instruction due to inattentiveness or being out of the classroom when receiving behavioral support. When students attempt to participate in instruction following disengagement, they become confused and frustrated, which leads to more behavior problems. Because of this cycle, students with EBD gradually fall further and further behind their peers, earn failing grades, and experience low graduation rates.

A popular belief among teachers is that behaviors must be under control before instruction can occur, but a different approach might prove more effective. The cycle of disengagement and poor academic out-

**Making Connections**

See Chapter 7 for more on PBIS and UDL.

comes can be disrupted by addressing instruction, classroom management, and individualized behavioral interventions simultaneously. Instruction should be designed to be responsive to individual learner strengths, needs, and preferences (Basham, Israel, Graden, Poth, & Winston, 2010). When students are interested and involved with the content through active responding, they are less likely to be engaged in problem behavior (Sutherland & Wehby, 2001). Additionally, effective classroom management strategies go a long way in preventing behavior problems (Simonsen, Fairbanks, Briesch, Myers, & Sugai, 2008), even among students with EBD; but yes, sometimes more intensive, individualized behavioral interventions are needed (Kern, George, & Weist, 2015).

The need for individualized behavioral interventions is determined through a functional behavioral assessment (FBA; Scott, Alter, & McQuillan, 2010), which is typically administered by a behavior support team. FBAs consist of teacher and student interviews and direct observations where data are collected on behaviors (including frequency, intensity, and duration), antecedents (i.e., triggers), and consequences (i.e., results). Data are analyzed to determine the function (i.e., reason) of the behavior. Once the function of the behavior is discovered, a replacement behavior (a desirable behavior that will result in the desired consequence) can be identified. Once the replacement behavior is identifed, an intervention can be selected or designed to help the student demonstrate the desired behavior instead of the undesired behavior when faced with the trigger. Several evidence-based behavioral interventions are available (consult the online resources listed at the end of the chapter) such as behavioral contracting, token economy systems, various reinforcement plans, and self-management.

**Key Concept**

**Replacement behavior** is an appropriate behavior that will provide the same *function* for the student as the problem behavior, but with a more desirable result.

**Behavioral contracting** is a positive reinforcement intervention in which teacher and student agree on behaviors that will be demonstrated and rewards that will be earned as a result. A tangible contract is written and signed, and progress is monitored. **A token economy system** allows the teacher to provide a primary reinforcer (i.e., a token) for demonstration of appropriate behavior. Students then exchange tokens for tangible

### STRATEGY SPOT
SELF-MANAGEMENT

1. Identify the undesired behavior and determine its function (e.g., student engages in verbal conflicts to defend himself when others make fun of him).
2. Identify acceptable replacement behavior (e.g., ask peer to stop, ignore, or seek adult support).
3. Design strategy for displaying replacement behavior (e.g., statements to say to peers instead of undesirable behavior of verbal conflict) when faced with trigger.
4. Teach strategy and monitoring process.
5. Practice strategy in "controlled" setting.
6. Practice strategy in context with support.
7. Practice strategy in context independently.
8. Monitor and reward progress.
9. Reflect, then adapt or maintain. (Fitzpatrick & Knowlton, 2009)

or activity-oriented rewards (e.g., ten tokens for five minutes of computer time), if that is what motivates that child.

**Reinforcement plans** are deliberate arrangements for when and how reinforcement is provided (e.g., differential reinforcement, non-contingent reinforcement, group contingencies). **Self-management** is an evidence-based behavioral intervention in which an individual engages in a specific process that includes self-monitoring, self-instruction, and self-reinforcement to increase a desirable behavior or decrease an undesirable behavior.

Although each of the evidence-based practices named above are effective and can easily be individualized using UDL guidelines to promote student voice and make choices available, we will focus on self-management in this chapter. Because self-management has maximum impact when it is individualized to incorporate student preferences, it is the perfect evidence-based strategy to model how UDL principles and guidelines can be used to increase intervention personalization.

We know that *teachers* can always make adaptations for *students*. We've done that for years. A process exists to adapt intensive behavioral interventions by varying certain parts of standard interventions (e.g., intensity, arrangement, content) according to students' needs, characteristics, and preferences (Danielson & Rosenquist, 2014). This would differentiate a standard intervention for a particular student's needs. In this chapter, we'll demonstrate how UDL can be used in conjunction with typical behavior intervention techniques.

However, to provide students more autonomy and choice, we offer a process that combines similar key ideas of the Universal Design for Learning–Implementation and Research Network's Critical Elements of Instruction (UDL-IRN, 2011), the UDL Cycle of Instructional Planning (Rao & Meo, 2016), and the Process of Adapting Behavior Intervention (Wehby & Kern, 2014). Think of how revolutionary it will be when students are taking more of a lead in helping shape their own behaviors!

## STEPS FOR DESIGNING OR ADAPTING INDIVIDUALIZED BEHAVIORAL INTERVENTIONS

### Step 1: Define Target Behavior and Replacement Behavior

The beginning of any behavior intervention requires first a clear description of the target behavior that needs to change and the identification of what the targeted behavior does for the student: *What is its function*? Completing this step in collaboration with the student provides a perfect opportunity for student voice in selecting a replacement behavior. See if the student even agrees with the data collection and determination of function: *It appears that you often yell out in order to get attention. Do you think that is accurate?* The replacement behavior goal is then written in measurable terms so both the teacher and student can accurately monitor progress.

## CASE IN POINT

Jeremy is a middle school student with EBD with externalizing behaviors. In settings where adults are not readily available to intervene, and when his peers make fun of him or his friends, Jeremy gets into verbal and physical conflicts in order to defend himself or his friends. Ms. Garrett and Jeremy identify the behavior goal: *Given a potential peer conflict, Jeremy will recognize triggers and employ one of three response strategies (ask the person to stop, ignore the person, seek support from an adult) four out of five times.* Jeremy wants to adjust this behavior so he can stay out of in-school suspension, which is impacting his grades, and so his mom will return his gaming system. He has been successful with self-management interventions in the past, so Jeremy and Ms. Garrett think this will be a good strategy for him.

### Step 2: Plan for Learner Variability and Critical Factors

Consider the student's individual strengths and weaknesses related to cognitive functioning, background knowledge and experience, progress with prior interventions, intervention preferences, level of motivation, and family support. Also consider contextual factors such as curriculum, classroom arrangement, and schedule.

### Step 3: Design or Adapt Intervention Through Flexible Methods and Materials

In this step, we apply the principles and guidelines of UDL. Following the recommendations of the National Center on UDL (Rose, 2012), we consider the guidelines first in horizontal rows (access, build, and internalize) to demonstrate how they build toward student ownership of their learning (see Figure 14.1). Then we consider the vertical columns (representation, action and expression, and engagement) to provide a more focused look at the UDL principles. In this chapter, we conceptualize the *access* row as providing access to the intervention, the *build* row as building the new behavior through use of the intervention, and the *internalize* row as internalizing the new behavior.

## Figure 14.1    UDL Guidelines to Access, Build, and Internalize Learning and Behavior

*Source:*  CAST (2018). Universal Design for Learning Guidelines version 2.2. Retrieved from http://udlguidelines.cast.org.

First, examine the top row of the UDL chart—*access*—and consider how the intervention can be customized so that students

- understand it (multiple means of *representation*—perception),
- "buy in" to it (multiple means of *engagement*—interest), and
- can do it (multiple means of *action and expression*—physical action).

## CASE IN POINT

In order to gain his interest or "buy in" (personalized for engagement), Ms. Garrett included Jeremy in the process of designing a self-management intervention to decrease his conflicts with peers. She and Jeremy discussed three strategies for responding to peer conflicts, and Jeremy ranked the options in order of preference (personalized for action and expression) and also made some adjustments to fit his personal "style" of interacting with peers. They also wrote self-instruction phrases that Jeremy could use when needed. Next, Ms. Garrett and Jeremy created a visual representation to which they could both refer (personalized for representation) and a sheet where Jeremy could self-monitor his use of the intervention and mark his progress with the new behavior.

Next, examine the middle row of the UDL chart—*build*—and consider how the intervention can be customized so that students

- clarify nuances of the expected behavior (multiple means of *representation*—language),
- expend effort on developing the new behavior (multiple means of *engagement*—effort), and
- can demonstrate the behavior (multiple means of *action and expression*—expression).

Last, examine the bottom row of the UDL chart—*internalize*—and consider how the intervention can be customized so that students

- analyze patterns and relationships related to the new behavior and generalize it to new situations (multiple means of *representation*),
- reflect on progress with the new behavior and make strategy adjustments as needed (multiple means of *engagement*), and
- monitor behavioral status, set new behavioral goals, and make plans to achieve them (multiple means of *action and expression*).

**CASE IN POINT**

After the intervention was designed, Ms. Garrett planned opportunities for Jeremy to build fluency with the new strategies for responding to peer conflicts. She directed Jeremy to discuss the strategies with his mom so she could reinforce them outside of school and provide encouragement for Jeremy's efforts. She practiced the strategies with Jeremy several times during the school day and asked the behavior interventionist, Mr. Hammond, to include role-plays of the strategies during social skills groups. The variety of practice opportunities and feedback (personalized for effort) provided him with clarification on the nuances of the new behavior (personalized for language). These opportunities also allowed him to "try out" his own style of the strategies (personalized for expression).

### Step 4: Monitor Progress of the Intervention

Collect data to monitor the student's progress and implementation fidelity of the intervention. It is critical that students also monitor their own progress. Students can choose how to record their data and teachers can use this to compare with their own data to ensure students are both measuring their progress and using the strategy correctly. The data can also be shared with students' families so that they can provide additional reinforcement and encouragement.

### Step 5: Reflect and Continue or Make Adaptations

Evaluate data in order to determine whether adaptations are needed. When adaptations are needed, consider predetermined criteria for mastery

**CASE IN POINT**

Once the intervention was underway, Ms. Garrett encouraged Jeremy to practice the intervention in mid- to high-probability areas (personalized for deep comprehension) when she or Mr. Hammond would be available to intervene. After these trials, she provided praise and feedback and facilitated Jeremy's personal reflection of his progress (personalized for self-regulation) and encouraged continued goal-setting/refinement based on current progress.

**CASE IN POINT**

After a period of time, the data revealed that Jeremy's discipline referrals were significantly reduced. He was not spending time in in-school suspension, and his grades were improving. Jeremy's mom was pleased with his progress, and Jeremy was happy to have his gaming system back. Ms. Garrett planned to work with Jeremy to continue maintenance of the new skill.

such as a required level of student progress or a required number of days where implementation fidelity is adequate.

While individualized behavioral interventions are necessary for only a few students in a typical inclusive classroom (i.e., students with EBD; Kern, Hilt-Panahon, & Sokol, 2009), teachers can adapt them for students without EBD who might benefit from a lower-level application of the intervention. This can be done by considering the intervention as it was originally designed and then running it through the same UDL-inspired considerations above. When we implement UDL in instructional design, our ultimate goal is to develop expert learners. Similarly, when we implement UDL in the design of individualized behavioral interventions, our goal is to develop expert self-managers.

**UDL v. DI**

## PUTTING UDL AND EBD INTO PRACTICE: REPRESENTATION

When designing or adapting behavioral interventions, consider the *access*, *build*, and *internalize* levels of the UDL guideline, **Multiple Means of Representation**.

1. **Access** = Understand the intervention.
2. **Build** = Clarify the nuances of the desired behavior.
3. **Internalize** = Analyze patterns and relationships related to the new behavior and generalize it to new situations.

When we consider the principle of representation in the context of developing or adapting behavioral interventions, our ultimate goal is for students to understand their behavior (both the unwanted behavior and the replacement behavior) well enough that they can analyze behavior patterns and relationships between triggers and consequences. With this understanding, they will be able to generalize what they have learned to new settings and situations.

In order for students to achieve this level of understanding, they first must be able to understand the intervention and develop clarity on the nuances of the desired behavior. We facilitate this process by providing multiple means of representation. We present (represent) the intervention in ways that align with individual students' preferences. One student might understand the intervention by hearing a simple verbal explanation while another student might need to see an example (e.g., a sample self-monitoring sheet) and walk through the intervention steps. We facilitate learning activities that allow students to leverage strengths and preferences. Students may choose to identify examples and nonexamples of the desired behavior via role-play activities with peers, video clips from YouTube, or even by creating scenes and story boards using animated characters. When students begin to develop the deep understanding of the behavior that we are looking for, we guide them to make meaningful connections with their life experiences.

**Tech Tip**

Use apps like *CrazyTalk7* to have students create their own cartoon or social story with the targeted and replacement behaviors.

- **GET TO KNOW YOUR STUDENTS** so you have information to draw upon when determining how to teach them about the intervention and the desired behavior.
- **EXPLICITLY TEACH THE STEPS OF THE INTERVENTION** and related strategies by providing models and guided practice.
- **CHECK FOR UNDERSTANDING OF THE INTERVENTION PROCESS** by having students explain the steps to you.
- **EXPLICITLY TEACH THE DESIRED BEHAVIOR** by providing models and guided practice.
- **CHECK FOR UNDERSTANDING OF THE DESIRED BEHAVIOR** by having students provide you with an example and nonexample.
- **FACILITATE STUDENTS' ANALYSIS OF THEIR OWN BEHAVIOR** by asking questions related to patterns that are evident.
- **PROMOTE STUDENTS' DEVELOPMENT OF INTERVENTION AND STRATEGY ADAPTATIONS** to promote generalization of the behavior from one situation to another.

## PUTTING UDL AND EBD INTO PRACTICE: ENGAGEMENT

When designing or adapting behavioral interventions, consider the *access, build,* and *internalize* levels of the UDL guideline, **Multiple Means of Engagement**.

1. **Access** = "Buy in" to the intervention.
2. **Build** = Expend effort to develop the new behavior.
3. **Internalize** = Reflect on progress with the new behavior and make strategy adjustments as needed.

When we consider the principle of engagement in the context of developing or adapting behavioral interventions, the ultimate goal is for students to engage with the intervention wholeheartedly so that they are not just invested in earning rewards (i.e., reinforcers), but more importantly, they see the benefit of the new behavior and the intervention that helped them to achieve it. In order for students to get to that point, they must first engage with the intervention and put forth the effort to develop the new behavior.

Educators can facilitate this process by making multiple means of engagement available. Teachers can gain initial interest for the intervention by offering choices related to many components of the intervention that suit student preferences and personal style. One student might choose a monitoring sheet where he circles Pikachu (a positive Pokémon character) when he is on-task and Gengar (a negative Pokémon character) when he is off-task. Another student might want simply to mark a plus or minus sign in her planner. Each student would likely also choose a different method for signaling intervals, such as a personal timer on an iPad (e.g., Repeat Timer) or a signal from the teacher (e.g., tap on the student's planner as she walks by the desk).

We can garner initial enthusiasm for the desired behavior by offering options for external motivations such as rewards from a class store. Facilitating learning opportunities where students have the opportunity to practice the new behavior in gradually more challenging situations provides opportunity for feedback. When students begin to take ownership of the new behavior and fully integrate it into their repertoire of behaviors, we can guide them toward self-reflection and behavioral adjustments that might impact multiple aspects of their lives.

- **THINK OUTSIDE THE BOX** when engaging students in the development or adaptation of the intervention. Get their input!
- **WORK WITH STUDENTS TO DESIGN INTERVENTION STRATEGIES** to match their personal "style."
- **INTEGRATE TECHNOLOGY** for the student to monitor and reflect on their progress.
- **LISTEN TO STUDENTS' CONCERNS** about standing out in front of peers.
- **VARY PRACTICE OPPORTUNITIES** to keep the development of the new behavior challenging and interesting and to align with practical situations.
- **FACILITATE COLLABORATION** and feedback opportunities with peers when appropriate.

## PUTTING UDL AND EBD INTO PRACTICE: ACTION AND EXPRESSION

When designing or adapting behavioral interventions, consider the *access*, *build*, and *internalize* levels of the UDL guideline, **Multiple Means of Action and Expression**.

1. **Access** = Participate actively in the intervention.
2. **Build** = Demonstrate the behavior.
3. **Internalize** = Monitor behavioral status, set new behavioral goals, and make plans to achieve them.

When we consider action and expression in the context of developing or adapting behavioral interventions, our ultimate goal is for students to continuously monitor their behavioral status, set behavioral goals, and make plans (i.e., develop and implement strategies) to achieve their goals. In order for students to reach this result, they must first have the ability to actively participate in the intervention and demonstrate the replacement behavior. We know you might be thinking that it is easier said than done with some students, and we agree. However, we also know that the more choice and voice students have, the more likely they are to be engaged in the intervention.

We can make options available for how students participate in the intervention and how they demonstrate the new behavior. We want to know our students well enough to anticipate some of their strengths and interests, but it is also acceptable to simply ask students, "What would make it possible for you to participate in this intervention or demonstrate this behavior?" as well as "What will make it difficult for you to participate in this intervention or demonstrate this behavior?" This allows students' voices to be heard loud and clear.

A student might prefer to check-in with a certain teacher, for example, and that simple choice can make the difference between the intervention being effective for the student or not. We can provide options for learning activities that include scaffolds as students build fluency and automaticity with the new behavior through practice opportunities. Once students begin to embrace the idea of monitoring and rewarding their own progress, we can guide them to consider new goals and interventions to achieve them.

- **BE OPEN TO ALL POSSIBILITIES for how students can participate in interventions.** Instead of saying "no" immediately, ask yourself: Why not?
- **BE OPEN TO ALL POSSIBILITIES of replacement behaviors.** Again, ask yourself: Why not?
- **OFFER OPTIONS AT EVERY POSSIBLE POINT of an intervention,** but don't offer an option beyond your means.

- **INCORPORATE INTERVENTIONS THAT UTILIZE TECHNOLOGY when available** (and when they add value).
- **BE OPEN TO STUDENTS' IDEAS about how they need to practice the new behavior.** See if you can incorporate family members and increase home to school collaboration.

**Making Connections**

See Chapter 16 for more on UDL with Home to School Collaboration.

## BRINGING IT ALL TOGETHER

As you develop behavioral interventions for your students, make sure they are genuinely involved in the steps of the process, even if they are very young. The student is the one who will most benefit from the new behavior; doesn't it make sense for them to partner in the process? Listen as they share their voice; then make choices available that respect that voice. To achieve the goal of developing expert self-managers, remember to help students access, build, and internalize. Facilitate students' *access* to the intervention by helping them personalize it. Create opportunities to practice the new behavior so they can *build* fluency and demonstrate the behavior in increasingly complex situations. Promote students' *internalization* of the new behavior through their involvement in progress monitoring and reflection opportunities. Take into consideration the cognitive ability level and developmental age of the student; the kindergarten "self-manager" will look very different than the adolescent "self-manager." Achieving this goal takes time and practice, but with persistence and student involvement it is possible.

**Table 14.1    Implementing UDL in Your Literacy Environment**

| *Individualized Intervention* |
|---|
| **Behavior goal:** |

**Behavior goal:**

Learner strengths, interests, preferences, barriers:

Evidence-Based Practice or Intervention:

> *Use this section to guide your note taking when you are working with a student to individualize an intervention using the UDL guidelines.*

**Access the Intervention:**

- Representation (facilitate basic understanding of intervention)
  After you have taught the intervention components, ask the student questions related to the intervention to check for accurate understanding and possible adaptations to address barriers.

- Engagement (promote buy-in)
  Ask questions about the student's interests (e.g., Marvel or DC?) to inform options related to the intervention logistics (e.g., self-monitoring form).

- Action & Expression (remove barriers to increase ability to participate)
  Ask the student, "What would keep you from being able to do your part of this intervention?"

**Build the New Behavior:**

- Representation (clarify the new behavior with examples/nonexamples)
  After you have agreed on a replacement behavior, ask the student questions related to examples and nonexamples to check for understanding and possible adaptations to address barriers.

- Engagement (expend effort to develop the new behavior)
  Find out what motivates the student. Ask about external motivators (rewards like extra computer time) and internal motivators (feeling happy when I have a good day).

- Action & Expression (demonstrate the new behavior)
  Ask the student, "What would keep you from being able to do this new behavior?"

  *Use this section to guide your note taking when considering steps for moving forward.*

**Internalize the New Behavior:**

- Representation (promote connections and generalization of the new behavior)
  Ask the student, "What did you learn about your patterns of triggers and responses that will allow you to choose the new behavior in the future?"

- Engagement (facilitate reflection and intervention/behavior adaptations)
  Ask student, "What have you learned in this process that will affect your behavioral choices moving forward?"

- Action & Expression (facilitate progress monitoring and goal setting)
  Ask students. "What did you learn from this process that will help you set and achieve behavioral goals in the future?"

## TOP FIVE WEBSITES TO SUPPORT EBD

→ http://www.behavioradvisor.com/

→ http://www.ccbd.net/teacherresources

→ https://charts.intensiveintervention.org/chart/behavioral-intervention-chart

→ http://ebi.missouri.edu/

→ http://www.interventioncentral.org/behavioral-intervention-modification

## APPS WE LOVE

→ BehaviorSnap

→ Choiceworks

→ CrazyTalk7

→ iReward

→ TrackCC

## RECOMMENDED READINGS

Hott, B. L., Walker, J. D., Robinson, A., & Raymond, L. (2017). Search for the miracle cure: Working with students with emotional and behavioral disorders. In Murawski, W. W., & Scott, K. L. (Eds.), *What really works with Universal Design for Learning.* Thousand Oaks, CA: Corwin.

Hughes, C. A., Ruhl, K. L., & Peterson, S. K. (1988). Teaching self-management skills. *TEACHING Exceptional Children, 20*(2), 70–72.

# REFERENCES

Basham, J. D., Israel, M., Graden, J., Poth, R., & Winston, M. (2010). A comprehensive approach to RTI: Embedding universal design for learning and technology. *Learning Disability Quarterly, 33*, 243–255.

CAST (2018). *Universal Design for Learning Guidelines* version 2.2. Retrieved from http://udlguidelines.cast.org

Danielson, L., & Rosenquist, C. (2014). Introduction to the TEC special issue on data-based individualization. *Teaching Exceptional Children, 46*(4), 45–53. doi:10.1177/0040059914522970

Edyburn, D. L. (2010). Would you recognize Universal Design for Learning if you saw it? Ten propositions for new directions for the second decade of UDL. *Learning Disability Quarterly, 33*(1), 33–41.

Fitzpatrick, M., & Knowlton, E. (2009). Bringing evidence-based self-directed intervention practices to the trenches for students with emotional and behavioral disorders. *Preventing School Failure, 53*(4), 253–266.

Kauffman, J. M., & Landrum, T. J. (2013). *Characteristics of emotional and behavioral disorders of children and youth* (10th ed.). Upper Saddle River, NJ: Pearson Education.

Kern, L., George, M. P., & Weist, M. D. (2015). *Supporting students with emotional and behavioral problems: Prevention and intervention strategies.* Baltimore, MD: Paul H. Brookes.

Kern, L., Hilt-Panahon, A., & Sokol, N. G. (2009). Further examining the triangle tip: Improving support for students with emotional and behavioral needs. *Psychology in the Schools, 46*(1), 18–32. doi:10.1002/pits.20351

Rao, K., & Meo, G. (2016). Using Universal Design for Learning to design standards-based lessons. *SAGE Open.* doi:10.1177/2158244016680688

Rose, D. (2012). *Videos from the National Center on Universal Design for Learning: UDL guidelines structure.* Retrieved from http://www.udlcenter.org/resource_library/videos/udlcenter/udl#video1

Scott, T. M., Alter, P. J., & McQuillan, K. (2010). Functional behavior assessment in classroom settings: Scaling down to scale up. *Intervention in School and Clinic, 46*(2), 87–94. doi:10.1177/1053451210374986

Simonsen, B., Fairbanks, S., Briesch, A., Myers, D., & Sugai, G. (2008). Evidence-based practices in classroom management: Considerations for research to practice. *Education and Treatment of Children, 31*(3), 351–380.

Sutherland, K. S., & Wehby, J. H. (2001). Exploring the relationship between increased opportunities to respond to academic requests and the academic and behavioral outcomes of students with EBD: A review. *Remedial and Special Education, 22*(2), 113–121. doi:10.1177/074193250102200205

UDL-IRN. (2011). *Critical elements of UDL in instruction* (Version 1.2). Lawrence, KS: Author. Retrieved from https://udl-irn.org/wp-content/uploads/2018/01/Critical-Elements.pdf

Wehby J. H., & Kern, L. (2014). Intensive behavior intervention: What is it, what is its evidence base, and why do we need to implement now? *TEACHING Exceptional Children, 46*, 38–44.

# SECTION V

*What Really Works Beyond the Classroom*

# 15

# *UDL and Administrators*

*Leading the Charge*

Amy Kramer
*Bowling Green State University*

## SETTING THE STAGE FOR UDL AND LEADERSHIP

If the title of this chapter caught your eye, you might be a leader. Are you a superintendent, principal, curriculum director, teacher, or professor? All of these titles clearly send the message that you are a leader. The decisions you make will certainly impact students in your district. If you are, however, the one at the "tippy-top," then you are charged with making decisions for the entire system. These decisions will inevitably impact everyone, from the school cooks to the teachers. Superintendents, principals, and directors are typically the change-agents who will lead their districts to greatness. Fullan (2010) recognizes how developing leadership skills is a precursor to tackling any challenge, organizational change, or accomplishing any collective goal. This most certainly applies to the school setting.

While what teachers do in the classroom holds the top spot for improving student achievement, school leadership is a close second (Leithwood, Harris, & Hopkins, 2006). Leaders have an immense responsibility to provide the type of leadership that will foster growth in a school setting. According to Day, Gu, and Sammons (2016), administrators can maximize their leadership potential by utilizing both *transformative* and *instructional* leadership skills. It is no longer enough to set a vision and think big. School administrators are called upon to serve as instructional leaders who can coach and model effective teaching skills.

There is no magic wand that will be a guaranteed win over the education system's standardized form of accountability. No matter how desperate we are to see our scores improve, there is no one program, instructional strategy, or method that works for all schools. Many schools fall prey to the "one-size-fits-all" promises that are provided in purchased curriculums. Lots of money is spent on such things, and when scores fall short of their expectations, everyone gets discouraged. Instead of spinning your wheels, focus your efforts on collaboratively using evidence-based practices, such as Universal Design for Learning, to identify strengths and opportunities within your district.

Evidence-based decision making accounts for more than just looking at the hard numbers (Novak & Rodriguez, 2016). Data are valuable, but insufficient on their own. Those individuals interpreting the data also need the critical context, historical implications, solid research backgrounds, and so on. Using all available evidence to make decisions on how to prioritize improvement efforts is more credible than looking at numbers alone. Universal Design for Learning (UDL) can be a catalyst for the type of improvements a district is seeking.

UDL is a framework for designing an educational environment that is accessible for all students (CAST, 2018). While most UDL literature focuses on how teachers can prepare their classroom and lessons, leaders should also consider the benefits it offers for system-wide improvements.

*Source:* Reprinted with permission from the Center for Mental Health in Schools at UCLA (2018)

When a school district wants to gain momentum toward systemic UDL implementation, using the principles as a guide can be a powerful tool. UDL can not only be modeled by leadership, it can also help educators connect and apply UDL to their everyday teaching. Before leadership can take a step toward fostering and encouraging UDL, a strategic plan must be carefully thought through (Novak & Rodriguez, 2016). This plan involves building awareness of UDL, the development of a vision and mission that closely aligns with the values of the community, development of teacher knowledge, implementation of UDL, continual support for staff, and ongoing communication.

## PUTTING UDL AND LEADERSHIP INTO PRACTICE: REPRESENTATION

UDL is a framework that can help provide a high level of support for all students. This type of framework is especially helpful for inclusive classrooms that seek to include all types and levels of learners. Leadership teams need to be well aware of what UDL is and the impact it can have on student learning, and then determine a systemic rollout plan. After the leadership team has invested time in their own understanding of UDL to make sure they are truly on board and know the potential impact on them, the district, and the personnel, the next step is to build awareness in the district for what UDL is and how to utilize the principles as a framework for developing lessons.

In part, building awareness means assessing district readiness for such an initiative. Keep in mind that just because a few teachers tell you, "That will never work here," doesn't necessarily mean you shouldn't move forward with an initiative on schoolwide propulsion of UDL. It simply means you might need to strategically think through how you are going to provide support. There will always be resistant participants. This is a timeless truth when it comes to educational change. It is more important for teachers to have sufficient opportunity to develop their knowledge and practice than it is for them to have ownership (or buy-in) on an idea (Nolan, 2007). Teachers have to understand what this change will personally mean to them. While the change-agents have had ample time to digest what this means and to strategize, teachers oftentimes have not been afforded this same opportunity.

There are many ways leaders can spread the word about UDL. Consider how having a wide range of options and methods for teaching educators about UDL, sharing information about UDL, and fielding questions about UDL will help to provide multiple means of representation as you work to bring UDL to your district. UDL might be new to some teachers, and others may have a more mature understanding. Within any given teaching staff, it will be important to vary how the teachers receive information on UDL and to give choice as they explore and learn the "what" of UDL. Below are suggestions for building awareness and knowledge around UDL.

- **EDUCATE THE LEADERS ON UDL.** Your first step is to prepare avenues for getting your leadership teams up to snuff on what UDL is and the benefits it can have for the students. This can be accomplished by offering onsite professional development, a retreat, and maybe even a group book study. Remember to model using UDL by not requiring a "one-size-fits-all" approach to your leadership team.
- **THINK BIG BUT START SMALL.** Too many people downplay the initiative to help teachers feel like they are already doing the things outlined in UDL; they want teachers to believe it won't impact their daily lives too much. First of all, why would someone believe in an initiative that is so similar to what they are already doing (Nolan, 2007)? What is the point of the initiative, then? Be honest and clear about what UDL will require from teachers. Second, UDL is a big deal, and we want it to be. That said, we do not want to scare anyone away. Think big, and don't be afraid to communicate the big vision. However, you should always start small. Keep the big vision for what UDL can be alive!
- **USE A SURVEY to examine staff attitudes on inclusive education.** Gather information on how comfortable teachers are with giving students voice and choice, with providing options, and with recognizing and valuing different learner profiles.
- **START WITH A SMALL GROUP of teachers and administrators.** Provide some professional development and have follow-up conversations about the feasibility for schoolwide implementation. Let these teachers help lead the way in the school.
- **FORM A UDL TASK FORCE to keep a pulse on staff attitudes, climate, and culture.** Collect data regularly and in a variety of ways to make sure all educators are represented.
- **ASSESS AVAILABLE RESOURCES.** Start with what you have!
- **SHARE TIDBITS OF INFORMATION ON UDL that are two to three sentences long.** Send them to staff once a week. Keep them short, sweet, useful, and to the point.
- **START MODELING UDL STRATEGIES IN YOUR STAFF MEETINGS so teachers can begin to see what they look like.** Be transparent about why you are using these strategies. Make a connection to how they might use the strategies in their classrooms with students.

- **TALK TO TEACHERS!** Never underestimate the power of a one-to-one conversation with a teacher. Connect with them and make sure they are heard. Be a better listener than talker. Use a variety of ways to ensure all your faculty have had a chance to share their opinions, to include surveys, small-group discussions, e-mails, interviews, and informal chats.

**STRATEGY SPOT**
FLIPPING THE CLASSROOM

Flipping the classroom was a concept made popular by Bergmann and Sams (2012). In a very simplified nutshell, these teachers recommended providing basic direct instruction to students via videos, webquests, and other online vehicles, and then doing the application aspect of the content with them in class. They suggested that the introduction of the content could be done without the instructor present, but that the application and "messy work" needed the teacher to ensure appropriate facilitation and learning.

So now consider doing this with the representation of UDL in your school! Why not introduce various readings, videos, and exemplars to teachers and ask them to come to a department or staff meeting having already read/watched the material? That would allow staff meeting time to be spent on discussions, arguments, debates, and application questions. This also allows teachers to select the methods by which they would prefer the material to be represented to them (e.g., video, book study, blog, journal article).

## PUTTING UDL AND LEADERSHIP INTO PRACTICE: ENGAGEMENT

When was the last time you looked at your district's vision and mission statements? Do you often bring them up at meetings, use them as a tool for decision making, or connect them with the work you are currently doing? Doubtful. But why not? Discussions around vision and mission statements can be deadly boring . . . or a way to engage faculty and staff at a truly deep and meaningful level. It's all in how you do it. And that is where UDL comes in!

## CASE IN POINT

In the 1990s, Howard Schultz, then CEO of Starbucks, was looking to grow and develop the Starbucks brand. One of the most critical things he and his team did was develop their mission statement. It was very important to them when developing their mission statement to (a) develop a strong sense of purpose and (b) listen to all levels of the organization (Linetsky, 2017). According to Schultz, this was a huge first step for them. This was followed by ongoing strategic planning and communication, all while keeping their mission statement a priority in everything they did. The mission statement they came up with was: "To inspire and nurture the human spirit—one person, one cup and one neighborhood at a time" (Starbucks Corporation, 2018). The company's efforts to put employees and customers first paid off . . . literally. The multimillion-dollar company continues to grow and open more and more franchises (Schultz & Yang, 1997).

Read the "Case in Point" about Starbucks. Impressive, isn't it? What, then, is the moral of the anecdote for educators? It is that we need to take a hard look at our vision and mission statements, and continue to revise as needed until our end result speaks to what we value as a district. Vision and mission statements can be powerful tools for decision making—though they are more often used as meaningless words on letterhead or websites. This is especially important when considering a UDL movement in your district. When the decision is made that UDL will be the framework that promotes success for all students, then a commitment needs to be made to develop a vision and mission that govern this philosophical understanding. Leaders have a powerful platform to engage stakeholders with the "why" of UDL.

Take a look—do your district's vision and mission statements already align to the principles set forth in UDL? If so, great. Your next step is to work as a team to outline all of the initiatives and strategies you are currently utilizing (Partee & Sammon, 2001) and rank them from most to least important. Discuss which of them already align with the UDL principles. From there you can start to connect several strategies to UDL and talk about next steps for further implementation. It is important to talk about how the vision for UDL implementation reflects your current vision and mission.

If your current vision and mission statements do not align with UDL principles, start there. Do not be disappointed. This is an opportunity to make real change—and that's what leaders do well! Want to get your leadership team and stakeholders *engaged* around UDL? Novak and Rodriguez

(2016) have several suggestions for reviewing your district's vision and mission statements:

- **EDUCATE, EDUCATE, EDUCATE.** Begin to educate stakeholders on what UDL is and how it can be a framework for conducting business within the district. Start small and don't assume even the most veteran of educators knows what you are talking about. Remember to model UDL by having various ways in which you share information with your stakeholders!

- **DEVELOP A REVIEW COMMITTEE that consists of all stakeholders** (teachers, parents, community members, and even students). Be sure to ask yourself, "Who needs to be at the table?" Remind yourself that this group will learn differently and represent the neurodiversity of the school.

- **CONSIDER THE HISTORY OF THE DISTRICT while envisioning a future.** It is difficult to move forward without knowing where you've been. Also, you may have "nay-sayers" who say, "We've already done that." Be prepared to show them how this is different through examples, strategies, videos, testimonies, and personal vignettes.

- **FIND OR DEVELOP A SURVEY that asks for input on the current vision and mission statements.** Share it liberally. Make sure you ask if the current vision and mission statements are all-encompassing and multidimensional, and whether they are shared, clear, rigorous, and meet the needs of *all* students in your district. Be sure to share the survey in multiple formats to remove barriers and increase accessibility.

- **ASK STAKEHOLDERS FOR FEEDBACK on any revisions before adopting.** Buy-in may not be mandatory, but it certainly helps! Remember that a key component of UDL is multiple means of engagement, so give a variety of ways for stakeholders to engage with the mission and vision statements. Do you have them on a website, e-mailed out, written in a flowchart, described in a video, and depicted in a visual representation?

- **RECEIVE FEEDBACK IN A VARIETY OF WAYS.** Have you asked for only written feedback, or have you also set up some focus groups, interviews, Twitter responses, and voice memo options? To communicate any new vision, consider all of the stakeholders and be sure you have multiple means of communication (audio, e-mail, television, print, social media, etc.).

- **DEVELOP A PLAN FOR ONGOING COMMUNICATION and connection to the new vision and mission.** In what manner will each of your stakeholders respond best? How do you know their preferred methods of communication? Rather than just posting a plan on a website only a few individuals might visit, consider all the other ways you can ensure communication and connection. "Coffee with the principal" meetings in the morning, reminders to give feedback through an app, Facebook videos, letters going home through students, TV or radio spots, and robo–phone calls are all ways to encourage engagement by a variety of stakeholders.


## PUTTING UDL AND LEADERSHIP INTO PRACTICE: ACTION AND EXPRESSION

Ongoing support for staff is critical. It is easy to convey a message to staff about a "great initiative" that will help all students learn. It is not as easy to keep the message going strong. Staff professional development will also need to offer choices for multiple means of engagement, representation, and expression (Novak & Rodriguez, 2016). We need to model what we are expecting of our faculty and staff!

UDL itself is an initiative within the district that needs strategic planning; however, *any* district initiative can embed the principles of UDL when it is rolled out. Regardless of whether your district initiatives are about UDL, positive behavioral supports to reduce negative student discipline, nonfiction comprehension, co-teaching, or vertically aligning curriculum, UDL can be used as a framework for strategic planning for any of these initiatives. Not only does UDL help reduce the barriers for learning for students, it also has the same impact on adult learning.

If the goal is for teachers to learn about UDL and then apply those principles to their own classrooms, multiple means of action and expression require that teachers have the ability to show their learning in a variety of ways. It has been well documented that regular teacher professional development does not always lead to changed behaviors and increased student outcomes. Why not? Potential barriers to teacher learning include difficult policies, lack of communication, lack of learning supports or resources, personal situations, lack of confidence, lack of time, lack of buy-in, and so on (Jarvis & Holford, 2007).

Understanding and removing possible barriers is important to a UDL initiative. Learning has fundamental components. Discovery learning, imitating, and trial and error are all important parts of adult learning (Jarvis, 2009). When committees are planning professional development, it is important to build in these opportunities for staff. Recognizing that teachers learn—and need to show that learning—in different ways is in complete alignment with the UDL principles.

Novak and Rodriguez (2016) outlined several strategies that can be used when developing a plan for professional learning. Table 15.1 showcases some of these examples. Keep in mind that many strategies that work well for engaging educators around UDL are also ones that can be used to help teachers demonstrate their learning through various actions and expressions.

**Table 15.1**   UDL-Infused Professional Development Strategies

| | |
|---|---|
| **Assess Needs** | Using evidence-based information, decide what the district needs are. This can be accomplished through a survey, schoolwide diagnostic assessment, standardized data, focus group discussions, etc. |
| **Professional Development Committee** | Form a professional development committee that consists of representatives from each area of the school. Make sure you have administrators, teachers, parents, community stakeholders, and even students (when applicable) on your committee. There might be others, depending on your unique situation. |
| **Professional Development Calendar** | When developing a new initiative, transparency is best. Teachers will be more willing to participate and engage if they see the vision. Developing a calendar of how and when the learning will take place will help with teacher understanding of the importance of the initiative. |
| **Multiple Offerings** | Make sure professional development on UDL is offered multiple times. Do not make this a "one and done" professional development. Have an initial launch to communicate the vision and mission and the benefits of UDL. After this point, break it up based on the UDL framework. |
| **Options for Representation** | Provide workshops, podcasts, articles/books to read, videos to watch, etc. Think of this as a "menu" of options teachers can choose from based on how they learn best. Giving teachers choice in their learning is key. See the "Tech Tip" on page 250 for an example of a menu of options. |
| **Options for Engagement** | Provide ample ways in which the importance of UDL is highlighted, minimize any barriers, and provide avenues for teachers to self-monitor (collaborate with others, video record their lessons for reflection, observe colleagues, etc.). |
| **Options for Action and Expression** | Provide teachers with a chance to implement their learning in the manner with which they feel comfortable starting. Give them choice on how they implement what they learned from the professional development, the goals they set, and the manner in how they receive feedback (verbal, written, etc.). |
| **Time** | One of the most important things an administrator can do is provide time for teachers to plan. Expecting teachers to embark on an important initiative (such as UDL) without providing the time to do so demonstrates a lack of commitment on an administrator's part. It has been noted through research that lower-performing schools provide less collaborative planning than higher-performing schools (Hixson, Stohr, & Hammer, 2013). It is an important reminder that staff development time is essential if we expect progress. |

**Tech Tip**

Ask educational consulting companies if they do more than just face-to-face professional development. Offer a menu of professional learning options, such as this one offered by 2 TEACH (https://2teachllc.com/resources).

## Leadership Tips for Ongoing Communication

"Studies show that more than two-thirds of change initiatives fail" (Roberto & Levesque, 2005, para. 3). Every district leader would like to see a change initiative move from "developing" to "institutionalized." Becoming a UDL district where leaders and teachers alike plan with the UDL framework is an ambitious, but attainable, goal. Fullan (2010) has several tips on how to build a community of learners where initiatives don't fade but become a part of a school's everyday way of doing business.

- **BE TRANSPARENT.** Teachers need to know how they are doing individually and as a team. Provide data and evidence for growth and areas to focus on and use various methods of sharing and discussing the data (Murawski & Lochner, 2018). Transparency will cultivate respect and earn trust. When using UDL principles, leaders should provide feedback through a variety of sources and in a variety of ways.
- **RESPECT TEACHERS AT ALL LEVELS OF UDL IMPLEMENTATION.** Remember that it is a journey, not a destination. UDL allows access to content at multiple points; do the same for teachers. Some will need longer than others to adopt and accept these concepts; that is fine.
- **HAVE PASSION.** UDL is a framework for giving all students the ability to learn by breaking down barriers. The notion that *all* students can learn through UDL implementation is an exciting endeavor. Continually show this passion to teachers!
- **COMMUNICATE, COMMUNICATE, COMMUNICATE.** Have constant, two-way communication with staff; stay close to the action; and offer different ways to seek feedback on implementation. Accept and consider even the most negative of information. Every bit of feedback is important communication.
- **RECOGNIZE AND VALUE PROGRESS.** Staff recognition is another important part of this process. Teachers need to be validated for the work they are doing. Vary the different ways in which you recognize teachers for their work on the UDL initiative. Customizing your approach in recognizing staff actions is important. While some teachers thrive on public recognition, others do not. Consider developing various ways

**Tech Tip**

Transparency is important when building trust and implementing change in your district. Consider livestreaming your staff meetings for any stakeholders who can't attend in person.

for staff to recognize each other. The possibilities are endless. To keep momentum on a UDL initiative, teachers need to see and hear about the progress they are making.

To keep communication alive, map out how often and in what manner you will share information with staff on UDL implementation. What will it look like? How often will it take place? In what manner(s) will it happen? Offer multiple means of engagement through online medium, audio recordings, and staff meetings. Change up your approach to communication—sometimes delivering straightforward content and sometimes being a bit more creative with your delivery.

Strategic plans may conjure up boring meetings and nonstop circular logic and discussions. Don't let this happen to you. Use strategic planning around UDL as an opportunity to represent, engage, and demonstrate learning in a variety of ways. When a strategic plan is developed and communicated with all stakeholders, there is more likelihood it will be followed. As many leaders know, whatever is calendarized will be prioritized! So put UDL on your calendar, create some strategic planning time, ask for feedback on mission and vision statements, and open the doors for real change.

## BRINGING IT ALL TOGETHER

Leaders can no longer afford to sit on the sidelines and hope the message of UDL sinks in. They need to be active participants in the process. By deeply immersing themselves in the process, they are utilizing transformational and instructional leadership to improve student learning. Leading with (or for) UDL requires both. The principles within the UDL framework need to be modeled for teachers. Otherwise, the concepts may seem abstract or unattainable.

To successfully guide teachers through a UDL initiative, leaders need to understand that this will be a personal journey for everyone. Each teacher will learn differently and in different ways. It will be important to offer choices and options for them to engage with UDL and decide how to implement the framework in their classrooms. The role of a leader in the UDL process is to be supportive, caring, knowledgeable, and understanding. UDL will be a wonderful, worthwhile journey filled with many great successes along the way. Take time to celebrate the journey!

## TOP FIVE WEBSITES TO SUPPORT UDL AND ADMINISTRATORS

→ www.animoto.com

→ www.dropbox.com

→ www.flipgrid.com

→ www.slideshare.net

→ www.voicethread.com

## APPS WE LOVE

→ Asana

→ Evernote

→ Forest

→ Nearpod

→ Notability

# REFERENCES

Bergmann, J., & Sams, A. (2012). *Flip your classroom: Reach every student in every class every day*. Alexandria, VA: International Society for Technology in Education.

CAST. (2018). *About Universal Design for Learning*. Retrieved from http://www .cast.org/our-work/about-udl.html#.W4L6LpNKjow

Day, C., Gu, Q., & Sammons, P. (2016). The impact of leadership on student outcomes: How successful school leaders use transformational and instructional strategies to make a difference. *Educational Administration Quarterly*, 52(2), 221–258.

Fullan, M. (2010). The awesome power of the principal. *Principal*, 89(4), 10–12, 14–15.

Hixson, N., Stohr, A. D., & Hammer, P. C. (2013). *Instructional planning time: A review of existing research and educator practice during the 2012–2013 school year*. East Charleston, WV: West Virginia Department of Education. Retrieved from https://wvde.us/wp-content/. . ./ExecutiveSummary_InstructionPlanning-Time2013.pdf

Jarvis, P. (2009). Developments in learning theory. *International Journal of Continuing Education and Lifelong Learning*, 2(1), 1–14.

Jarvis, P., & Holford, J. (2007). Adult learning: It is never too late to learn. *International Journal of Lifelong Education*, 26(2), 117–118.

JPAssociates. (2013). *Leadership: Instructional, transformational or both?* Retrieved from http://www.jponline.com/jp-blog/leadership-instructional-transformational-or-both

Leithwood, K., Harris, A., & Hopkins, D. (2006). *Seven strong claims about successful school leadership*. Retrieved from http://dera.ioe.ac.uk/6967/1/download%3 Fid%3D17387%26filename%3Dseven-claims-about-successful-school-leader-ship.pdf

Linetsky, B. (2017, November 29). *Starbucks' Howard Schultz on the importance of a business mission*. Retrieved from http://barrylinetsky.com/blog/schultz-importance-of-a-business-mission/

Murawski, W. W., & Lochner, W. W. (2018). *Beyond co-teaching basics: A data-driven, no-fail model for continuous improvement*. Alexandria, VA: Association for Supervision and Curriculum Development.

Nolan, J. F. (2007). Five basic principles to facilitate *change in schools. Catalyst for Change*, 35(1), 3–8.

Novak, K., & Rodriguez, K. (2016). *Universally Designed Leadership: Applying UDL to systems and schools*. Wakefield, MA: CAST Professional Publishing.

Partee, G. L., & Sammon, G. (2001). A strategic approach to staff development. *Principal Leadership: High School Edition*, 1(6), 14–17.

Roberto, M. A., & Levesque, L. C. (2005). The art of making change initiatives stick. *MIT Sloan Management Review*, 46(4). Retrieved from https://sloanreview.mit .edu/article/the-art-of-making-change-initiatives-stick/

Schultz, H., & Yang, D. J. (1997). *Pour your heart into it: How Starbucks built a company one cup at a time*. New York, NY: Hyperion.

Starbucks Corporation. (2018). *Starbucks mission statement*. Retrieved from https://www.starbucks.com/about-us/company-information/mission-statement

University of California, Los Angeles. (2004). Educational reform strategies [cartoon]. In *Systemic change for school improvement: Designing, implementing, and sustaining prototypes and going to scale*. Retrieved from http://smhp.psych.ucla.edu/pdfdocs/systemic/systemicreport.pdf

# 16

# UDL and Home School Collaboration

## Partnering for Empowerment

Tesha Fritzgerald

*East Cleveland City School District*

## SETTING THE STAGE FOR UDL AND HOME TO SCHOOL COLLABORATION

Learning about what really works in UDL sparks images of classrooms and students who are embarking upon memorable journeys, but why stop there? When envisioning the ideal implementation of UDL, you may think about reaching all students, trying various methods of delivery, giving students choice, and meeting students' needs. Now, imagine extending the reach of UDL. Imagine extending the choices and strategies beyond the teacher's desk, then just past the students' learning environment. What if the reach of UDL went beyond the busy hallways, into the administrators' offices, and kept going past the cafeteria and out of the doors of every learning institution? What if UDL followed learners home? What would that look like?

Home to school collaboration can be a daunting, multifaceted topic. The power of actualizing and solidifying a partnership of UDL that spans the distance from school to home and back again creates powerful learning experiences that yield results that can lengthen those connective paths wider than what we can imagine. Home to school collaboration through a UDL lens is the purposeful partnership between parents/family members and school personnel for the transformation of every setting into a flexible, powerful learning environment for all. Traditionally, school settings have looked at family involvement as a way to simply engage families with activities that support a student's learning process (Drake, 2000; Khanh & Rush, 2016). "Engaging" families for some meant just having parents show up.

While presence is a part of engagement, it is definitely not the ultimate goal when it comes to measuring the impact of this approach on academic achievement. Using UDL as a strategy to connect schools and homes shifts the conversation from simply involvement as engagement to shared strategic empowerment.

*Empowerment* (n.d.) is defined as "authority or power given to someone to do something." With UDL, schools empower homes by handing over tools, resources, and choices to build unique educational connections—not just asking families to complete prescribed activities. Homes empower schools by entrusting that the time their children spend in our care will help move them closer to their academic and life goals. Strategic empowerment means that we share information, resources, plans, dreams, and insights to reach a common goal for a child we have collaborated to shape together.

This image of a never-ending cord that follows the students through every location brings about the connectivity that is most powerful. It is already well documented that home to school collaboration manifests positive gains not only in student achievement, but also in the areas of increasing attendance, improving behavior, earning higher grades and test scores, and evidencing a command of social skills (Garcia & Thornton, 2015). Simply put, when family is engaged in the educational process, the results are positive.

If home to school collaboration is such a powerful factor, why aren't more parents and families involved? This question has been posed many times . . . what keeps school to home collaboration from blossoming?

Some overarching common barriers to home to school collaboration include:

- **Time**—Teachers have numerous responsibilities, including designing academic lessons and assessments, classroom management, addressing the behavioral and social/emotional needs of students, administrative duties, providing feedback to students, and participating in additional school extracurricular activities. Parental/family involvement is one more responsibility that educators may struggle to fit into an already busy schedule. Families are equally busy and may also find it difficult to make time for involvement (Caplan, 2000).
- **Beliefs**—"Teachers believe that parents can't help their children because they have limited educational backgrounds" (Barriers to Parent Involvement, n.d.). The beliefs and attitudes of both families and staff can become barriers or enhancers (Mapp & Kuttner, 2013). Also, there are some teachers who may perceive that parents

do not respect them and who may encourage their children to disrespect them as well (Metropolitan St. Louis, 2004). Similarly, some families may feel disrespected and devalued by teachers.

- **Communication Styles**—The communication styles of parents and families can be disconnected from the culture and language of schools (Caplan, 2000; Murawski, Carter, Sileo, & Prater, 2012). Communication can make or break a collaboration.
- **Lack of Resources**—Child care and transportation issues can limit the availability of—and the amount of time families have to spend with—schools and family/parents (Caplan, 2000).
- **Relational Issues**—Negative experiences early on can mar the relationship between parents and teachers. Feelings of unfamiliarity, inadequacy, suspicion, and anger are barriers to parents and families partnering with schools (Baker, 2000; Caplan, 2000; Jones, 2001).

UDL confronts barriers by designing strategies to empower schools and families to use the barriers as springboards to increase academic achievement for all students. Overcoming the barriers to learning encourages teachers and leaders to consider the variability of learners. The way that each person learns changes based on "biology, family context, cultural background, history with schooling, socioeconomic status, moment to moment internal and external changes, and the context with the learning" (Meyer, Rose, & Gordon, 2014, p. 100). Just as students are learners, so too are we, as parents and as educators.

Because home to school collaboration yields such powerful results, every student deserves a learning environment that locks arms with the home support system, regardless of impending barriers. Transforming home to school collaboration with UDL means both teaching parents about the UDL guidelines and creating environments for them to experience the power of it for themselves. UDL strategically empowers home to school collaboration through representation, engagement, and expression.

## PUTTING UDL AND HOME TO SCHOOL COLLABORATION INTO PRACTICE: REPRESENTATION

Providing families multiple means of representation can help mitigate the barriers of communication style and relational issues. Providing options for comprehension for each communication item that is sent home with the student may bridge the communication gap and allow for communication between school and home to flow freely. Let's take a look at how to provide multiple means of representation in common tools used frequently to communicate with families.

Class newsletters are often used to update parents and families on upcoming units of study, classroom events, and generally important

**Tech Tip**

www.mailchimp.com empowers parents to choose the language of the communications sent to them. See how it works in this YouTube video: https://youtu.be/N7me2T-DIVw

information. If print is a barrier for parents, consider giving options on how the newsletter is consumed. Perhaps there is a printed version available, but the same information can also be captured in video format or in a voice message that can also be accessed. Keep in mind while crafting these communicative features that educational jargon is a barrier to home and family communication. Try to stay away from terms that only educators would understand. It is important to note that families must be able to

choose which options work best for them. In differentiated instruction, the teacher makes the choice on what option is the best fit for the families, and that is the option they receive. For example, the teacher might translate the newsletter into Spanish for one family, not realizing there are other families who might benefit from it. In UDL, all options are presented and the families get to make the choice. Make the same options available for permission slips, sign-up campaigns, fund-raising overviews, and/or general announcements.

In order for home and school to solidify a fruitful partnership, content-specific supports must be available for parents and families as well. Providing options for language, mathematical expressions, and symbols gives families the flexibility to provide support for their child. Parents don't have to just learn "the teacher way" of doing the work—they can see a variety of ways and select the one that works the best with them and their child! Providing options for different ways to interact with material is optimal to overcome communication barriers with families.

Consider the fact that even the media used to communicate will either bridge the gap or widen the chasm. If all a school ever does is send written notices home, a large group of families may be disenfranchised. The same holds true if the only notifications are done through a group text, e-mail, or phone call. The more variety there is in the representation of information, the more families can access the information and, in turn, collaborate with the school.

Customizing the display of information can help too. Customization may look like sharing a product that a student created to capture the main concepts of the lesson. A family member will be much more likely to want to see what is happening in the classroom if they are able to see their own child's work. Families also appreciate the value of other voices in the learning community, those who are not always the teachers or adults. If a picture is posted on the teacher's website, perhaps the student who is featured could explain the activity and the learning goals in his or her own words. Creative teachers can share poems, raps, comics, YouTube videos, songs, and other techniques that illustrate and highlight the important content on which families can focus. Consider how much more engaged a parent will be with his or her child if visuals of everyday items or mnemonics are sent home to help make connections—rather than boring old worksheets or notes from a lecture!

Use of multiple means of representation provides choices for parents and families to understand and experience communication and content in a way that works best for them. When they see that the teacher has offered these options rather than just one mandated method, the barriers of communication and relationship begin to diminish and collaboration can flourish (Baker, 2000; Caplan, 2000; Jones, 2001). Looking for concrete examples that demonstrate how multiple means of representation can improve home to school collaboration? Try these:

- **MIX IT UP.** Write a blurb about what's happening in your school or class. Translate it immediately into the top three languages at the school—either through Google Translate, a colleague, or an app. Read what you've written into your phone while videotaping

## CASE IN POINT

Mr. Anderson decided to use a specific writing strategy with students. In an effort to provide support to students in class and at home, he had his students write a song featuring the key components of the writing strategy. The song was recorded and students filmed a music video to use at home. The music video featured both audio and visual support, with the lyrics appearing on the screen. Any time students had a writing assignment they were working on for school, parents had a quick reference that featured the expectations for writing for their child at their disposal. The video explained key vocabulary, and gave plain examples to clarify the goals of the final product. Utilizing multiple media like audio, video, music, and print gives more students and families access to the information needed to meet the learning goal. Because the students created the lyrics and helped decide what would be featured in the video, they were excited to share it in the video. The production of the video featured teachers, leaders, parents, and prominent community members working together. Who doesn't want to capture their principal rapping in a video? Parents who were not able to attend the videotaping were still able to see the final product. Mr. Anderson was able to provide parents with a ready resource they could use to support their child, bolster their own writing skills, or share with other family members, which would only increase the use of the writing strategy overall.

yourself. Upload your video to YouTube and get it captioned. Make all versions available via e-mail, a QR code, a phone call, putting it on your website, and/or a group text.

- **SPONSOR Q&A SESSIONS.** However, instead of just offering "Coffee With the Principal" once a month at the same time in the morning, offer those as well as "Chai in the Afternoon" and "Virtual Chats Online" at varying times. This will let parents and families ask questions at different times of day and in different forums. Have interpreters available and consider even having a "Suggestion Box" online or a "Q&A Box" in the main office.

# PUTTING UDL AND HOME TO SCHOOL COLLABORATION INTO PRACTICE: ENGAGEMENT

## Overcoming Barriers Related to Lack of Resources

Engaging parents happens in the affective networks of the brain. The CAST guidelines remind us that this is where parents and families, just like their student learners, "get engaged and stay motivated . . . they are challenged, excited or interested" (Meyer et al., 2014, p. 90). If schools want families to collaborate (really collaborate—not just in name only), they need to be clear as to what the purpose of the collaboration is! When parents feel there is a real purpose and it is a shared purpose, they will find a path into collaboration with their child's school that works for them. It is not a path that can be forced, but through strategic empowerment, a path can be forged as a team. Using UDL to provide options for self-regulation, options for sustaining effort and persistence, and options for recruiting interest should result in increased interest by families in partnering with schools, as well as increasing the motivation to stay connected.

Plan surveys to ask what is needed, wanted, and expected by parents and families. Also, find out the areas in which family members are skilled—in both content knowledge and supportive information—that will enhance the entire school community. Giving parents, families, students, and teachers the opportunity to nominate other parents or colleagues to present or guest lecture at schools may help cultivate family-to-family connections, as well as optimize motivation. When offering different types of programming, consider streaming the material live and sharing the name of the families who suggested the topic. It is a small gesture, but it sends a message to the families and parents that suggestions are valued, taken seriously, and used. This provides a link back to engaging parents in a purposeful way.

Providing options for recruiting interest is key to empowering parents and families to connect with schools. Uncovering strategies that put

**CASE IN POINT**

Each year, the Family Engagement Policy is reviewed in New Star School District. For years, a meeting would be scheduled from 6:00 p.m. to 8:00 p.m. on the last Thursday of April in the cafeteria of the district's largest high school. Though the district served about 12,000 students, only about fourteen to twenty parents would show up. In an effort to try a different tactic, the parent engagement specialist decided that this year the policy review would take place via several methods. She hosted meetings at each school that ran about fifteen to twenty minutes in length. She coordinated them close to dismissal time so parents would only have to make one trip to participate. She also sent a link in an e-mail to every parent and family contact in the district database. She offered a print copy to any family who requested one, and every secretary in the district offered to read and record answers for families who needed that service. The engagement policy was reviewed, but suggestions for programming were also welcomed. A local restaurant offered a free ice cream cone to every family member who completed a survey. The results were compiled and shared with all stakeholders. The names of all participants were placed on a graphic design that was posted prominently on the district website. Each school received its own graphic to display both on the website and in its buildings. The programming for the following year was based on the feedback from the parents and families. There were choices to attend in person, programming was made available online, computers were set up for families to research, and various changes were made to the time and delivery models districtwide. In the first year of implementation, approximately 35 percent of the families participated. The second year, close to 50 percent of parents completed the survey.

parents in the driver's seat when it comes to content is important. Too often, teachers try to "do it all" without validating the real expertise that families might be able to provide. Find out where parents feel confident and invite that expertise into your classroom.

One way to do this is by reframing homework. Reframing is a practice that asks participants to take a practice that causes stress or strain and retell the story to themselves in a way that changes the meaning, the belief, and lastly, the behavior. Comaford (2018) explains: "We form our own reality based on visual, auditory, and kinesthetic cues. These cues recall our beliefs about the world and ourselves (our identity), which results in either feeling good or feeling bad." How would you imagine most parents feel about the word *homework*? What feelings do the word conjure up about your own experience in school? Reframing is defined as,

**STRATEGY SPOT**
REFRAME HOMEWORK

**Five Ideas to Reframe Homework:**

1. Recycle objects.
2. Design a comic strip.
3. Draw with sidewalk chalk.
4. Scout animals like a scientist.
5. Play improvisational games. (Hudgel, 2017)

"A way of viewing and experiencing events, ideas, concepts, and emotions to find more useful alternatives" (Comaford, 2018, para.3). If homework from your schooling experience still leaves a nasty taste in your mouth, as it does for many, then it is time to reframe homework to serve as a bridge builder, not a bridge buster. What does that look like? Transform homework into work that can only be done with the people *at home*.

To reframe homework, begin by reconsidering what is asked of students. In the past, homework was typically practice work that replicated or mirrored classwork. Instead, replace that work with options that will build community, increase connection to the material, and optimize relevance, value, and authenticity. Interestingly, those things are exactly what the UDL Guidelines for Engagement outline!

Homework for many usually means lugging multiple books home, trying to carve out an interruption-free location (which often does not exist), struggling for too long on one's own, and only asking for help to avoid bedtime. Needless to say, homework does not strike up happy memories. Is it possible to have homework be meaningful, and—dare we even imagine—fun? Instead of projects and assignments that increase stress, what if students were empowered with discussion questions they could ask parents, siblings, grandparents, or neighbors? What if options were provided to students and parents for how to send or record their replies? Students could write the answer, or use their cell phones to record the interactions, or they could make audio recordings, or fill in graphic organizers with pictures. Perhaps they could use Tic-Tac-Toe boards to choose from various options to diversify their interactions each week. Here are a few ways to reframe homework:

- **HOME ENGAGEMENT WITH ENGLISH** (e.g., pre-reading homework for *Romeo and Juliet*): Ask five adults—at least one must be in your household—the following questions: Do you believe in love at first sight? Why or why not?

- **HOME ENGAGEMENT WITH MATH** (e.g., introducing right angles): Send each student home with a cutout of a right angle. Ask them to choose one room in their home or apartment. How many right angles can they find? How do they know if it is a right angle?
- **HOME ENGAGEMENT WITH SCIENCE** (e.g., at the start of a chemistry unit on molecules): What kind of laundry detergent is used in your home? Has anyone at your home used a different one? Why did they make the switch?
- **HOME ENGAGEMENT WITH SOCIAL STUDIES** (e.g., with early geography): What landmarks would people be able to use to get to your home?

Are parents and families able to participate in these conversation starters? Yes. Do they have to have an in-depth content knowledge to do so? No. If games and discussion questions help families to make meaning of content, then it is likely to empower them to ask questions, utilize resources, and find a personal connection to the content and perhaps to the school. Reframing homework means recreating the work that goes home from individual practice to family communication.

## PUTTING UDL AND HOME TO SCHOOL COLLABORATION INTO PRACTICE: EXPRESSION

Multiple means of expression will give schools and families a way to connect with goal setting, communication, and physical action. Connecting with parents and families to set goals is encouraged by research. The act of setting a goal results in that goal getting more effort, focus, and persistence (Kinicki & Kreitner, 2009). The benefit of applying goal theory research to home to school collaboration is to increase desired outcome performance in individuals, teams, and organizations (Bipp & Kleingeld, 2011; DuBrin, 2004). Educators and families are supposed to be a team and, in order to center the work, they must share a common goal. What are some ways to set a common goal to establish the direction of all action this team takes? Use the multiple means of expression to take A.C.T.I.O.N. offered on Table 16.1. on page 266.

Following the ACTION steps will

- **INCREASE POSITIVE INTERACTIONS.** Research has been clear that positive interactions between home and school must be plentiful in order for there to be trust on a team (Mapp & Kuttner, 2013).
- **MITIGATE THE LACK OF RESOURCES.** When families and educators decide together which tools and supports are feasible and accessible, both tend to agree with the outcomes. Creative use of resources is also more likely when families and schools collaborate.

- **ADDRESS BARRIERS, SUCH AS TIME AND DIFFER-ING BELIEFS.** Rather than one side dominating and dictating, using the ACTION steps enables both educators and families to jointly determine goals, as well as how they will be achieved. This results in conversations about belief systems, how time will be used, who will do what, and other logistical decisions. School and home will collaborate using UDL methods to guide appropriate goal setting, support planning and strategy development, and enhance capacity for monitoring progress.

## CASE IN POINT

One small change of plans helped Dietrich, an intelligent fifth grader who was having a tough time with his course work. At a meeting to try to identify and break down barriers, two solutions emerged:

1. Dietrich wanted to be an entrepreneur.
2. School would be better if he could approach his studies as a business owner approaches profit.

Dietrich, his teachers, and parents came up with a "business plan." His goals included choices on how to consume content and express learning. He would receive a productivity report, just like a business owner, that shared how many points were available for "profit" versus how many points were available. He would pose questions to the team and the team would also pose questions to him to ensure that progress toward the desired outcome was actualizing. An incentive that fueled his motivation was the opportunity to pitch an entrepreneurial idea to the youth Shark Tank, if he ended the quarter with enough profit to meet his goal.

Parents opted to check the progress software biweekly and communicate with the teacher via that software. They watched the weekly newsletter bulletin and posed questions to both Dietrich and the teacher to participate in his learning and shape his Shark Tank pitch as much as possible. Finding creative ways to use a team approach to connect helped to shape Dietrich's experience and foster a strong strategic partnership between home and school.

Instead of parents asking the ubiquitous question, "What did you learn today?" educators can support students' action and expression by sending a daily text, e-mail, or voice message with content-specific questions that family members could ask their child. A bonus support feature would also be to include a link with a short video, picture, or audio clip of some of the answers. Ask family members to reply to the prompt, "Did your child explain that answer correctly?" This will serve as an informal assessment that reveals whether or not the child understands the concept or if he or she needs more practice. The link empowers the family member to follow-up at home and to communicate with the teacher. This super strategy solidifies ongoing two-way communication and collaboration between school and home.

## BRINGING IT ALL TOGETHER

Families are diverse, as are their experiences with the educational system. Some trust teachers, while others do not; some want to work alongside their children's teachers, while others believe it is the teachers' job to educate. With multiple means of representation, engagement, and expression, parents and other family members will be able to interact at their level of readiness. Providing options eliminates a forced—and possibly fake—collaboration, and instead provides various entries for collaboration in ways that parents and families choose for themselves. Being offered various ways to get information from—and give information to—schools, as well as a variety of ways to participate in the students' learning activities, are all concrete examples of how UDL can make the home to school collaboration more successful. Experiencing UDL in their own interactions will help families see the value of Universal Design for Learning in their child's educational training. The more options and ways to collaborate, the more likely it is that meaningful collaboration will actually occur. The ultimate beneficiaries of this collaboration are the students themselves.

Table 16.1   Taking ACTION to Set Goals Between Educators and Families

| ACTION Step | Explanation |
|---|---|
| A **Ask** parents and families what their goals are for their children. | Make sure to provide various methods for expression. Parents may want to share their goals in a hashtag (e.g., #teamgraduation), or there may be a family picture, a story, or a song. Whatever method they would like to use to communicate their dream or goal for their child, use it. Share your goal only in response to theirs. Connect the school to home circle by synthesizing the two goals into one mutual one. Make sure to hear input from the child, no matter how young or how old. |
| C **Communicate** progress toward the goal from the home and from the school. | Decide the method of communication that will eliminate the most barriers and be most effective for all parties. Use a variety, if possible. Consider using an app like Classroom Dojo or build communication into parent/teacher conferences. Plan to check-in at events the parent will attend or talk via video conference apps. |
| T **Tips** for success generated by the team will promote sharing and foster relational collaboration. | If a strategy is highly successful at home, encourage family members to share it with the school. If a strategy is successful at school, teachers should share it with home. This conversation will be "win" based instead of problem based. |
| I **Initiate** change as a team if there is no progress. | The team will think ahead for ways to make changes for the success of the student. The school, family, or the student can initiate the conversation for change. This initiation should be open, clear, and nonthreatening. |
| O **Organize** supports, plans, incentives, and strategies to energize the path toward the goal. | Celebrate short-term wins together, rather than waiting for the long-term ones. Utilize visual, written, and verbal supports for the plan. Identify strategies that both parties feel will aid the organization. |
| N **Needs** assessments keep the conversation going. | Plan in advance to conduct regular needs assessments. Needs assessments at the end of the agreed-upon time will help to clarify next steps toward the goal, celebrate progress, and record improvements. All of this information will help both parents and teachers to execute additional actions strategically in the future. |

## TOP FIVE WEBSITES TO SUPPORT UDL AND HOME TO SCHOOL COLLABORATION

→ https://www.ed.gov/parent-and-family-engagement
→ https://www.playworks.org/resource/34-conversation-starters-for-your-family/
→ http://www.projectappleseed.org/
→ https://www.pta.org/
→ https://www.youtube.com/watch?v=af5A1F2AGN8

## APPS WE LOVE

→ Bloomz
→ Classdojo
→ Flyer
→ Remind
→ Seesaw

## RECOMMENDED READINGS

34 conversation starters for your family. (2012). Retrieved from https://www.playworks.org/resource/34-conversation-starters-for-your-family

CAST. (2010). *UDL at a glance*. Retrieved from https://youtu.be/bDvKnY0g6e4

CAST. (2018). *Let them thrive webinar with author Katie Novak*. Retrieved from https://www.youtube.com/watch?v=af5A1F2AGN8

Fritzgerald, T. (n.d.). *UDL and urban education: An expressway to success*. Wakefield, MA: CAST Professional Publishing. [Work forthcoming]

Katz, J. (n.d.). *UDL for parents*. Retrieved from http://www.threeblockmodel.com/udl-for-parents.html

Novak, K. (2017). *Let them thrive: A playbook for helping your child succeed in school and in life*. Wakefield, MA: CAST Professional Publishing.

# REFERENCES

Baker, A. J. L. (2000). Making the promise of parent involvement a reality. *The High School Magazine, 7*(5), 14–17.

Barriers to Parent Involvement | Project Appleseed. (n.d.). Retrieved from http://www.projectappleseed.org/barriers

Bipp, T., & Kleingeld, A. (2011). Goal-setting in practice: The effects of personality and perceptions of the goal-setting process on job satisfaction and goal commitment. *Personnel Review, 40*(3), 306–323. doi:10.1108/00483481111118630

Caplan, J. G. (2000). Building strong family–school partnerships to support high student achievement. *The Informed Educator Series*. Arlington, VA: Educational Research Service.

Comaford, C. (2018). *Reframing: Change the story, change the result*. Retrieved from https://www.thriveglobal.com/stories/26695-reframing-change-the-story-change-the-result

Drake, D. D. (2000). *Parents and families as partners in the education process: Collaboration for the success of students in public schools* [Electronic version]. *ERS Spectrum, 18*(2), 34–39.

DuBrin, A. J. (2004). *Applying psychology: Individual and organizational effectiveness* (6th ed.). Upper Saddle River, NJ: Pearson Education.

Empowerment. (n.d.). In *Dictionary.com*. Retrieved from https://www.dictionary.com/browse/empowerment?s=t

Garcia, L. E., & Thornton, O. (2015). *The enduring importance of parental involvement*. Retrieved from http://neatoday.org/2014/11/18/the-enduring-importance-of-parental-involvement-2/

Hudgel, M. (2017). *10 after-school activities and games for kids*. Retrieved from https://www.care.com/c/stories/3176/10-after-school-activities-and-games-for-kids/

Jones, R. (2001). How parents can support learning. *American School Board Journal, 188*(9), 18–22.

Khanh, B., & Rush, R. A. (2016). Parental involvement in middle school predicting college attendance for first-generation students. *Education, 136*(4), 473–489.

Kinicki, A., & Kreitner, R. (2009). *Organizational behavior: Key concepts, skills and best practices* (4th ed.). Boston, MA: McGraw-Hill.

Mapp, K. L., & Kuttner, P. J. (2013). *Partners in education: A dual capacity building framework for family–school partnerships*. Retrieved from https://www2.ed.gov/documents/family-community/partners-education.pdf

Metropolitan St. Louis. (2004). *Increasing parental involvement*. Retrieved from http://www.mstl.org

Meyer, A., Rose, D. H., & Gordon, D. T. (2014). *Universal Design for Learning: Theory and practice*. Wakefield, MA: CAST Professional Publishing.

Murawski, W. W., Carter, N., Sileo, N., & Prater, M. A. (2012). Communicating and collaborating with families (pp. 59–90). In N. M. Sileo and M. A. Prater (Eds.), *Working with families of children with special needs: Family and professional partnerships and roles*. New York, NY: Pearson.

# 17

## UDL and Policy

### Considering Legal Implications

Jacqueline Rodriguez

*American Association of Colleges for Teacher Education*

## SETTING THE STAGE FOR UDL AND POLICY

Why is Universal Design for Learning (UDL) represented in education policy? To create expert learners who are purposeful and motivated. Preparing expert learners begins with the preparation of their teachers. In a "Foundations of Education" course, or other similarly related course, professors often introduce the concept of evidence-based practices. To the layperson, this concept may be referred to simply as "good teaching"; however, the field of education places an infinite value on what we constitute "good teaching" by identifying practices that are scientifically validated to produce positive outcomes. While our field staunchly defends the scientific process to develop evidence-based practices, the principles of peer review, and the replication of research for generalization and operationalization, policy makers can become enamored by trendy ideas and stylish programs that have little, if any, basis in research. It's simply not enough to review an interesting program by evaluating what search results are offered by Google!

The initial confidence in the principles of UDL originated, in part, with a conviction that broadening educational access to a swath of students who struggled in traditional learning environments was, of course, a splendid concept to champion. The last two-plus decades worth of research, however, have broadened the scientific foundation of UDL with research in promising practices and application of UDL principles in U.S. preK–12 schools (Cooper-Martin & Wolanin, 2014), international baccalaureate schools (Rao, Currie-Ruben, & Logli, 2016), institutes of higher education (Parker, 2012), and international school systems (British Columbia Ministry of Education, 2015). While more research is required to increase the fidelity of implementation, we can identify UDL not as a trendy program, but as a means to level the playing field for all students, including students with disabilities, for whom many of the policy campaigns were launched. When your principal, superintendent, school board, or group of parents asks "why" you are a proponent of UDL in schools, you will have a plethora of research and policy to back you up. This is not a fly-by-night initiative or here-today-gone-tomorrow trend.

To date, many components of our local, state, and federal education policies acknowledge and encourage the use of universal design principles and the framework of Universal Design for Learning. These concepts, with historical foundations that span decades (Hehir, 2009), are now distributed across some of our nation's most influential educational legislation. In addition to specifically addressing the use of UDL within our legislation, other federally mandated practices such as Multi-Tiered Systems of Support (MTSS) and School Wide Positive Behavioral Interventions and Supports (PBIS) can be addressed

**Making Connections**

See Chapter 7 for more on UDL with PBIS.

through the UDL framework (Basham, Israel, Graden, Poth, & Winston, 2010; Edyburn, 2010). They fit together and support one another; they are not "yet another stand-alone initiative" that many teachers fear. Each of these approaches is universally designed to include all students where they are with an individual path forward toward an identified outcome. In noting these intersections, we recognize the value policy makers, researchers, and practitioners place on the principles of the UDL framework. With the support of national and international networks, including the UDL National Task Force, the UDL principles are also promoted and included within our global education community.

This chapter uses the UDL framework as a guide to answer the questions: (a) *Why* have researchers and practitioners advocated for the application of UDL in federal, state, and local education policy?, (b) *What* do you need to know about UDL's inclusion in policy and the associated legal implications?, (c) *How* have we seen the practical and legal

applications of UDL take hold?, and (d) *What* strategies can you implement in your own schools and districts to increase the understanding
and use of UDL?

## PUTTING UDL AND POLICY INTO PRACTICE: REPRESENTATION

### The Argument for UDL in PreK–12 Classrooms

Free and appropriate public education (FAPE) is the right of every
child and a legal obligation of every preK–12 public school in our nation
(IDEIA, 2004; Rehabilitation Act, 1973). Through the successful implementation of UDL, all students are given access and opportunity to learning,
ensuring all students are on the path to receiving FAPE. A fantastic meta-
phor for the application of UDL in preserving FAPE for every student can
be found in Rose and Gravel's 2009 article paralleling UDL with a GPS
(global positioning system). A GPS is designed to help an individual get to
a location on time. In the same manner that a GPS differentiates directions
based on an individual's current location and any roadblocks that may lie
ahead, the principles of UDL take into account a student's current level of
performance, the potential challenges that gaps in prior knowledge or a
disability may create, or a language barrier may impose, and then offers
the best route to navigate the student to get from one place to the next, on
time. Given every student's unique set of experiences, the UDL framework
is an affirmation of their background and the distinctive path they may
take as they navigate the curriculum.

Some preK–12 teachers, however, question the idea of adding student
choice and voice, not to mention multiple means of expressing learning
and competency attainment in their classrooms. They worry that students
will not be able to have these "luxuries" in college or in "the real world."
Nothing could be further from the truth!

### CASE IN POINT

The 2001 passage of No Child Left Behind (NCLB) and the 2004 reauthorization of IDEA held states accountable for the learning gains of students
traditionally left out of annual yearly progress due to small sample sizes
or the significance of their disability. In many ways, UDL offers a seamless
response to higher standards for student learning. By designing multiple
pathways to access, engage, and assess student learning, UDL lays the
foundation for schools to adhere to the increased accountability.

At the postsecondary level and even in the job market, accessibility discussions are often rooted in addressing supports for students with identified disabilities per Section 504 of the Rehabilitation Act (1973) and the reauthorization of the Americans with Disabilities Act (ADA, 2008). In a nutshell, universities and employers also must legally provide accessible learning materials and environments to individuals with disabilities as needed. But shouldn't learning be accessible to everyone, regardless of an identified disability? The UDL framework provides the mechanism for constructing accessible learning materials rather than retrofitting learning materials to make them accessible to learners (Nepo, 2017). That means that universally designed classes are merely proactively setting students up for success, rather than waiting for a law or legal piece of paper to mandate specific adaptations.

Even though Section 504 and ADA legally support necessary accommodations, "the real world" supports UDL. Think about it . . . if you are bad at spelling, don't you use your computer for spellcheck—even though your show-off sister can spell everything perfectly without the spellcheck? When you are calculating tax, do you grab your phone for the calculator app? Do you read a hardcover book while some of the folks in your book club listen to the book on Audible? Our world offers options; classrooms can *and should* do the same.

The more that stakeholders know about UDL success stories like the Maryland Learning Links, and resources like British Columbia's UDL Resource Center, the more we can start changing mindsets and building skills toward a more universally designed, equitable, and inclusive educational system. You can represent your advocacy to colleagues, administrators, policy makers, parents, students, and beyond:

- **CHALLENGE STUDENTS to identify various ways that UDL is apparent in various jobs, careers, and hobbies.** Encourage older students to share these options with their parents and peers.
- **SHARE ON SOCIAL MEDIA positive stories that promote UDL in various classroom settings.** Invite schools and educators to "like" your posts.
- **INVITE MEDIA OR POLICY MAKERS to come visit a universally designed classroom.** Be explicit about what they are seeing and what makes the lesson UDL.

## PUTTING UDL AND POLICY INTO PRACTICE: ENGAGEMENT

### Early Advocacy Successes

Remember CAST (the Center for Applied Special Technology) that Katie Novak discussed in this book's Introduction? CAST is the clear

## CASE IN POINT

In 2001, David Rose, co-founder of CAST, testified before the Senate Appropriations Subcommittee on Labor, Health and Human Services, Education, and Related Agencies (Rose, 2009). His testimony addressed how digital technology could bridge the learning divide for students who required assistive technology. Additionally, he testified to the value of digital technology in all learning environments. While addressing concerns related to copyright, Dr. Rose influenced congressional leaders as they considered the great need for accessible learning materials for students with print disabilities. Within three years, the National Instructional Materials Accessibility Standard (NIMAS) was developed and then mandated in IDEA (National Center on Accessing the General Curriculum, 2004).

leader in the UDL movement. How did CAST encourage schools, districts, state departments of education, curriculum providers, and other stakeholders to take the time necessary to reconstruct the way in which we teach, assess, and engage our students? They began by orienting our congressional leaders.

During congressional testimony, UDL misconceptions were addressed, learning supports were detailed, and examples of UDL in practice were introduced by practitioners demonstrating how advocacy can work.

CAST also galvanized a critical mass of organizations with strong voices and large memberships to advocate together on behalf of UDL. The National Universal Design for Learning Task Force, which includes more than forty national and international organizations, encourages policy makers to include UDL in education-related activities and policies. Professional

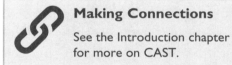

**Making Connections**

See the Introduction chapter for more on CAST.

organizations such as the Universal Design for Learning Implementation and Research Network (UDL-IRN) offer additional communities of practice that encourage UDL research, practice, and implementation in schools, higher education, and global education networks.

Here are two strategies in which you or your school can engage to continue to advocate for UDL policy and implementation:

- **INVITE PARENTS TO A COMMUNITY FORUM to discuss how UDL is being implemented within the school in a holistic manner.** Make sure to provide examples from administrative practices to classroom practices, as well as practices supporting social-emotional well-being. Try to offer parents the option of participating in the meeting via webinar or video record to allow them access at a later date and time.

- • WRITE AN OP-ED TO YOUR LOCAL NEWSPAPER highlighting the positive outcomes of students when they are engaged in classroom practices that embed the principles of UDL. Remember to emphasize the contributions that strong UDL professional development has on the teaching practices of the faculty in your school. Finally, commend your teachers for their investment in the learning gains of their students!

### Where Is UDL Represented in Federal Policy?

As noted by Gordon, Gravel, and Shifter (2009), UDL is best represented in federal-level policy. Table 17.1 provides highlights of policies that refer to Universal Design, Universal Design Principles, and Universal Design for Learning at the federal level. Feel free to share this information with school administrators, other educators, parents, and community leaders who are unfamiliar with UDL and its place in federal legislation.

**Table 17.1**   Policies That Relate to UDL

| Year | Policy | Description |
| --- | --- | --- |
| 1998 | Assistive Technology Act of 1998. Pub. L. 105-394 | States, "the use of universal design principles reduces the need for many specific kinds of assistive technology devices and assistive technology services by building in accommodations for individuals with disabilities before rather than after production" (PL 105-394, 1998). |
| 2004 | Assistive Technology Act of 2004. Pub. L.108-364 | Was amended and included a definition for UDL: "a concept or philosophy for designing and delivering products and services that are usable by people with the widest possible range of functional capabilities, which include products and services that are directly accessible (without requiring assistive technologies) and products and services that are interoperable with assistive technologies" (PL 108-364).tgh |

| 2004 | National Instructional Materials Accessibility Standard (NIMAS) | The National File Format Technical Panel, which consisted of members from the U.S. Department of Education, the CAST/National Center on Accessing the General Curriculum (NCAC), consumer/advocacy groups, and feasibility groups developed technical specifications for NIMAS, emphasizing standardization of a digital file format to create multiple versions of a text to be accessible by a variety of students. |
|------|------|------|
| 2004 | Individuals with Disabilities Education Act (IDEA) of 2004. Pub. L. 94-142 | This reauthorization requires state and districtwide tests to adhere to universal design principles to the extent possible. It also encourages the use of accessible technology to increase access and participation of more students in the general education environment. It also allows states to use professional development funds to focus on implementing UDL with fidelity. NIMAS was included within Part B of IDEA, moving the standard from voluntary to mandated for all states. |
| 2006 | Final regulations of NIMAS in IDEA | States, "Adopt the National Instructional Materials Accessibility Standard (NIMAS), published as appendix C to part 300, for the purposes of providing instructional materials to blind persons or other persons with print disabilities, in a timely manner after publication of the NIMAS in the *Federal Register* on July 19, 2006 (71 FR 41084)" (§ 300.172). |
| 2008 | Higher Education Opportunity Act (HEOA) of 2008, Pub. L. 110-315 | Provides the first definition for UDL in federal legislation. Targeted recipients of Title II, Part A and B funds, requiring them to teach the principles of UDL and UD, describe the activities that integrate and use technology effectively and how they are consistent with the |

*(Continued)*

**Table 17.1**    (Continued)

| Year | Policy | Description |
|------|--------|-------------|
| | | principles of UDL, assess students' understanding of the principles, and report on these activities annually. Part B also requires that teacher preparation programs "assess the effectiveness of . . . institutions of higher education in preparing teacher candidates for successful implementation of . . . environments consistent with the principles of UDL that enable K–12 students to develop learning skills to succeed in higher education and to enter the workforce." (PL 110-315 Section 231). HEOA established an advisory commission on accessible instructional learning materials in postsecondary education for students with disabilities, as well as a technical assistance center to support the professional development of faculty at institutions of higher education. Finally, HEOA requires that any grant recipient use a portion of their funds to conduct awareness, outreach, and training for faculty, staff, and students. |
| 2015 | Every Student Succeeds Act (ESSA) of 2015, Pub. L. 114-95 | Addressed UDL in four separate sections. ESSA requires that state plans include challenging assessments in the content areas of reading or language arts, mathematics, and science, as well as any other content areas the states chooses, and "(xiii) be developed, to the extent practicable, using the principles of UDL." States must also describe how they have included UDL in alternative assessments. States may apply to use an "Innovative Assessment System" as their state accountability measure. In their state plans, applicants must identify how they have met various criteria including "(vi) be accessible to all students, such as by incorporating the principles of UDL." States are |

| | | |
|---|---|---|
| | | required to "revise, develop, or update their comprehensive literacy instruction plans" to include, among other items, the principles of UDL. Finally, ESSA provides technical assistance to states to support the "use of technology, consistent with the principles of UDL, to support the learning needs of all students, including children with disabilities and English learners." |
| 2010, 2016, and 2017 | National Education Technology Plans (NETP) | Includes references to UDL. In particular, the 2017 plan includes the recommendation that, "Education stakeholders should develop a born accessible standard of learning resource design to help educators select and evaluate learning resources for accessibility and equity of learning experience." To be born accessible is to be accessible from inception. For example, a piece of technology, a teaching practice, an intervention has to be developed, crafted, and disseminated in an accessible manner from its inception; ergo, born accessible. The plan encourages the use of UD and UDL principles in crafting born accessible technologies (U.S. Department of Education, 2017). |

## PUTTING UDL AND POLICY INTO PRACTICE: EXPRESSION

In preK–12 schools, the adoption of the UDL framework has grown exponentially since 2010. One reason for this initial growth was schools' allocation of the American Recovery and Reinvestment Act of 2009 (ARRA) funds toward the adoption of UDL. In 2010, the Common Core State Standards (CCSS) officially included UDL in the "application to students with disabilities" section. (It is critically important to note, however, that UDL is for all students and should not be remanded to a supplementary section for a subgroup of students who are struggling or have an identified disability!) Additionally, the National Education Technology Plan of 2010 included UDL for the first time, specifically addressing special populations considered underserved and "digitally excluded," including low-income and minority students, English language learners, learners with disabilities, early childhood, adult workforce, and seniors (U.S. Department of Education, 2010).

UDL v. DI

UDL's focus on Action and Expression helps educators understand there should be multiple means of determining if a student has truly mastered the material. When applying Action and Expression to UDL and Policy, we must look to ways that schools, districts, or state departments have demonstrated their understanding of UDL. The concept of UDL is not just one of policy and rhetoric to be admired or regurgitated; for UDL to be successful, it must be implemented, and then its implementation must be assessed.

Some schools and districts have successfully implemented UDL in their preK–12 schools and found various ways to assess and then disseminate their successes. These assessments include surveys, interviews, observations, focus groups, empirical research studies, and case studies. Dissemination has occurred through journal articles, dissertations, school board reports, conference presentations, informal discussions, and other means of expression. It is these successful efforts that have encouraged stakeholders to fund, train, and provide ongoing professional development for practitioners in the field, have encouraged policy makers to continue to write UDL into federal and state policy, and have encouraged school administrators to embrace UDL initiatives.

## CASE IN POINT

Within Bartholomew Consolidated School Corporation (BCSC), a district with sixteen schools in Indiana, UDL is a way of life. Over the course of the last ten years, BCSC has embedded its teacher practices, its school procedures, and its district professional development in the UDL framework. But what's really exciting about BCSC is its outreach and collaboration with external audiences! BCSC's Dr. George Van Horn, the special education director, and Rhonda Laswell, the UDL coordinator, highlight the importance of aligning the UDL framework across all learning environments, beginning with a student's initial learning environment: the pre-school classroom. To that end, Rhonda reached out and provided professional development to before care and aftercare programs to ensure the district continued a student's instruction utilizing the UDL framework. Looking beyond a student's school experience, BCSC established a business advisory committee, which meets regularly to discuss gaps employers are noticing in their workforce. To develop this relationship, the BCSC director of secondary education identified UDL's characteristics of an expert learner as a means of addressing those gaps. BCSC is undoubtedly a hallmark UDL school system, so check out the resources it has developed to support UDL implementation in your school! http://www.bcsc.k12.in.us/UDL

Another concrete example of taking policy to practice is the work of the state of Maryland. Maryland's State Department of Education developed a task force to study the adoption of UDL (Maryland State Department of Education UDL Task Force, 2011) and "to develop a more comprehensive knowledge base and scalable framework for school-level implementation of UDL" (Cooper-Martin & Wolanin, 2014, p. 1). In evaluating the elementary school and middle school projects, the Office of Shared Accountability published four recommendations. Its recommendations encourage teachers to

1. Increase the use of choices and variety they provide to students;
2. Use stations or centers as choice routines so that students have more options and are more active during class;
3. Engage in formal lesson planning on how to increase student choice, as that has not been a traditional part of teacher education in the past; and
4. Increase collaboration with other teachers through greater access and shared materials.

Consider the variety of ways a school or district can use multiple means of action and expression to share UDL results and thereby influence policy. These may include

- **HAVING FOCUS GROUPS OF STAKEHOLDERS** and collecting data on their experiences with UDL.
- **PUBLISHING METRICS (e.g., GRADUATION RATES OR GPAs)** from before and after the implementation of a UDL policy.
- **ENCOURAGING MEDIA INTERVIEWS** with individual students and families regarding how a universally designed school or classroom impacted their lives.

## BRINGING IT ALL TOGETHER

Given the progress students have achieved through successful UDL implementation and the legal and policy support behind UDL, it is only surprising that more schools have not jumped on the UDL train. As our nation creates more inclusive schools, UDL will be the equalizer to help with equity, diversity, and meeting individual students' needs without having to segregate students or create separate lessons. Having more options in learning and assessing is not just a smart choice, it is the legal one. As more schools embrace UDL principles, the research base on UDL in classrooms will also increase. Currently, there is still a need to increase the professional development required for fidelity of implementation, as teachers seek to incorporate UDL principles in classrooms beyond the content areas of reading, mathematics, science, and the social sciences. The more we know, the more we can continue to advocate for real change in schools and in the policies that govern our schools.

## TOP FIVE WEBSITES TO SUPPORT YOUR UNDERSTANDING OF UDL POLICY

→ http://www.udlcenter.org/advocacy/referencestoUDL

→ http://www.udlcenter.org/advocacy/taskforce

→ https://udl-irn.org/network/

→ http://www.udlnet-project.eu/about-udlnet-project

→ http://udloncampus.cast.org/page/policy_legal#.WxbbdlMvxQI

## APPS WE LOVE

→ The Congressional Record

→ Countable

→ CQ (CQ Roll Call)

→ Roll Call News

→ SCOTUS Blog

# REFERENCES

American Recovery and Reinvestment Act of 2009 Pub. L. 111-5.

Americans with Disabilities Act of 2008. Pub. L. 110-325.

Basham, J. D., Israel, M., Graden, J., Poth, R., & Winston, M. (2010). A comprehensive approach to RTI: Embedding universal design for learning and technology. *Learning Disability Quarterly, 33,* 243–255.

British Columbia Ministry of Education. (2015). *Introduction to British Columbia's redesigned curriculum.* Retrieved from https://curriculum.gov.bc.ca/sites/curriculum.gov.bc.ca/files/pdf/curriculum_intro.pdf

Cooper-Martin, E., & Wolanin, N. (2014) *Evaluation of the Universal Design for Learning projects.* Report for the Office of Shared Accountability of Montgomery County Public Schools. Retrieved from http://montgomeryschoolsmd.org/departments/sharedaccountability/reports/2014/UDL%20report_Final.pdf

Edyburn, D. L. (2010). Would you recognize Universal Design for Learning if you saw it? Ten propositions for new directions for the second decade of UDL. *Learning Disability Quarterly, 33*(1), 33–41.

Gordon, D. T., Gravel, J. W., & Shifter, L. A. (Eds.). (2009). *A policy reader in Universal Design for Learning.* Cambridge, MA: Harvard Education Press.

Hehir, T. (2009). Policy foundations of Universal Design for Learning. In D. T. Gordon, J. W. Gravel, & L. A. Schifter (Eds.), *A policy reader in Universal Design for Learning* (pp. 35–45). Cambridge, MA: Harvard Education Press.

Maryland State Department of Education UDL Task Force. (2011). *A route for every learner: Recommendations from the task force to explore the incorporation of the principles of Universal Design for Learning into the education systems in Maryland.* Retrieved from http://www.udlcenter.org/sites/udlcenter.org/files/Route_for_Every_%20Learner_Report_NSG_%2032511.pdf

National Center on Accessing the General Curriculum. (2004). *National Instructional Materials Accessibility Standard Report—Version 1.0* (National File Format). Wakefield, MA: Author. Retrieved from http://aem.cast.org/about/publications/2004/ncac-nimas-report-national-file-format.html

Nepo, K. (2017). The use of technology to improve education. *Child and Youth Care Forum, 46*(2), 207–221. doi:10.1007/s10566-016-9386-6

Parker, H. B. (2012). Learning starts with design: Using Universal Design for Learning (UDL) in higher education course redesign. In S. Myran, A. H. Normore, F. S. Miller, & K. L. Sanzo (Eds.), *Transforming learning environments: Strategies to shape the next generation* (pp. 109–136). Bingley, England: Emerald.

Rao, K., Currie-Rubin, R., & Logli, C. (2016). *UDL and inclusive practices in IB schools worldwide.* Wakefield, MA: CAST Professional Learning. Retrieved from https://www.ibo.org/contentassets/318968269ae5441d8df5ae76542817a0/research-udl-full-report-en.pdf

Rehabilitation Act of 1973. Pub. L. 93-112.

Rose, D. H. (2009). Saving resources . . . and saving children. Testimony to the U.S. Senate Committee on Appropriations, Subcommittee on Labor, Health, Human Services, Education and Related Agencies, July 25, 2001. In D. T. Gordon, J. W. Gravel, & L. A. Schifter (Eds.), *A policy reader in Universal Design for Learning* (pp. 83–92). Cambridge, MA: Harvard Education Press.

Rose, D. H., & Gravel, J. W. (2009). Getting from here to there: UDL, global positioning systems, and lessons for improving education. In D. T. Gordon, J. W. Gravel, & L. A. Schifter (Eds.), *A policy reader in Universal Design for Learning* (pp. 5–18). Cambridge, MA: Harvard Education Press.

U.S. Department of Education, Office of Educational Technology. (2010). *Transforming American education: Learning powered by technology*. Washington, DC.

U.S. Department of Education, Office of Educational Technology. (2017). *Reimagining the role of technology in higher education*: *A supplement to the National Education Technology Plan*. Washington, DC.

# 18

# *UDL and Change*

## *Taking Baby Steps to Success*

Wendy W. Murawski
*California State University, Northridge*

Katie Novak
*Groton–Dunstable Regional School District*

## SETTING THE STAGE FOR UDL AND CHANGE

How can we pull all of these strategies together? Each of these chapters has described how embracing the concept of Universal Design for Learning (UDL) helps design learning experiences so all students, regardless of variability, can become knowledgeable, strategic, and motivated. Each chapter addressed the three core principles of UDL and related them to a specific area: to

**Tech Tip**

Want to learn more about student variability and how to design to the edges? Watch Todd Rose discuss "The Myth of Average" during his TEDx Talk: https://www.youtube.com/watch?v=4eBmyttcfU4

provide multiple means of representation (the "what" of learning), to provide multiple means of engagement (the "why" of learning), and to provide multiple means of action and expression (the "how" of learning; Novak, 2016). Using these three principles when working with all students helps to build a foundation for educators who are interested in creating classrooms or even schools that provide a "buffet" of teaching and learning options so all students can customize their learning experience.

We believe most readers will quickly embrace the concept and rationale behind UDL. They will appreciate and want to use the various strategies provided throughout this text. They will want to jump into designing UDL lessons . . . and then they might get a deer-in-the-headlights look as they worry about where to even begin! We decided to end this book with a chapter on just exactly that—how to pull all of this together in a way that is not overwhelming. We provide you with some templates and scaffolds for dipping a toe in the UDL waters so that you can be successful and want to continue to wade in until you are swimming in options, strategies, choice, and variability!

First, it's important to know that anything worth achieving will require a journey, and that journey is far more critical than the destination. Just think back to when you first learned to shoot a basketball, bake a pie, or play the guitar. You've come a long way from those first attempts, and a part of the reason why you're now an expert is because you took it step by step. LeBron James, Julia Child, and Jimi Hendrix weren't born experts. They became them through a long journey of trial and error and effort and persistence. Neither will you become a UDL expert overnight, and that is okay. Each day, you will make a choice, try something new, and reflect on the success with your students. Over time, this process of "choose-do-review" will help you to become an expert teacher who can meet the needs of all learners (Anderson, 2016).

Wondering where to start? Many educators begin by reviewing the UDL Guidelines. For example, when looking at providing students with multiple means of engagement, the first checkpoint reminds us to optimize individual choice and autonomy so students can choose their pathway. That's pretty wide open though! Where can we provide those choices? What are the first steps to take? What lesson planning template should we use? What types of choices should we consider? Glad you asked. . . .

**Key Concept**

The *UDL Guidelines* should be familiar to you by now, but we want to emphasize the need to keep them handy. Print off page 15 from the Introduction chapter and keep it in your lesson planner for daily motivation.

## STARTING YOUR UDL LESSON PLANNING

A Google search for UDL lesson planning templates, examples, and strategies results in a plethora of results—so many that it can be difficult to determine any real consistent guideline for ensuring a universally designed lesson planning process. In her book *UDL Now!*, Novak (2016) cautions that there is no one specific template for planning universally designed lessons; rather, she reminds readers that UDL is a philosophy that has guidelines.

These guidelines remind us to design lessons so that all students can reach the same goals (or objectives) while taking different pathways in *how* they learn (our instructional methods), *what* they use to learn (our instructional materials), and how they *express* what they know (our assessments). So, as an educator, you get to decide where to start! We recognize, however, that guidelines won't be sufficient for some of you; you will be seeking something a bit more concrete as a way to scaffold your entrée into the UDL world. So as long as we are all clear that there is no one "right way" to create a universally designed lesson or to assess student learning, we'll provide four basic steps you can use to begin your work.

1. **REWRITE YOUR OBJECTIVES.** Within the UDL framework, goals or objectives should be articulated in a way that acknowledges learner variability. Oftentimes, though, teachers create objectives that include embedded methods. For example, "All students will learn how to write arguments *by giving a persuasive speech about which new club belongs in our school.*" When you can step back and see that your real objective is for students to "write arguments," it is easy to provide numerous choices for students to achieve that goal that doesn't require all students to stand up in class and read a speech about a club.

   *Ask yourself this:* Is the standard actually requiring that students all do the exact same thing in the same way? (The answer should always be *no*!) In fact, in the example above, we would also question if students really have to "write" arguments or if they could be required instead to "craft" an argument. Already, you've opened up the possibilities just by rewriting the objective.

2. **REEXAMINE YOUR PROCEDURES.** The instructional decisions, approaches, procedures, or routines that expert teachers

use to accelerate or enhance learning are considered instructional methods. Oftentimes, however, all students are expected to follow the same procedures in how they learn or express their knowledge. They need to sit in the same places, write the headings on their papers in the same fashion, use a pencil, take the same types of notes, and so on.

*Ask yourself this:* Why? How important are these procedures for learning? Once you've established a structure to your class, could more choice be provided in simple procedures or instructional methods? Does it really matter where students are sitting as long as they are paying attention and learning?

3. **MIX UP YOUR MATERIALS.** Materials are usually seen as the media used to present learning content and what the learner uses to demonstrate knowledge. Unfortunately, yet again, the same materials are provided to all students. We call this "packet syndrome." CAST calls it "one-size-fits-all" teaching and learning. In UDL, educators provide students with multiple materials so they can personalize the resources, scaffolds, and materials they need to meet the goal.

*Ask yourself this:* Do you like to do the same things the same way as all your friends? Would you choose paper and pencil, the web, a comic book, a song, or a piece of art if you could spend your time on something? How difficult would it be to ask your students to bring in ideas for different materials or even the materials themselves so you can mix the process up a bit?

4. **ASK FOR EVIDENCE.** Assessments are an expression of student learning. When designing assessments, it's critical that teachers consider exactly what students need to know and do and then strip away any specific methods or materials that have been tied to the goal. We'd like to emphasize that last part—*strip away any specific methods or materials that have been tied to the goal.* Simply ask for evidence that the student met the learning objective . . . without requiring a specific way of doing so.

*Ask yourself this:* How will students provide evidence that they met the objective? Can they have a choice in doing so? How can you ensure your students are on the same page with you in terms of exactly what the objective is, so you can assess their mastery effectively?

**STRATEGY SPOT**

OPME

Take baby steps to UDL implementation by remembering your OPME (Objectives, Procedures, Materials, and Evidence). As you think through your next lesson, really challenge yourself to make sure your OPME have as much choice and variability as possible:

- **O**bjectives are broad.
- **P**rocedures are open.
- **M**aterials are varied.
- **E**vidence matches the objective.

## BABY STEPS USING THE UDL PROGRESSION MATRIX

Are you most comfortable providing students with options in the goals they set (multiple means of engagement)? In how they learn (multiple means of representation)? In what materials they choose to use? Or in how they express what they know (multiple means of action and expression)? Once you start, how will you begin to provide students with more autonomy so they can begin to know themselves as learners? Just as our students need to take personalized steps to create their own learning journey, so do we as practitioners.

One resource to self-assess your UDL practice and decide on your first steps is the UDL Progression Rubric (Novak & Rodriguez, 2018). For each UDL guideline and checkpoint, the authors identify teacher progress as Emerging, Proficient, and Progressing toward expert practice. Using this tool can help you to recognize your UDL strengths and where you're already progressing, as well as areas in which you can take your next baby steps.

For example, the first UDL checkpoint, which we referenced above, reminds us to optimize individual choice and autonomy. But what does that look like when we are taking our first steps? Table 18.1, an excerpt from the UDL Progression Rubric, shares a typical progression when teachers personalize education for students through UDL. Using the rubric as a first step provides educators with an opportunity to create their own universally designed journey to implement UDL with students.

You will note that in "emerging practice," teachers begin to provide students with small choices in the goals they set, the methods they use to learn, the materials they use, and/or the assessments they use to express knowledge. If you would like some examples of the types of options to consider, you may want to review Table 18.2, which outlines possible choices for each of the UDL Principles. Remember that UDL is not an all-or-nothing

Table 18.1    Excerpt From UDL Progression Rubric

| | Emerging | Proficient | Progressing Toward Expert Practice |
|---|---|---|---|
| Optimize individual choice and autonomy (7.1) | Offer choices in what students learn (e.g., "choose a country to study" rather than "study France"), how students learn (e.g., use books, videos, and/or teacher instruction to build understanding), and how they express what they know (e.g., "you can create poster or write a paragraph"). | Encourage students to choose from multiple options to determine what they learn (guided by standards), how they learn, and how they express what they know. Encourage students to suggest additional options if they can still meet the standard. | Empower students to make choices or suggest alternatives for what they will learn, how they will learn, and how they will express what they know in authentic ways. Free them to self-monitor and reflect on their choices with teacher facilitation and feedback but not explicit direction. |

*Source: UDL Progression Rubric,* by K. Novak and K. Rodriguez, 2018.

*Note:* Go to http://castpublishing.org/novak-rodriguez-udl-progression-rubric/ for access to the entire rubric.

framework; rather, it is one where educators begin to think about providing students with multiple pathways to reach standards. They may seem like a lot of work for you as an educator, but that doesn't have to be the case.

Consider all the technological tools that can provide options and choices for students. Newsela, for example, allows students to choose their own text, which increases engagement and accessibility. Additionally, there are a number of embedded web tools that allow students to use a built-in screen reader to provide an auditory option to comprehend text. VoiceOver is one such app, which is the built-in screen reader for iOS, while ChromeVox and Announcify are available on Chromebooks. Table 18.2 provides additional ways to begin to select options, in all areas of representation, engagement, and action and expression.

**Tech Tip**

Newsela (www.newsela.com) is a free Instructional Content Platform that provides updated content daily so students have personalized text choices that interest them, are culturally responsive, and are linguistically appropriate. Each article is written at multiple readability levels so all students can access rigorous content that is appropriately challenging so they can work toward meaningful content standards.

**Table 18.2**   Menu of UDL Teaching Options

| *A Universally Designed UDL Lesson Planning Checklist* |
| --- |
| UDL doesn't have to be overwhelming. Take baby steps to ensure you have multiple means of representation, engagement, and action and expression. Start small and keep adding options! |

*Clear lesson goal/objective:*

*Multiple Means of Representation:*

☐ Mini-lecture   ☐ PowerPoint   ☐ Visuals   ☐ Realia   ☐ Kinesthetic movement
☐ Humor   ☐ Art   ☐ Music   ☐ Video   ☐ Technology
☐ Reading   ☐ Writing   ☐ Numbers   ☐ KWL Chart   ☐ Individual/group work
☐ Web-Quest   ☐ Social media   ☐ Hands-on   ☐ Real world   ☐ Cultural examples

*Multiple Means of Engagement:*

☐ Parallel Teaching   ☐ Station Teaching   ☐ Alternative Teaching   ☐ Team Teaching
☐ Partner work   ☐ Individual work   ☐ Small-group work   ☐ Online work
☐ Choose your seat   ☐ Choose your topic   ☐ Choose your partner(s)   ☐ Choose your medium

☐ Read about it   ☐ Write about it   ☐ Talk about it   ☐ Draw about it
☐ Blog about it   ☐ Tweet about it   ☐ Think about it   ☐ Act about it
☐ App about it   ☐ Game about it   ☐ Problem-solve about it   ☐ Sing about it
☐ Connect personally   ☐ Connect culturally   ☐ Connect academically   ☐ Connect emotionally

*Multiple Means of Action/Expression:*

☐ Oral presentation   ☐ PowerPoint/Prezi   ☐ Visual presentation
☐ Artistic presentation
☐ Quiz/test   ☐ Ticket in the door   ☐ Ticket out the door
☐ Homework
☐ Design something   ☐ Discuss something   ☐ Present something
☐ Analyze something
☐ Compare something   ☐ Solve something   ☐ Write something
☐ Show something
☐ Choose your own self-assessment   ☐ Peer feedback   ☐ Expert feedback

*Reflection on this lesson:*

*Goal for making the next lesson even more UDL:*

## BABY STEPS TO UDL: USING THE WHAT/WHY/ HOW/WHO APPROACH

The UDL Progression Rubric isn't the only scaffold that will support you in the first steps of your UDL journey. Another possible starting point is to consider the What/Why/How/Who scaffold for designing lessons (Tables 18.3–18.5). Murawski (2012) shared the What/How/Who approach to lesson planning for co-teachers, and we found that by adding a "Why," all teachers could use this framework for designing UDL lessons. These scaffolds can be used when considering representation, engagement, and action and expression as you reflect on questions that will help you to take your first steps into UDL. Consider highlighting a single question, and let that be the focus of your practice for the week! Using the What/Why/ How/Who scaffold, when coupled with the UDL Progression Rubric and all the amazing examples in this text, will give you multiple materials to begin your UDL journey. What/Why/How/Who can be applied to all three principles of UDL, but in a nutshell, you are continuing to ask yourself the following questions:

- *WHAT* **IS THE OVERALL GOAL OR OBJECTIVE? What are you really trying to accomplish with students?** This will help you to identify the true purpose of the lesson. So often, teachers begin planning lessons by thinking about their content before considering the goal. For example, a teacher may decide to plan for a lesson on sea turtles in an elementary science class, but sea turtles are not the goal. The standard is that students understand that animals depend on their surroundings for survival. Once you identify the standard, you may realize that the lesson doesn't have to be about sea turtles. Instead, you could give students the option to choose any animal and examine through videos, articles, and books how the animal depends on its environment to survive. Using UDL, the *what* provides options for students even when the goal is the same.
- *WHY* **IS IT CRITICAL TO BE DONE IN A PARTICULAR WAY? Or is it?** We strongly recommend discussing why a particular standard is important to achieve with a colleague who has a different frame of reference from you (e.g., a special educator, a coach, a teacher who teaches the grade above yours). This will lead you to consider why the knowledge or skill is relevant or valuable to *all* students. Why is it valuable for students to learn about animal adaptation? This information needs to be shared with students so they understand that the lesson is relevant, authentic, and meaningful to them and

their future. If *you* are struggling to find the value, it's going to be a tough sell to an inclusive classroom full of students. When you universally design the "what," students will be more engaged in this process because they will be able to choose an animal that interests them and they will care more about the *why*. This will also help with student motivation and engagement.

- *HOW* **CAN YOU LET STUDENTS HAVE VOICE IN WHAT IS DONE AND CHOICE IN HOW TO MEET THE GOAL?** You already know *what* the standard is and *why* it is important, but *how* will you know if students have reached it? This is a great time to consider which assessment options you have available to ensure that students are meeting the standard. Teachers often design a single assessment. For example, using the lesson on how animals use their surroundings to survive, teachers may require all students to create a poster or write a paragraph. Instead, realize that students may have the option to share a report orally, make a poster, create a children's book, or write a short essay, as this will increase student engagement! In this example, any of the options would in fact allow students to meet the same standard. An assessment like this allows teachers really to vary the level of challenge so the assessment both challenges and meets the needs of all students.

- *WHO* **MAY STILL REQUIRE SPECIALLY DESIGNED INSTRUCTION TO BRIDGE SOME REMAINING GAPS?** We like to use the term *UDL-topia* to describe a classroom in which teachers consider every possible need that students have and proactively create options to eliminate barriers. The reality is that students need the support from teachers to learn how to become expert learners, and specific students sometimes need accommodations and modifications that simply are not available to, or appropriate for, their peers. During the planning process, it is important to review Individualized Education Programs (IEPs) and ensure that options are available to meet these needs. A student who is blind, for example, will need access to books in Braille about animals and their environment when other students will not. That being said, it's important to note that we ask you to consider the individual needs of students only *after* proactively designing a lesson for an entire inclusive classroom. UDL removes barriers and will greatly minimize the need for additional adaptations, accommodations, or specially designed instruction.

UDL
v. DI

Table 18.3    UDL Planning Template Using the What/Why/How/Who
                     Approach: **Representation**

| UDL Principle | Driving Question | UDL Alignment |
|---|---|---|
| Planning for Instruction and Multiple Means of **Representation** | **WHAT** do students need to know in order to achieve the standard and be successful on the assessment? | Once your goal is clear, decide *what* instructional methods you will utilize throughout the lesson. How can you represent the information in a variety of ways with which you are already comfortable (e.g., PowerPoint, lecture, visuals) and still include more options for helping students truly learn the material you are sharing so that everyone can achieve the objective? |
| | **WHY** are you selecting particular instructional approaches to teach this content and these skills? | When deciding on an instructional approach, it may be tempting to choose one randomly, but we ask you to consider the rationale for choosing each approach. As you're deciding on your instructional approaches, consider the goal of the lesson, the needs and interests of the students, and the different instructional experiences and resources to which students should have access. If you are co-teaching, be sure to consider different regrouping options that can help students learn the content! |
| | **HOW** will you challenge and support all students to foster individualized growth? | First, be proactive about creating an environment that maximizes choice. In order to optimize the power of UDL, teachers have to proactively create an environment that allows students to "choose their own adventure" to get exactly what they need by creating conditions for nurture (Anderson, 2016). You do not want to create an environment where students who struggle are embarrassed to choose a more accessible option, or where students only choose a particular resource so they can sit with their friends. |

| UDL Principle | Driving Question | UDL Alignment |
|---|---|---|
| | **WHO** will be accessing these additional supports or challenges/ enrichment? | During the planning process, it is important to review Individualized Education Programs (IEPs) and ensure that options are available to meet these needs. A student who is deaf, for example, may need access to a sign language interpreter while others do not. That being said, it's important to note that we ask you to consider the individual needs of students only *after* proactively designing a lesson for an entire inclusive classroom. |

**Table 18.4**    UDL Planning Template Using the What/Why/How/Who Approach: **Engagement**

| UDL Principle | Driving Question | UDL Alignment |
|---|---|---|
| Planning for Multiple Means of **Engagement** | **WHAT** is the goal or standard of the lesson? | Identify the standard(s) or goal(s) that you want all students to reach. Do this with your partner if you are co-teaching. Essential questions can help teachers realize that using UDL, the *what* provides options for students even when the goal is the same. For example, a goal might be to "demonstrate an understanding of persuasive writing" as opposed to "write a persuasive essay." A clear, open goal now allows for far more student engagement around meeting the objective! |
| | **WHY** do students need to achieve this standard? | Critically analyzing all objectives to determine why (or even *if!*) the knowledge or skill is relevant or valuable to *all* students will help educators focus on only the most salient of goals. If you feel too wedded to your own content, ask a colleague, co-teacher, administrator, parent, or even the students to weigh in on what is most important. Focusing on the most important components of a lesson allows for more time to engage with them. |
| | **HOW** will you provide scaffolds and supports so all students can maintain effort and persistence? | During this step, consider what materials you will need to provide students as they work toward the standard. What resources will help students maintain effort and persistence (e.g., books, videos, graphic organizers, scaffolds, exemplars)? Consider encouraging the use of apps, like Popplet, which allow students to create concept maps to provide visual support of concepts. Don't worry if you can't get all of the resources you identify—take baby steps! |
| | **WHO** may need additional support to access the lesson, and how can these supports be embedded into lesson design? | In the perfect UDL classroom, teachers consider every possible need that students have and proactively create options to eliminate barriers. In the real world, however, some students will still need additional supports. Specific students may need accommodations and modifications that simply are not available to, or appropriate for, their peers. Use IEPs and collaboration with colleagues and parents to determine how to meet those needs. |

**Table 18.5**   UDL Planning Template Using the What/Why/How/Who Approach: **Action and Expression**

| Planning for **Action and Expression** (Assessment) | **WHAT** formative assessments will you use to monitor their progress? | There are many different types of assessments that teachers may select based on the objective of the lesson and of the assessment. Using the UDL lens, select or design assessments with embedded options so all students can access the same assessment and personalize their learning experience. These assessments may include norm-referenced, criterion-referenced, individual-referenced, curriculum-based, performance-based self-assessments, and even alternative assessments. |
| --- | --- | --- |
| | **WHY** are the selected universally designed assessments considered authentic measures of student performance? | Most teachers are used to relying on a single assessment to complete a unit or lesson. Even those assessments that are "creative" in nature (e.g., write a song, draw a poster, create a PowerPoint) tend to be required of all students. Asking the same actions and expression from all students may actually work against them showing their mastery of content. A student may not be a strong artist, and therefore the poster option is not an authentic measure of his or her ability or knowledge. |
| | **HOW** will teachers reflect on student data and feedback and communicate student progress to one another so the team can make important instructional decisions? | Time is precious . . . and scarce! You probably do not have unlimited time to reflect upon and discuss every student's progress on every aspect of a lesson, and we respect that. However, teachers obviously are expected to know how students are doing in order to make any necessary changes to instruction and be more proactive about planning the next UDL lesson. You may need to share information with co-teachers, paraprofessionals, parents, a Professional Learning Community (PLC), other grade or subject-level teachers, or even a coach or administrator to support your own professional growth and provide you with more options and choices to design instruction in the next lesson. |

*(Continued)*

**Table 18.5** (Continued)

| | | |
|---|---|---|
| | **WHO** may need a unique adaptation to their assessment in order to address IEP goals and objectives or other unique needs? | It's important to reflect on the needs of students so you are ready to provide feedback and support them if they don't make choices that allow them to be successful. For example, if all students are asked to solve an equation, students may have the choice of using math reference sheets, manipulatives, calculators, scratch paper, small groups, partners, etc. . . . If students are working toward a written task, they may have the choice of writing on paper, using a device, accessing a graphic organizer, exemplar, rubric, etc. . . . But what if students need additional support or don't choose the supports they need? Be prepared to offer support to these students in the way of specially designed instruction, accommodations, modifications, and mini-lessons on self-monitoring or self-advocating. |

## BRINGING IT ALL TOGETHER

Creating universally designed lessons can help all students to become expert learners who are motivated to achieve goals, self-assess, and self-direct their learning. In UDL-topia, students have choices in what they are learning, how they are learning, what materials they use, and how they express what they know. Furthermore, these choices are both engaging and accessible. But early UDL implementation, at the emerging level, may be only focused on providing choices in one or more areas, and that's okay. We repeat—*it is absolutely acceptable to start small*. If you're not sure where to start, another option is to **ask your students**!

In UDL, student voice is optimized. Strong UDL practice starts with collaborating with students to ask them what they need to be successful. We truly believe that students know what they need to be successful and that everything they need to follow their passion and achieve their dreams is inside of them. We as educators have a tremendous opportunity to learn more about our teaching from our students if we are open to them. We need to ask the right questions and listen to our students' answers. Only then can we proactively design lessons that embrace the incredible variability of our students.

## TOP FIVE WEBSITES TO SUPPORT BABY STEPS TO UDL

→ http://castpublishing.org/novak-rodriguez-udl-progression-rubric/
→ www.dcmp.org
→ www.onlineeducation.net
→ www.udlcenter.org
→ www.visuwords.com

## APPS WE LOVE

→ Announcify
→ Blinkist
→ Bookly
→ ChromeVox
→ VoiceOver

## RECOMMENDED READINGS

Ralabate, P. K. (2016). *Your UDL lesson planner: The step-by-step guide for teaching all learners.* Baltimore, MD: Paul H. Brookes.

## REFERENCES

Anderson, M. (2016). *Learning to choose, choosing to learn: The key to student motivation and achievement.* Alexandria, VA: ASCD.

Murawski, W. W. (2012). 10 tips for using co-planning time more efficiently. *Teaching Exceptional Children, 44*(4), 8–15.

Novak, K. (2016). *UDL now! A teacher's guide to applying Universal Design for Learning in today's classrooms.* Wakefield, MA: CAST Professional Publications.

Novak, K., & Rodriguez, K. (2018). *UDL Progression Rubric.* Retrieved from http://castpublishing.org/novak-rodriguez-udl-progression-rubric/

# Index

CORWIN
A SAGE Publishing Company

**Helping educators make the greatest impact**

**CORWIN HAS ONE MISSION:** to enhance education through intentional professional learning.

We build long-term relationships with our authors, educators, clients, and associations who partner with us to develop and continuously improve the best evidence-based practices that establish and support lifelong learning.

# Solutions YOU WANT | Experts YOU TRUST | Results YOU NEED

EVENTS

> > > **INSTITUTES**

Corwin Institutes provide large regional events where educators collaborate with peers and learn from industry experts. Prepare to be recharged and motivated!

**corwin.com/institutes**

ON-SITE PD

> > > **ON-SITE PROFESSIONAL LEARNING**

Corwin on-site PD is delivered through high-energy keynotes, practical workshops, and custom coaching services designed to support knowledge development and implementation.

**corwin.com/pd**

> > > **PROFESSIONAL DEVELOPMENT RESOURCE CENTER**

The PD Resource Center provides school and district PD facilitators with the tools and resources needed to deliver effective PD.

**corwin.com/pdrc**

ONLINE

> > > **ADVANCE**

Designed for K–12 teachers, Advance offers a range of online learning options that can qualify for graduate-level credit and apply toward license renewal.

**corwin.com/advance**

Contact a PD Advisor at (800) 831-6640 or
visit www.corwin.com for more information